Christianity in Culture

A Historical Quest

John R. Sommerfeldt

For Jay and Gene, my ever dearer friends.
John

University Press of America,® Inc.
Lanham · Boulder · New York · Toronto · Plymouth, UK

Copyright © 2009 by
University Press of America,® Inc.
4501 Forbes Boulevard
Suite 200
Lanham, Maryland 20706
UPA Acquisitions Department (301) 459-3366

Estover Road
Plymouth PL6 7PY
United Kingdom

All rights reserved
Printed in the United States of America
British Library Cataloging in Publication Information Available

Library of Congress Control Number: 2009926538
ISBN-13: 978-0-7618-4671-0 (paperback : alk. paper)
ISBN-10: 0-7618-4671-9 (paperback : alk. paper)
eISBN-13: 978-0-7618-4672-7
eISBN-10: 0-7618-4672-7

∞™ The paper used in this publication meets the minimum
requirements of American National Standard for Information
Sciences—Permanence of Paper for Printed Library Materials,
ANSI Z39.48-1992

This volume is dedicated to the readers
of its many versions, readers who
became my collaborators:

Christopher M. Bellitto Kean University	Robert Kugelmann University of Dallas
E. Rozanne Elder Western Michigan University	Daniel M. La Corte Saint Ambrose University
Mariann Garrity, O.C.S.O. Mount Saint Mary's Abbey	Timothy Mahoney Providence College
Mark Goodwin University of Dallas	Gregory Roper University of Dallas
James E. Grace, Jr. Wallingford, Connecticut	Edith Scholl, O.C.S.O. Mount Saint Mary's Abbey
Mary Grace Kalamazoo, Michigan	James M. Sommerfeldt Grand Haven, Michigan
Wendell Harrison Irving, Texas	Marilyn J. Sommerfeldt Elk Rapids, Michigan
Timothy J. Heines Frisco, Texas	Thomas Sommerfeldt Elk Rapids, Michigan
Ann M. Kamm Battle Creek, Michigan	Charles Sullivan University of Dallas

Francis Swietek
University of Dallas

On January 27, 2008, died my best and dearest collaborator,
my wife Patricia. To her this book is especially dedicated.

CONTENTS

Preface	ix
I. Christianity and Culture	1
A. Christianity	1
B. Culture	3
C. The Story of Christianity and Culture	4
II. Christianity and the Culture of the Ancient World	7
A. Pagan Culture and Christian Faith	8
1. Christian Virtue and Pagan Learning	9
2. The Seven Liberal Arts	11
B. Discovering Christianity	13
1. The Divine Teacher	14
2. Scripture	16
3. Inspiration	17
4. Tradition	18
5. Reason	19
6. Apostolic Authority	19
C. Early Christian Spirituality	22
D. Christianity as the Imperial Religion	24
E. The Cultures of Christian Monasticism	26
III. Creating a New Christian Culture	29
A. A Clash of Cultures	30
B. Clovis and His Franks: The Demise of Germanic Values	32
C. The Meeting of Christian and Germanic Cultures	33
D. Missionary Activity and Cultural Continuity	34
E. Baptizing Germanic Culture	36
F. Rome and the Conversion of Germany	38
G. Charles the Great and the New Synthesis	39
IV. Feudal and Imperial Christianity, Church, and Culture	43
A. Invasion	44
B. Feudalism and the Church	46
C. Reviving the Roman Empire	48
D. A Vision of Christendom	50
E. A Technological and Cultural Revolution	51
V. The Medieval Reformation	55
A. The Cluniac Reform	56
B. The Reform Captures Rome	58
C. The Gregorian Reform	59
D. Compromise and Continued Reform	61
E. The Crusades	63

VI. High Medieval Culture and Society I: The Regulars	67
A. The Saintly Ideal: Bernard of Clairvaux	69
B. The Spiritual Foundation of Society	71
C. Society as Church	73
D. Cistercian Monks and the Third Wave of Reform	73
E. Regular Canons and the Philosophy of History	75
F. The Friars: A New Reform Idea and Institution	77
G. Women of the Cloister	79
VII. High Medieval Culture and Society II: The Seculars	81
A. The Secular Clergy	82
B. The Lay Leaders of Society	83
C. Chivalry	84
D. Courtly Love	86
E. The Middle Class	87
F. Farmers and the Value of Labor	89
G. The Dissidents	90
H. Heresy and Heretics	91
VIII. The Mind of the High Middle Ages	97
A. The Revival of Learning .	98
B. Education and the Universities	100
C. Scholasticism	102
D. Faith, Science, and Philosophy .	104
E. Nature and History	105
F. New Developments in Theology	106
G. Canon Law and the Growth of Papal Monarchy	107
IX. A Christian Culture Coming Apart: Late Medieval Church, State, and Society	109
A. The Failure of the Institutional Church	110
1. Boniface VIII	111
2. The Babylonian Captivity at Avignon	112
3. The Great Schism	115
4. The Conciliar Epoch	115
5. The Papal Restoration	116
B. The Failure of the State	117
1. The Dissolution of the Empire	118
2. The Strengths and Weaknesses of the French Monarchy	118
3. English Successes and Failures	119
C. Economic and Social Upheaval	120
X. The Mind of the Late Middle Ages	123
A. Political Thought and Papal Power	124
B. Late Medieval Religious Life	127
C. The Scandal of Indulgences	129
D. Renaissance and Humanism	130

1. Humanism in Literature: Petrarch	131
2. Humanism in Art: Michelangelo	132
3. Humanism and Science: Sandro Botticelli and Leonardo da Vinci	133
XI. The Protestant Reformation and European Culture	135
A. Martin Luther	136
B. Luther and Erasmus	140
C. John Calvin	143
D. Cultural Influences and Consequences	144
E. A New Approach to Politics	146
F. The English Reformation and the Growth of Secularism	147
XII. Catholic Reformation and Counter-reformation	151
A. The Range of Papal Reaction	152
B. Three Reforming Cardinals	154
C. The Council of Trent	157
D. The Society of Jesus	159
E. Matteo Ricci and the Mission to China	161
F. The Condemnation of Galileo	162
XIII. Movements Toward Modernity	165
A. Antecedents of the New World	166
B. Gallicanism, Febronianism, and the Jesuits	168
C. The King as Christ	169
D. A Revived Caesaropapism	170
E. Pietism and Protestant Spiritual Life	171
F. Methodists and English Evangelicals	173
G. Early Modern Catholicism	174
XIV. Enlightenment and Revolution	179
A. The Notion of Progress	180
B. Enlightened Cosmology and Anthropology	181
C. The Origin of Evil	182
D. Religious Intolerance and Enlightened Toleration	183
E. Enlightened Politics	183
F. New Forms of Religion	185
G. The French Revolutions	187
H. The New Force	190
XV. Religion in Conservative and Romantic Culture	193
A. The Conservative Response	194
1. The Politics of Edmund Burke	194
2. Conservative Culture and Religion	195
B. The Romantic Revolution	196
1. Goethe and the Daemonic	196
2. Science and the Origins of Romanticism	198
3. The World of Simple Beauty	198
4. The Restless Quest for Happiness	199

5. Romantic Culture and Religion	200
XVI. Religion and Reactions to the Industrial Revolution	203
A. The Human Cost	204
B. The Liberal Response	205
C. Marxism	206
D. Social Democracy	209
E. A Catholic Response: Pope Leo XIII	209
F. A Protestant Response: Otto von Bismarck	210
XVII. Religion in a Scientific Age	213
A. Evolution	214
B. Religious Reactions to Darwinism	215
C. The Neo-Enlightenment	216
D. Comte and Positivism	217
E. Nationalism	218
F. The Protestant Engagement with Modernity	219
XVIII. The Catholic Church Faces the Modern World	223
A. Traditionalists and Progressives	224
B. Ultramontanism and Infallibility.	224
C. The Pope as Absolute Monarch	226
D. The Progressive View of the Church and Its Demise	228
E. Pope Paul VI on Birth Control	230
F. The Church and the Life of the Mind	230
G. John Paul II	234
H. A Church Deeply Divided	234
XIX. Religion and Culture in Today's World	237
A. The Phenomenon of Fundamentalism	238
B. The Collapse of Communism	239
C. The Metamorphosis of Liberalism	240
D. Science and Religion	242
E. A Brief Postscript	244
Index of Persons	245
Index of Topics	249

PREFACE

The book is intended for people with intelligence and curiosity but no specialized training in historical scholarship. Aiming at what is for me a new audience requires an approach also new to me, and so I have asked for help from a number of people. To keep my story accurate, I have requested the service of the sharp eyes and equally sharp pens of a number of scholars: historians, biblical scholars, theologians, philosophers, and psychologists. To make sure my story is comprehensible to, and enjoyable for, "real people," I have enlisted a "reality corps" to support and correct me. My brother Tom, a mechanical engineer, informed me from the start that if I employed one of my favorite "scholarly" words, "epistemology," even once, he would not read another line. My sister Mary and my wife Pat have counted–quite independently–the number of times I have used and, they believe, overused the word "folk." So I have used "people" more often than I would have preferred.

I have listened gratefully to the scholars who have read the first versions of this book. Timothy Mahoney, a professor of philosophy at Providence College in Rhode Island, is a kind, gentle, and patient man, whose only idiosyncracy is his loyalty to baseball's Toledo Mudhens. Tim sent me a three-page commentary on a philosophical movement, Nominalism, that I had described in Chapter X. He kindly, gently, and patiently suggested that I had got it wrong. With Tim's help–and additional information supplied by Christopher Bellitto, a professor of history at Kean University in New Jersey–I was able to discover that I had indeed got it wrong. It seems that several scholars have slowly but surely attacked all the common wisdom on Nominalism–to the point that it seems doubtful there was such a movement. Tim and Chris have demonstrated to me once more that scholarship must be a cooperative venture. They have saved me from embarrassment and you from misinformation.

I have followed faithfully all–or nearly all–the suggestions of my readers. Only one major idea I have not included–and that not because I have failed to appreciate it, but because I know myself incapable of its realization. A former student, and now as then my friend, is Father Timothy Heines, the pastor of Saint Francis of Assisi Church in Frisco, Texas. After reading Chapter II, Christianity and the Culture of the Ancient World, Timothy shared with me an insightful thought. He wrote that "the issue of Christianity and culture devolves naturally from the internal struggle of first-century Judaism to reconcile culture and religious heritage, which was itself a struggle to identify the 'true' meaning of being Jewish." Timothy explained this to me at some length and concluded: "Since Christianity was born of this kind of conflict, I believe that the issue of culture versus secularism is in the DNA of Christianity (at least in its foundational documents)."

I am sure Timothy is correct in asserting that the whole of Jesus' message and ministry must be re-evaluated in the light of "Jewish questions of culture and enculturation." This, I fear, is beyond my ability–even beyond my command of the vocabulary on the question. What is necessary in the case of Timothy's response is a book on the subject–a book probably as long or longer than the one I have written. I wish Timothy would write it, but I am sure his devotion to his flock makes such a project impossible. But perhaps he may when he is as old as I.

This is the seventh book which Cathy Carol has typed for me. Each of them has been better for her expert care.

John R. Sommerfeldt
University of Dallas

I. CHRISTIANITY AND CULTURE

A. Christianity

Christianity is, of course, a religion. But what is a religion? We all have an awareness–more or less vague–of what constitutes a religion, but coming up with a definition is a challenge–at least it has been a challenge for me. The definition I have settled on, after considering this question for years, is not at all unique. I agree with whoever said–surely from a Christian perspective–that a religion has three components: a creed, a code, and a cult.

I understand "creed" to mean a set of beliefs about reality, about what is and what is not. Whether that set of beliefs is based on what God has revealed on a mountain or in my heart, on what Mother taught me as a child, or on what I have reasoned out from experience, it provides me a picture of the world. We all need such a picture; the alternative is the sheer horror of meaninglessness.

Even though a religion must have a creed, a creed need not be religious. In the course of this book we shall encounter several powerful sets of belief that do not include a god or the supernatural in their understanding of reality. We shall spend a good deal of time on the set of beliefs called the Enlightenment–an eighteenth-century creed that provides by far the most important basis for modern culture. We shall meet and discuss three more world-views, creeds that arose in the nineteenth century: Marxism, nationalism, and the sociological system of Auguste Comte. Because these four creeds are, in the end, based on faith–though they do not admit this–we shall treat them as religions. They are religions that are powerfully alive today and are active rivals of the Christianity they intend to overcome and replace.

A "code," as we are using the word here, is a more or less detailed list of what we must or must not do. The code may have been inscribed on tablets of stone on Mount Sinai or it may be based on the talks Jesus delivered on the Sabbath in the synagogue at Capernaum. The code may claim to be derived exclusively from reason or science. But a code is an essential component of a religion, for behavior both reveals and best expresses one's deeply held beliefs.

The presence or absence of a code is what constitutes the difference between magic and religion. The word "magic" calls up–in my mind at least–an image of frenzied dancing, endlessly protracted chanting, and the powerful presence of a priestess or priest–the *mambo* or *oungan*–in the rites of Haitian voodoo. The world of the voodoo believer is inhabited by *loa*, spirits that reside in trees, waterfalls, springs, and ponds. To better their lot, pilgrims to these places offer eggs, rice, beans, chickens, and other gifts pleasing to the spirits. I ask myself: does the belief in *loa* (a creed) and the sacrifices made to them (cultic behavior) make voodoo "magic" or "religion"? I think the answer depends on something I do not know: whether in bestowing favors the spirits require adherence to a moral code. If yes, then it seems to me Haitian voodoo is a religion. If the offerings are means of pleasing and, more importantly, of controlling spirits who do not require me to alter any bad behavior, then I would call the practice magic.

The third defining component of religion is "cult." Cult refers to the response believers make to their creed. Cultic behavior can take all sorts of forms: the singing of psalms or the baptism of babies. The reenactment of the Last Supper in a eucharistic meal, also called communion or the Lord's Supper, is a widely practiced Christian cultic or liturgical practice. Cultic practices or liturgies vary widely, and that diversity has always been heavily influenced by the culture of the time and place in which the specific liturgical practice was developed.

While we shall speak no more of voodoo cultic practices in this book, I shall more than once describe the cultic practices of Christians that have been more magical than religious. The deal that the sixth-century Germanic chieftain Clovis thought he made with God, described in some detail later in this volume, was surely magic–at least as I have defined the term. The late medieval practice of purchasing indulgences for the release of relatives from Purgatory was surely magic, since virtue was not required of the purchaser.

Using the same criterion, I believe that, no matter how firmly the basic precepts of science are held, science is not ever a religion. Science does indeed have a set of beliefs. It trusts that truth will result from applying logic or reason to mathematically measured sensory observation. But scientific results are not dependent on the moral or ethical stature of the scientist. A good scientist is not necessarily a good person. A saint will not necessarily be a more successful scientist than will a sinner.

Time is more important to Christianity than to most religions. Like the Israelites' Yahweh and the Muslims' Allah, the Christian God acts in time. This God creates and sustains a world that changes with time, and Christians believe he enters into time by becoming a human being. So it is not surprising that many Christians are not dismayed by developing doctrines, the fine-tuning of moral stances, and organizational changes that sometimes seem to onlookers to assume the proportions of revolutions. All of these cultural and religious phenomena we shall investigate.

B. Culture

Having looked briefly at creed, code, and cult, the "inside" characteristics of religion, we need now to explore the world "outside," the cultural world surrounding religious beliefs and practices. We tend to think of the word "culture" as a description of activities loftily intellectual or intensely artistic. That is not at all the way I shall be using the word. My concept of culture is much broader. It makes sense to me to speak of material culture as well as the cultural world of ideas. A common-sense, down-to-earth approach to humans and their history should take seriously both thought and things.

This means that, in the pages that follow, we shall observe the interaction of ideas and institutions. I believe that both insightful ideas and favorable material environments–including weather–can give rise to new and impressive social structures. Societies reflect both the values of real people and the realities of the material world in which those real people find themselves. So too, the social structures that humans create can lead to ever newer modes of thought and still more clever and effective methods and machines through which they respond to the environment.

Let me offer an example about which we shall speak more extensively in a later chapter: the Agricultural Revolution. About the year 1000, the climate of Europe grew gradually warmer. The part of that continent lying north and west of the Alps, a wide expanse of unused or underused land, offered pioneering opportunities to enterprising people. This climatological and geographical opportunity was seized by a people whose Christianity taught them to value the dignity and worth of each human being. Idea and opportunity combined. The combination led to the invention of a startling array of labor-saving devices: the mold-board plow, the horse shoe and horse collar, the windmill and the watermill, and a host of new farming techniques. Food production increased greatly, and, as a result, people grew healthier, they lived longer, and many more of their babies survived the dangers of disease. Populations grew radically, and so did the confidence of Europeans in their ability to face the forces of nature and triumph over them.

Ideas and institutions interact with one another. Institutions result from attempts to bring ideals and values into the real, the material world. Conversely, the success or failure of institutions can lead to new ideas. It seems only common sense to think that social structures are born from the marriage of ideas and material opportunities or limitations. These are the notions that underlie my reflections on the interaction of Christianity and culture, the subject of this book.

Its subject is *not* Church history, although the history of the Church is often conspicuous in the following pages. The Church is an institution devised to realize–to make real and tangible–the complex of ideas called Christianity. In its structure and organization, the Church–like all institutions–changes over time. It grows and shrinks. It sometimes shatters, as it did during the reformations of the sixteenth century, so that today it is no longer possible to speak simply of "the Church" without recognizing its fragmentation. The history of the institution or the institutions we call "church" is important to our story here because the Church, like all institutions, becomes a component of culture and thus both reflects and influences ideas.

C. Story of Christianity and Culture

In the year 2005, I finished yet another book intended primarily for scholars. At that point I sat down, without much prior reflection, to tell a story instead of continuing to rehearse the fruits of my ongoing research. For some fifty years I have been telling my students the story of the interaction between Christianity and culture. It seemed to me that, through telling and retelling the story, I had learned enough about that story that I could share it with a wider audience. And that is how this book began.

Of course, I cannot tell the whole story within the compass of this very small book. The story contained in chapters II through IV of this volume takes me fifteen weeks to tell in a course labeled Medieval Europe I. Chapters VI, VII, and VIII require another semester's course: Medieval Europe II. Chapters IX and X are radical condensations of a course I call–with a deception I shall later explain–the Renaissance. And so it goes, through a number of undergraduate and graduate courses, through several graduate seminars, and through a host of doctoral dissertations and master's theses. From the students in each of these I have learned much about the story I keep telling, so my story, I trust, gets better and better and, I sincerely hope, more and more faithful to the facts. This is the reason I keep on teaching, though I am well beyond retirement age.

I have always found that the lives and thoughts of people are more exciting than either abstract ideas or historical dates and facts. So, whenever possible, I have tried to tell the Christianity-and-culture story through the lives and thoughts of real individuals. Some of these people are well known: Charlemagne and Saint Francis, Martin Luther and Henry VIII, Galileo and Karl Marx, for example. Others who will appear whom almost no one knows, among them Ovid and Clovis, Bernard of Clairvaux and Walter von der Vogelweide, Matteo Ricci and Samuel Smiles. Some of them you will like; some not. But, it is their story, and I hope, the story will be better told through them.

The subject of my story–the interaction between Christianity and culture–is vast and complicated. Components of that interaction are controversial. Some early Christian and medieval thinkers relied on Plato to supply the philosophical framework for their theology. They saw their religion from a radically different perspective than did those Christians who looked to Aristotle for the same sort of help. Sixteenth-century Protestants who desired to reform the Church chose different and often opposing ways of accomplishing their goal. In our own day, Catholics see themselves divided into camps called–inaccurately, I think–"liberal" and "conservative." Protestants are similarly divided: some see a literal reading of Scripture as the unerring source of Christian knowledge; some would reinterpret Scripture by "demythologizing" it. My goal in describing these competing ideas has not been to support–let alone prove–one side or the other.

My intention is, rather, to provide the cultural and historical background that will enable the reader to understand these differing positions. Through that understanding, I hope to assist all of us in overcoming our natural tendency to "demonize" people who hold positions at odds with our own. I do hope this small volume will help us all to season our disagreements with charity, courtesy, and good humor.

II. CHRISTIANITY AND THE CULTURE OF THE ANCIENT WORLD

Some Useful Data

106-43 B.C.	Cicero, Roman orator and statesman
43 B.C.-18 A.D.	Ovid, Roman poet
54-68	reign of Nero, emperor
60-70?	Gospel of Mark
90?	Pauline Letter to the Ephesians
c. 35-95	Quintilian, Roman rhetorician
c. 95	Clement of Rome's Letter to the Corinthians
100?	Gospel of John
c. 50-c. 107	Ignatius, bishop of Antioch
c. 130	writing of Papias, bishop of Hierapolis
c. 100-c. 165	Justin Martyr, Christian apologist
c. 125-c. 200	Irenaeus, bishop of Lyon
c. 215	Clement of Alexandria, Christian theologian
c. 160-c. 220	Tertullian, Christian theologian
258	death of Cyprian, bishop of Carthage
205-270	Plotinus, neo-platonic philosopher
233-303	Porphyry, neo-platonic philosopher
284-305	reign of Diocletian, emperor
306-337	reign of Constantine I, emperor
329?-379	Basil, bishop of Caesarea
379-395	reign of Theodosius I, emperor
c. 340-397	Ambrose, bishop of Milan
354-430	Augustine, bishop of Hippo
c. 439	death of Martianus Capella, poet
440-461	reign of Leo I, bishop of Rome
410-485	Proclus, neoplatonic philosopher
492-496	reign of Gelasius I, bishop of Rome
c. 475-525	Boëthius, philosopher and theologian
c. 480-547	Benedict of Nursia, abbot
c. 490-580	Cassiodorus, monk and educator

A. Pagan Culture and Christian Faith

Nearby the city of Nazareth, in which Jesus spent most of his life, stood the city of Sepphoris, a larger and far more impressive city than Jesus' home town. Sepphoris was, or was to become, a center of Greco-Roman culture. The geographic juxtaposition of Nazareth and Sepphoris neatly symbolizes the two great cultural systems with which the earliest Christians had to deal.

The first of these was the religion of the Church's founder: Judaism. The problem for potential converts was: must I, as a gentile, adhere to the Law of Moses to be a follower of Jesus? This is scarcely an insignificant issue, for, if the answer is yes–that one must become a Jew to follow Christ–then the consequence for approximately fifty percent of new adherents to the faith is an extremely painful operation, circumcision. Fortunately, the answer, recorded in the biblical books of Acts, Galatians, and Romans, is that one need not observe the Old Covenant in order to embrace the New. Gentiles can remain Greeks and Romans throughout their lifelong external and internal conversion.

But the fact that virtually all early Christians were Greeks and Romans forced them to face another formidable barrier. Does Christianity demand rejection of the Greco-Roman cultural heritage: its literature, its philosophy, and its science–its whole way of looking at and living in the world? The values which Greek and Roman converts had derived from their classical culture were, after all, not Christian but pagan: their literature was pagan, their philosophy was pagan, and their science took no account of the new religion.

The answer to this monumental problem came early in the life of the Church and was, perhaps, best embodied in the "apologies" of Justin Martyr, written to defend Christianity against pagan attacks. Justin was a splendidly educated, Greek-speaking school master in Rome, both philosopher and convert to Christianity. The latter led to a martyr's death about the year 165. In his first *Apology* (c. 150), Justin asserted that "...Christ is the first-born of God, and...he is the Reason [the Word or, in Greek, the *Logos*] of which the whole of humanity partakes." "And so," Justin continued, "those who live according to reason are truly Christians, even though they are thought to be atheists. Of this sort are Socrates and Heraclitus among the Greeks, and the other philosophers like them...." Here we see Justin's startling stance: Socrates was really a Christian–even though he did not know it.

The first premise of Justin's position is that the universe was created according to the pattern of reason, which pattern is the Son of God himself. As the gospel of John says: "Through him [the Word, the *Logos*, the Reason] all things came into being...." Human beings, the argument goes on, are created in the image and likeness of the God who is Reason, and thus, through the exercise of their reason, human beings–all human beings–are able to recognize reality, to know God. Thus, for Justin, "...the teachings of Plato are not contrary to those of Christ..., and this is true too of other philosophers, like the Stoics, as well as the authors of both poetry and prose." To the company of the philosophers Socrates and Plato, we can now have the audacity to consider as Christians the pagan poets Homer and Vergil.

"Each of these," Justin claimed, "discoursed rightly....They saw what was Christian because they shared the life-giving and divine Reason [again, the Word or *Logos*]." With surety Justin made the sweeping statement, in his second *Apology*, that "whatever has been correctly said by any person from any place belongs to us Christians." Why? "Because, next to God, we worship and love the Reason [the *Logos* who is Christ], who is from the unbegotten and ineffable God." And thus, as Clement, the saintly bishop of Alexandria wrote, about the year 200, "philosophy is a preparation [for the mind], paving the way toward perfection in Christ." God had given the Greeks philosophy so that they could be brought to Christ, just as he had given the Law to Jews.

1. Christian Virtue and Pagan Learning

To incorporate Justin and Clement's view of classical culture into an educational system required a decision about leadership qualifications within the emerging Christian Church. That decision quickly came: early Christian leaders were to be virtuous and learned. The virtues meant were, of course, faith, hope and love–with the greatest of these love. Christian leaders were to exemplify the virtues required of their flock. All this is surely easy to understand. What is less clear is why early Christian clergy were required to be learned–especially since the only learning available was classical learning, which was, of course, pagan learning.

We learn much from the treatment early Christians gave to Publius Ovidius Naso, the great storyteller and sometime jokester who lived from 43 B.C. to 18 A.D. and whom we call Ovid. Ovid was tremendously popular among early Christian and medieval readers. Some modern students, especially the few who are of my generation, remember reading Ovid in third- or fourth-year Latin class. But, if they do, I dare say that the Ovid they remember is the Ovid of the *Metamorphoses*, a series of pleasant tales of how things came to be the way they are, rather like Rudyard Kipling's *Just So* stories. But the Ovid to whom I refer and who was surely denied most students by censorious Latin teachers is the Ovid of the *Ars amatoria*. Ovid's *Art of Love* is no romantic novel; it is a manual of seduction. This how-to-do-it book leaves no aspect of sexual intercourse unexamined–and it was a best-seller among medieval monks, at least judging by the enormous number of manuscripts of this work which they copied and recopied. Ovid, banished for his urbane immorality to the shores of the Black Sea by the Emperor Augustus, was brought back from exile in triumph by medieval copyists.

Copying a manuscript is a formidable task. It is as remote from our taking notes on a professor's lecture as climbing Mount Kilimanjaro is from stepping on an ant hill. Let us suppose we wish to copy a manuscript as monks once did. One or more of our company must first engage in the lengthy and tedious task of raising a flock of sheep. After the bloody business of butchery is completed, some of us must stretch, cure, scrape, and otherwise care for the skin which will furnish us the parchment on which we shall write. Actually, we shall not write at all; we shall draw. With our model on one easel, we shall draw each letter of our text–slowly and painstakingly–onto the leather stretched out on another easel. Often we will employ a drawing stick to support the pen. But, with or without such an aid, our copying process is laborious and demanding–both mentally and physically. So tiring is this process that we sometimes find marginal notes in medieval manuscripts which contain messages like: "Thank God it's the Vespers bell" or "Oh hell my hand hurts"–a rather free translation from the Latin.

You would think that this painful process would be reserved only for the most treasured works of antiquity–and in this you would be right. But why then did medieval monks copy dirty old books like Ovid's? Is it possible that they were dirty old men, as a student of mine once suggested? Perhaps a few were, but, for the vast majority, copying Ovid was part of a grand plan to preserve the literary and philosophical works of classical antiquity.

The learning demanded of early Christian leaders had a purpose: the reading and understanding of the book that was their source and standard for both belief and practice. It did not take much learning for early Christians to read the Bible; after all it was written in or early translated into both the principal languages of the Roman Empire: Greek and Latin. But understanding the Bible is something different altogether.

The Bible is not a book; it is a collection of books in a wide variety of genres: laws, hymns, parables, letters, narratives that purport to be histories, collections of pithy and sometimes witty sayings. The Bible contains prophetic literature, vision literature, books which seem to challenge God's ordering of the universe, and some powerfully erotic Jewish love poetry. How is one to understand this bewildering variety of literature? What is to be taken literally? What figuratively? The only way early Christians–and we too–can learn how to interpret this literature is by practice. We do this today. We take courses in English, French, German, or Russian literature and try to understand that literature. (Most of us try to understand it the way we think the professor does.) In short, literary interpretation requires practice. And the only literature available in the Greek- and Latin-speaking world was classical literature, which thus became essential to Christianity's understanding of itself and which therefore had to be copied and recopied, just as was the Bible. If we are to understand the intensely erotic poem which is Solomon's Song of Songs–a poem believed to be part of God's revelation–then it surely helps to have had practice reading and understanding erotic literature–like Ovid's *Art of Love*. Medieval scholars and saints read Ovid allegorically and were thus helped to read the Song of Songs equally allegorically–seeing in the sexual union of the Bridegroom and the bride the spiritual union of God and the soul, a soul (*anima*) conveniently feminine in Latin.

2. The Seven Liberal Arts

And thus were born the Seven Liberal Arts. A curriculum invented in ancient Greece to foster good citizenship had developed into a program of studies for Imperial Roman bureaucrats, providing them the intellectual tools needed for governance. And this curriculum received its final fine tuning in a design for the education of early Christian clergymen. Eventually, through the agency of Martianus Capella (died c. 439) and his long (and tedious) allegorical poem *The Marriage of Philology and Mercury*, even more through the work of Cassiodorus' (c. 447-583) *On Divine and Human Readings*, the arts curriculum provided the design for the education of all Europeans and their offspring down to and sometimes into the twentieth century.

These most powerful vehicles for transmitting western culture, the seven liberal arts, are conventionally divided into two parts. The first part consists of three disciplines: grammar, rhetoric, and dialectic. Medieval scholars called these three paths to the truth the *trivium*. We now call them the humanities. The remaining four paths to the truth, the *quadrivium*, are mathematics, music (by which they understood acoustics, the physics of sound), geometry, and astronomy–what we call the sciences.

Through the art of grammar we study language as a means to, or method for, gaining a reasonably sophisticated understanding of literature in all its many modes–including history. This understanding enabled early Christians to gain insight into the profound depths of Scripture, the basis for their understanding of the meaning of life. A few of the texts read were the grand epics of Homer, the *Iliad* and the *Odyssey*, and the equally sweeping Roman epic, Vergil's *Aeneid*. Christians did not wince at Vergil's description of the seduction of Aeneas by Queen Dido of Carthage, despite its obvious inconsistency with the sexual standards of Saint Paul. They knew that both Vergil and their old friend Ovid were really Christian and would tell the same truths as Paul if but understood allegorically.

The purpose of rhetoric is easy to see. The knowledge of God and his ways must be communicated by Christian leaders called on to preach and to instruct their flocks. Here the techniques of speech and written communication are learned by a study of the work of the master orator of all times, Cicero (106-43 B.C.), and by noting the sometimes differing approach of the rhetorician and schoolmaster Quintilian (c. 35-95 A.D.).

Dialectic is the third of the arts. Its method is logic, taught to early Christians by Aristotle (384-322 B.C.) through the commentaries of another Greek philosopher, Porphyry (233-303), and the translations of the sixth-century Roman, Boëthius. The content of their discipline is, of course, philosophy, in which the Greeks Aristotle and Plato reigned supreme. Plato's metaphysics, delivered through his splendid dialogue, the *Timaeus*, was most read in the early Christian centuries and the Early Middle Ages, but Aristotle's thought enjoyed increasing popularity and much influence later, in the twelfth and thirteenth centuries, in the thought of

Bernard of Clairvaux, Peter Abelard, and Thomas Aquinas.

Dialectic offered Christians two essential services. As Justin Martyr and Clement of Alexandria had vigorously affirmed, the ancient philosophers told the truth, and the Truth is God. The Second Person of the Trinity *is* Reason, and so through the ancients one can know God.

And yet there is still more benefit to be derived from dialectic. The very Bible which Christians held so dear is filled, as we shall see, with apparent inconsistencies. The solutions to these inconsistencies are not found in Scripture. There is no mention of the Trinity in the New Testament. The doctrines at which early Christians arrived were, in large part, the result of the application of the logic of dialectic to the content of revelation. If we were somehow able to listen in on the debate at the Council of Nicaea in 325, we would be able to overhear assertions pro and con on the Son's "coeternity" and "consubstantiality" with the Father. This is not the language of Luke's gospel. Were we able to listen to the triumphal proclamation which concluded the Council of Chalcedon in 451, we would hear language like this:

> The one and the same Jesus Christ, the only-begotten Son of God, must be confessed in two natures, unconfusedly, immutably, indivisibly, inseparably united, and that without the distinction of natures being taken away by such union, but rather the peculiar property of each nature being preserved and being united in one Person and substance, not separated or divided into two persons but one and the same Son....

Surely, the Council Fathers, the bishops at Chalcedon, could not have understood their own declaration without a thorough and sophisticated knowledge of Greek philosophy. Words like "nature," "person," and "substance" have their origin Greek thought, not in Scripture.

The *quadrivium*, what we would call the sciences, can be considered together. Why, we might ask, should early Christian leaders know science? Augustine of Hippo (354-430) offered an answer in his *Commentary on Genesis Literally Interpreted*. At one level, surely a very low level, Augustine maintained that if we make mistakes in science, potential converts to Christianity will mistrust our message. But, in the end, Augustine would have us know science because God has written two books, the Bible and nature, and we can discover much about him by reading both books.

Early Christian leaders, then, were not merely to be virtuous but learned, learned in the liberal arts, a pagan curriculum which they enthusiastically baptized. Medieval monks embraced this curriculum and copied the texts which made it possible. Without them we would not know that Socrates or Plato or Aristotle had existed, that Homer and Vergil and Ovid had ever written.

There were some early Christian thinkers who seemed to reject this synthesis of Christianity and classical culture. About the year 197, for example, this protest was trumpeted: "What does Athens have to do with Jerusalem? ...Away with all projects for a 'Stoic,' a 'Platonic,' or a 'logical' Christianity! After Christ Jesus we desire no subtle theories about, no probing enquiries into, the gospel...." The protestor's name was Tertullian. He was a Christian from Carthage in North Africa (today Tunisia), whose prodigious output of theological works spanned the years from about 195 to 220. Tertullian's pugnacious protest was seemingly directed against the use of Greek philosophy in the development of Christian doctrine. That protest has been viewed by scholars through the centuries as the quintessential assertion of Christian obscurantism, of the view that "worldly wisdom" has no place in Christian thought.

I think we can better understand Tertullian when we remember that, although he had an excellent education in Greek thought, the language of his many works was Latin, his native tongue. Tertullian wrote as he thought, as a Roman not a Greek–and in his works he employed all the tools of Latin rhetoric.

I suspect that when most of us think about Greek culture we picture mentally the Parthenon in Athens, we recall the philosophical contributions of the great minds of Socrates, Plato, and Aristotle. But when we think about the Roman contributions to culture, we tend to recall the Colosseum and other wonders of Roman engineering, such as roads, bridges, and aqueducts. We see the genius of Romans at work in law and politics, in the mastery of rhetoric rather than philosophy. And this popular view of the differences between Greeks and Romans is basically correct, even though insufficiently nuanced.

It is in this cultural context that we can best understand Tertullian. His was a protest not against classical culture or its use by Christians. His protest was a marvelous example of hyperbole, of rhetorical exaggeration directed against unnecessarily abstract Greek thought in favor of down-to-earth Roman concerns. It was the practical questions of daily religious life that most interested Roman Christians, even though Latin theologians like Tertullian contributed significantly to the development of Christian doctrine. The different cultural worlds of Greek East and Latin West are reflected even in the different sorts of heresies propounded in the two parts of the Roman Empire. In the Greek East, metaphysical questions, questions about the nature of ultimate reality, about God and the Trinity, provided the substance of theological debate. In the Latin West, the questions which concerned Christians were, for example, the effects of baptism, the practice of prayer, and the reconciliation of Christians who had renounced their faith when threatened by persecution. In its very earliest days, Christianity responded to, and hence reflected, the various cultural worlds of the people who gave it their allegiance.

B. Discovering Christianity

Despite the apparent misgivings of thinkers like Tertullian–misgivings based on the cultural variations within the Roman world–most early Christians eagerly embraced the synthesis of their religion with the thought of both Greek and Latin culture. As we have seen, that culture provided Christians with various means to assist them in discerning the truths of their religion, with sophisticated ways of speaking about and teaching that truth. *Why* Christians needed to appropriate the culture of the pagan world in which they lived requires a brief historical background.

Christianity had an inauspicious origin. Sometime about 5 B.C., we think, a baby was born in an animal stall in a backwater area of the Roman Empire called Palestine. The Jewish boy was called Yeshua, and he spent the bulk of his life in an obscure hamlet, Nazareth. After a brief public career as a wandering teacher, he was condemned for blasphemy by the Jewish leaders in Jerusalem and was flogged and crucified by the Roman authorities there–suffering the same ignominious death as a host of dangerous criminals, troublesome rabble-rousers, and small-time thieves of the day.

Of course, this crucifixion was not the end of the matter, as both Jewish and Roman authorities had devoutly hoped. The followers of Yeshua (or Jesus, as Greek-speaking Jews called him) went about preaching that he was the anointed one of God, the Messiah or Christ, whom God had promised to humankind almost at the beginning of time. Due to the efforts of Saul of Tarsus (known as Saint Paul to subsequent ages) and others who shared his missionary enterprise, not only did the Jews of Palestine hear of the Christ, but Jews and gentiles of the entire Roman world as well.

Despite the opposition of Jewish religious authorities and the Roman government, which as early as the reign of the Emperor Nero (57-68 A.D.) began to imprison and execute Christians, the disciples of Jesus met with astonishing success. Christianity spread through Palestine, Syria, and Egypt, through Asia Minor and Greece, and to the West where it found a home in Italy, North Africa, Spain, Gaul, and the rest of the Roman world. In the first century A.D., Christian communities were concentrated in cities in the East–like Alexandria, Antioch, and Athens. In the second century, not only had the number of church communities in the East been multiplied manyfold, but the West had become an increasingly fruitful field for missionary endeavors. By the third century, Christianity was established in all the principal cities of the Empire–and most of the lesser towns. Still, less than ten percent of the Roman population was Christian in 313 when the Emperor Constantine (c. 288-337) embraced the faith and forbade future persecutions of Christians. The subsequent years saw a remarkable increase in the number of followers of Jesus, and, in 380, the Emperor Theodosius (c. 346-395) proclaimed Christianity the official religion of the Empire. Henceforth, paganism was almost entirely relegated to a few rural areas. Indeed the Latin word for a country dweller or "hick" was *paganus* (from which we get "pagan").

1. *The Divine Teacher*

What was this Christianity which the people of the Roman Empire were embracing? Why were Greeks and Romans accepting the teachings of Jesus? One important reason that they believed was because they thought Jesus was sent by God and therefore spoke with God's authority. We can see this claim reflected throughout early Christian literature, and a story in the gospel of Mark–written, many scholars think, between 60 and 70 A.D.–illustrates the claim well:

> After some days, when Jesus returned to Capernaum, the news spread that he was back home. So many people gathered together there that there was no room left, not even at the door. While he was delivering his message to them, a man who was paralyzed was brought to him. Four men were carrying him, but because of the crowd they could not bring him near. So they opened up a hole in the roof above Jesus and lowered the man on his stretcher. When Jesus saw their faith, he said to the paralyzed man: "My son, your sins are forgiven."

Some among the crowd, scholars who knew Jewish law, silently mused: "How can this man talk like this? He is blaspheming, for who other than God can forgive sins?" Jesus, aware of what they were thinking, said to them:

> "Why do you think this way? Is it easier to say to the paralyzed man: 'Your sins are forgiven' or to say: 'Stand up, take your bed, and walk away'? But I shall show you that the Son of Man has authority on earth to forgive sins. Then, turning to the paralyzed man, he said: "I tell you: stand up, take up your stretcher, and go home." Then immediately the man got up, took up his bed, and left.

The result of this event, Mark told his early Christian audience, is that the onlookers "were astounded and praised God," for they had "never seen anything like this." Mark's account surely implies that Jesus possessed divine power and, perhaps, was himself somehow divine.

The gospel of John goes much farther. This gospel–written, perhaps, about 100 A.D.–begins with an early Christian hymn which affirms not merely that Jesus possesses divine power, but that he is, in truth, God:

> In the beginning was the Word. The Word was in God's presence, and the Word was God....The Word became flesh and made his dwelling among us. And we have seen his glory, the glory of an only Son coming from the Father, filled with enduring love.

John's gospel goes on to record Jesus' affirmation that "I and the Father are one." The response of his hearers was to gather rocks with which to stone him, "for you, who are only a man, make yourself God."

Early Christians, then, believed Jesus to be divine. And it is surely understandable that they, who were being persecuted and executed for their beliefs, should desire assurance of Jesus' divinity. If Jesus claimed to be divine and was not, he was a fraud, and dying for his teachings was absurd.

But the assertion that Jesus was divine brought early Christians all sorts of deeply troubling difficulties. Moving from Jesus the man, who died nailed to a cross, to Jesus as an omnipotent God is a giant step indeed. The Jesus who prayed to God in the Garden of Gethsemane is a far cry, it would seem, from Jesus as an all-powerful God. The gospel of Mark reports that Jesus' final words were: "My God, my God, why have you forsaken me?" This seems hardly consistent with John's claim that Jesus, the Word, is God. First-century Christians venerated Jesus as Lord–alongside of God. This surely posed a serious question concerning Christian monotheism. For centuries to come, Christians would wonder what was the relationship of Jesus to the Father, who, as Jesus declared, is God. How could Jesus the Word be *with* God and, at the same time, *be* God? Are there two Gods? Perhaps there are three, for the gospel of Matthew reports that Jesus commissioned his followers to "make disciples of all nations, baptizing them in the name of the Father and of the Son and of the Holy Spirit." These problems had to be addressed and answered if people of even average intelligence were to become or remain Christians.

Subsequent history has been modified greatly by the answers Christians gave to the problem of Jesus' divinity. Even more important for the development of western culture have been the *ways* Christians went about trying to solve this crucial question. The problem can be stated this way: granted, as Christians do, that Jesus has the answer to the question how he can be both God and "with God." And granted further that Jesus wishes to convey this answer to Christians, how can those Christians discover the mind of Jesus on this or any other topic?

2. Scripture

The source to which most modern Christians would turn is the Bible, in which, they think, they can discover answers by reading about Jesus' life and teachings. But this source presented early Christians with two principal difficulties. The first stems from the fact that, as we have seen, the Bible is not one book; it is, rather, a collection of books. In the Christian Scriptures (the New Testament) are contained books which purport to be biographies (the four gospels), an impressive historical account of the first days of the Christian community (Acts), a large number of letters, and a grand vision of end times (Revelation). But there were several other gospels written in the early days of Christianity with which most of us are not familiar: the gospel of the Hebrews, of the Ebionites, of James, of Bartholomew, of Nicodemus, of Thomas–among others. Which of these widely diverging gospels should be taken as authentic? By what authority did Christians include but four gospels in their canon, their list of authentic sources of God's revelation? The complexity of the problem is revealed by the fact that in the sixth century doubts were still being expressed about the authenticity of some seven of the books now accepted by Christians. But even if one knows which biblical books are authoritative, which contain authentic information about the life and teachings of Jesus, a formidable obstacle to the search for that truth, for the basis of Christian identity and its definition, still remains.

Although early Christians eagerly accepted the teachings of Jesus recorded in the New Testament, they disputed the meaning of many biblical passages. They wondered whether each word in the Scriptures should be taken literally, whether all passages should be read figuratively, or whether some passages were meant to be taken literally and others figuratively. If they chose the last option–which they usually did–they had to face the problem of identifying which passages to take literally and which figuratively. And when they believed a passage was best interpreted figuratively, they had to decide which of the many possible figures, metaphors, or similes was the correct one.

3. *Inspiration*

One of the ways through which early Christians sought to discover what to believe was to rely on the inspiration–the breathing in–of the Holy Spirit, the same Breath of God that, as the book of Acts reports, had rushed like a mighty wind through the upper room at Pentecost and filled the earliest Christian disciples with wondrous knowledge. A reference to this source of truth seems to be contained in a letter, commonly attributed to Paul, to the Christian community at Ephesus. About the year 90 A.D., the author wrote: "When I mention you in my prayers, I ask that the God of our Lord Jesus Christ, the all-glorious Father, give you the Spirit of wisdom and revelation so that you may know him. I ask that he illumine the eyes of your hearts...." Throughout the ages, this way of knowing has been called inspiration, the gift which results in charismatic (from the Greek for "inspired") knowledge. The meaning of inspiration is illuminated when one remembers that the "spir" part of the word comes from the Latin *spirare*, to breathe. Very early on, evidently, Christians came to believe that the "breath" of the Spirit could inspire them both to know the truth (charismatic knowledge) and to perform extraordinary, sometimes miraculous feats (charismatic power).

Those who believe that God inspires humans to know the true Christian teaching must face a consequent problem: ascertaining who is inspired and thus knows the truth. In the fourth century, for example, one of the burning issues among Christians was the nature of the relationship of Jesus to the Father. Some, led by Arius, a priest of the great Egyptian city of Alexandria, taught that Jesus is a created being and thus not the equal of the Father. Their source was, of course, their interpretation of Scripture–an interpretation they thought inspired. But the same appeal was made by Arius' opponents, led by another Alexandrian clergyman, Athanasius, who taught that Jesus is of the same nature as the Father. How could Christians decide between these conflicting claims unless they were themselves inspired by God? But those who claim a certainty coming from God are, at least, open to the danger of self-deception. The history of Christianity is rife with conflicts–sometimes bloody–between opposing Christians, each side "knowing" itself inspired by God and counting themselves his agents.

4. Tradition

Early Christians, then, having accepted both Scripture and inspiration as sources of truth, were still faced with unsettling uncertainties about authentic Christian teaching. Their Teacher was no longer present among them, and his disciples, his students, were, at least by the end of the first century, no longer available as sources of Christian doctrine. What of *their* disciples, asked Papias, the leader of the church at Hierapolis? Very early on, about the year 130, Papias wrote:

> I shall not hesitate to set down for you ...all those teachings which I learned from the elders. I recorded these carefully, because I was convinced of their truth....Indeed, I took pleasure not from those who had much to say, but from those who taught the truth. I listened carefully not to those who recorded strange precepts, but to those who related those teachings given to the faithful by the Lord and thus derived from the Truth itself.

Papias then turned to the method by which we can learn of this Truth from the Lord:

> So, if any one came to us who had been a follower of the elders, I would inquire about the sayings of those elders. I would ask what Andrew had said, or Peter, or Philip, Thomas or James, John or Matthew, or any other of the Lord's disciples. For I did not think to get as much profit from books as from the utterances of a living voice.

Papias, then, thought to discover the authentic teachings of Jesus by consulting the living tradition which had its origins in those teachings and was transmitted orally through the succeeding generations of Jesus' disciples. Indeed, thought Papias, since the Scriptures were themselves the products of oral tradition, their meaning could be ascertained by consulting the tradition which out of which they came.

The difficulty with tradition is obvious to anyone who has played the parlor game in which one whispers a story to one's neighbor, who then whispers it to his or her neighbor–and so around the circle. The story that emerges is often only a pale reflection of the original tale; indeed, it may contradict the original intent. To return to our Arius–Athanasius example, both were members of the same Christian community at Alexandria and should have been guided by the same tradition. Traditionally, the first overseer of their church was the gospel writer Mark, who–again according to tradition–was the disciple of the apostle Peter. Clearly, the tradition extending from Peter to Arius and Athanasius had suffered some distortion. Early Christians truly believed in tradition, but they were confronted by a host of diverse and differing traditions that had undergone complex development. Sincere Christians were often hard pressed to identify which version of the tradition was authentic.

5. Reason

Another solution offered as a means to authentic Christian teaching was an appeal to reason. We have seen how Justin Martyr and Clement of Alexandria baptized Greek philosophy–and did so already in the second century. Following the views of Justin and Clement, early Christian thinkers, with few exceptions, embraced philosophy because they thought it told the truth. Then again, Christians discovered that the philosopher's tool, reason or logic, was indispensable in their search for the sense of Christianity. For example, they employed Aristotle's logic to avoid picturing the Father, Son, and Spirit as merely three manifestations of a single God (Sabellianism). To sidestep the notion that there were three gods whose only unity was in their common divinity (tritheism), early Christians also employed Greek philosophical categories. They concluded that God is a Trinity–a word not found in the Bible–in which there are three persons (Father, Son, and Holy Spirit) and one nature (divinity). "Person" and "nature," used in this technical sense, are words not found in Scripture.

Augustine, bishop of Hippo (in North Africa) from 395 to his death in 430, is an outstanding example of someone who applied the logic of reason to many questions that perplexed early Christians. As one case among very many, he wrote a treatise *On the Trinity* in which he employed the extensive knowledge of philosophy, especially of Plato and the platonic tradition, which he had acquired in his youth. Augustine saw the Father as an Infinite Thinker whose reflection on himself is an Infinite Thought which, because infinite, includes all the dimensions of reality, including consciousness, and is thus itself a person. The Word, the Reason, the Thought of God is, consequently, himself a thinker, a person. The relationship between these two Persons is one of Infinite Love. That love, because infinite, is also a person, the Spirit. These three Persons share the same divine nature of which there is only one.

Though not a proof of the Trinity, this is a rational explanation of the doctrine. But Arius' idea of God as the Father with two lesser divinities is as rational a construct as Augustine's presentation of the Trinity. For that matter, the Sabellian and tritheistic explanations of the three and one biblical descriptions are equally rational. Which of these rational explanations is the correct one? Early Christians did indeed recognize reason as a divine tool, the use of which is a participation in the very nature of God. But, they thought, there are clearly some concerns, such as a proof of the Trinity, which lie beyond the scope of a finite mind.

6. Apostolic Authority

Despite its limitations, early Christians did indeed accept and employ reason in their efforts to discover the content and elaborate the implications of their faith. They accepted, as well, the authority of Scripture, inspiration, and tradition–despite the sometimes ambiguous and even conflicting answers which each of these provided. We have already alluded to some of the supporters of these means to truth: Papias of Hierapolis, Clement of Alexandria, and Augustine of Hippo. Their authority was undoubtedly recognized because of their incisive intellects and cogent arguments, but it would seem that their teachings derived at least some authority from their role as institutional leaders in the various Christian communities.

Even in the earliest days of Christianity some elementary organization was necessary. The preaching of Paul, for example, led to the formation of small communities which required some structural basis for carrying on their Christian commitment when the preacher moved on. Paul's first letter to the Corinthians tells us that members of that community were called by the Spirit to serve as teachers, healers, helpers, and administrators, among other ministries. Presbyters (or elders) were assigned to conduct worship services, and, at least sometimes, Paul ordained them to this ministry by laying his hands on their heads. The elders of the congregation at Ephesus received a pauline letter appointing them overseers of the community. The word used is *episkopoi*, which today we translate as bishops, but "supervisors" would probably convey better the original meaning. At any rate, "elders" and "supervisors" were names for the same function.

Paul also reminded the community at Corinth that they are members of the body of Christ and thus responsible for the well-being of all other communities. This responsibility was often met by letters from one Christian community to its sister Church. Very early in the history of Christianity (c. 95), the church community of Rome addressed a letter of support and advice to its sister Church at Corinth. The letter was written by the bishop of Rome, Clement, on behalf of his community. Clement, it would seem, was the sole overseer of the Roman community. An affirmation of this sort of structure is explicit in a letter of the year 110 by Ignatius, the overseer (or bishop) of the congregation of Antioch.

Ignatius' letter to the community at Ephesus was written while he was a prisoner on his way to be fed to the wild beasts of the Roman Colosseum. In this epistle Ignatius endorsed a church organization expanding to meet the needs of growing communities. Ignatius first exhorted the Ephesians "to live in harmony with the mind of God." "As Jesus Christ," he continued, "is the mind of the Father, so the bishops represent the mind of Jesus Christ." And thus, Ignatius argued, "it is proper for you to act in agreement with the mind of the bishop." Ignatius then employed a musical metaphor to evoke an arresting harmony in the Ephesian church. In it the presbyters are in harmony with the bishop "as completely as the strings with a harp." In it the rest of the folk "...form a choir, so that, joining the symphony by your concord, and by your unity taking the key note from God, you may with one voice sing a song to the Father through Jesus Christ." In Ignatius' time it is clear that the bishop was thought to be the representative of Christ in his service to the community. He presided at the celebratory reenactment of the Last Supper, sometimes called the Eucharist, sometimes communion. The bishop baptized initiates and led the congregation in witnessing marriages. He spoke to his congregation as its teacher, and he spoke for his community through his letters to other Christian communities. What was the source of this acknowledged authority?

Toward the end of the second century, sometime about 185 or so, Irenaeus, bishop of Lyon (in modern day France), gave an answer to this question which became universally accepted. Faced with varied interpretations, with differing traditions and rational explanations, Irenaeus urged "those who wish to discern the truth to consult the tradition of the Apostles made manifest in every Church throughout the whole world." According to Irenaeus, the Apostles had learned the basic truths of Christianity from Jesus Christ himself. They had then appointed and ordained bishops in the Churches of the world, in the process conveying to them fundamental Christian teachings. These bishops had handed down to their successors their apostolic authority. The advantages of apostolic authority over inspiration or oral tradition are clear. In the early Church, bishops were elected by the clergy and people of their area, their diocese. Bishops of neighboring areas were called in, often to observe and guide the process, but always to lay their hands on the head of the newly elect. This historical event made it clear to everyone who was the authentic holder of apostolic authority.

This answer was not, however, foolproof. Bishops could, and did, disagree, even about fundamental doctrinal matters. Local and regional consensus was often reached by bishops meeting together in synods or councils. But sometimes disagreements over fundamental questions–like the Trinity or the relationship of Christ's humanity to his divinity–were so divisive and disruptive to political as well as religious order that the Roman emperors, themselves Christian from the fourth century on, would call a council representing the universal Church, an ecumenical council. The first of these councils was held at Nicaea in 325, and it adopted a strongly trinitarian position. This position was reiterated in 381, at the Council of Constantinople, and this doctrinal statement, or creed, is today affirmed by most Christian Churches.

Conflicting factions in the Church led, however, to holding two councils in quick and contentious succession. One, the so-called robber council, was held at Ephesus in 449, the other at Chalcedon in 451. Both claimed to be ecumenical, though they held radically differing positions on whether Jesus was truly human. Attempting to secure and maintain the unity of the Church, many early Christians, understanding Peter as the leader of the apostles, located that leadership in the bishop of Rome, whom they saw as Peter's successor. In 251, Cyprian, bishop of Carthage (in North Africa) wrote that the authority of the bishops was "one and undivided." All the apostles and, hence, all their successors, the bishops, had been sent out by Christ, and thus received the same, equal "dignity and power." Nevertheless, Christ had designated a symbol of unity in Peter and his successors–although Cyprian was hardly deferential in his sometimes stormy relations with Rome. In 381, the ecumenical Council of Constantinople affirmed the primacy of Rome as the seat of the "first bishop" of the Church. The year before, the emperor Theodosius had decreed that, to be authentic, a creed must meet the approval of the Roman bishop. Leo I, bishop of Rome from 440 to 461, went much further and claimed that, as the successor, heir, and representative of Peter, he was the head bishop of the Church. It is clear that Leo's contemporaries allowed the bishop of Rome a leading role in the determination of doctrine, but they would have surely contested his right to make policy or administrative decisions affecting Churches other than his own. Leo was neither the infallible pope nor the "supreme pontiff" of the nineteenth- and twentieth-century papacy.

By luck or design, early Christians had worked out methods through which the teachings of Jesus could be discovered and the doctrinal consequences made clear. Early Christians esteemed the written word of Scripture, believed in the inspiration of the Holy Spirit, accepted the truth of tradition, applied the reason learned from philosophers, and deferred to the authority they thought resided in their bishops as a legacy of the apostles. Christians came to rely on all these means of discovering the contents of their faith, and the conclusions of each method impinged on and influenced the answers given by the others. Christians also came to believe that the conclusions provided by all these methods were complementary and ultimately one. It had taken some 400 years to work all this out, but by that time Christians were confident they had at their disposal the means of discovering Christian truth.

C. Early Christian Spirituality

Almost all early Christian thinkers, as we have seen, accepted everyone who lived according to Reason as a fellow Christian. By this standard, pagan philosophers and their philosophies were easily baptized and employed in the quest for authentic Christian doctrine. Foremost among these philosophers were, of course, Plato and Aristotle. Early Christian thinkers found Greek categories–like substance, accident, and, as we have seen, person and nature–essential tools in the discovery and explication of Christian doctrine. But faced with a choice between Aristotle and Plato's very different approaches to fundamental reality, early Christian thinkers chose Plato. Or, rather, they chose the form of Platonism widely held in the second through fifth centuries of the Christian era. That Neo-platonism had produced the splendid system of Plotinus (205-270) and was well communicated to Christians by the thought of Proclus (410-485).

According to the Neo-platonic view of reality, there exists a totally transcendent "One," pure spirit whose being overflows into a series of lesser beings. All that is spiritual in nature is arranged hierarchically according to its degree of likeness to the One. At the bottom of the hierarchy of being, just above nothingness, are matter and material things. Midway between lowly matter and pure spirit are humans, who occupy that position because they are both material and spiritual. Neo-platonists saw the human body as immensely inferior to the human spirit. Christian Neo-platonists substituted "God" for the "One" and insisted that God was the active Creator of all lesser beings. But they kept the hierarchy of spiritual beings, eventually assigning them names drawn from Jewish and Christian sources, like angels and archangels and a whole host of superior angelic beings called seraphim and cherubim, thrones and dominations, principalities and powers.

The impact of Neo-platonism on Christian spirituality was profound. Since the universe is arranged hierarchically, with spirit immeasurably superior to matter, the goal of the Christian must be to transcend his or her material nature by overcoming the "flesh." Rigorous asceticism is necessary to overcome the material body, and free the soul or spirit. Harsh fasting, extended sleeplessness, and the rigid rejection of any sort of sex were all practices widespread among early Christians, especially among monks who fled to the deserts of Egypt, Palestine, and Syria to escape the enticements of the flesh and contamination by the world.

This early Christian view of the path to perfection was supported and reinforced by an essentially Neo-platonic anthropology–or view of human nature. Clearly, if the spiritual journey is a pursuit of perfection, then that perfection is determined by the nature of the being that is to be perfected. The happiness of human beings necessarily depends on what human beings are.

Augustine of Hippo (354-430), whom we have met before, offers a splendidly sophisticated version of Christian anthropology in its Neo-platonic form. By far the most important component of the human being is, for Augustine, the soul. That soul has, in turn, three components or faculties: the intellect which knows, the memory which remembers, and the will which chooses. What is missing from this description of the soul is any mention of passion or emotion, despite the fact that Augustine's autobiography, *The Confessions*, reveals him as an intensely passionate man. That work also reveals a man whose overriding goal is union with God, but who sees that as possible only through liberation from human passion and its source in the material body. Indeed, one gets the distinct impression from Augustine–and from many other Christian Neo-platonists as well–that a human being is a soul incidentally, accidentally, and unfortunately inhabiting a body.

Augustine's life-long struggle to overcome his own material being and physical impulses is well illustrated by his attitude toward sex. Sexual desire was for him a "disease of the flesh," "a lust that could never be sated." Even non-venereal vice was often described by Augustine in sexual terms, and thus sexual desire became a compelling metaphor for all sin. Moral conversion was seen by Augustine largely in terms of the rejection of sexual activity. And thus, even for spouses to seek sexual pleasure is sinful–though somewhat less serious than sexual activity outside of marriage. However, Augustine advised against marriage, which he saw as excusable only as an alternative to fornication.

Virtually all early Christian teaching on the nature of the Church–at least from the fourth century on–followed logically from a Neo-platonic understanding of the hierarchical nature of the universe and its derivative anthropology and spirituality. The Church itself was seen as hierarchical, though the hierarchy here is not that of which we ordinarily think. At the summit of the early Christian hierarchy were monks, "holy and inspired men," those who through their rigorous asceticism had distanced their spirits from the world, the flesh, and the devil. Below monks came the clergy, respected because of their ministry, but too involved in the world to be intensely spiritual. At the bottom of the hierarchy were the laity, living in the world with their spouses, and thus still less spiritual. The function of these marginally spiritual people was to pray, pay, and obey. And, of course, to procreate chastely–for from what other source could come the holy monks at the top of this hierarchy?

The Neo-platonic world-view is also reflected in early Christian Christology, their thinking about Jesus. After the Council of Chalcedon (451), most Christians had agreed that Jesus is one person with two natures: divine and human. But among early Christians it was surely the divine nature of Christ which received the most attention–and his divinity continues to be the focus of the Christology of the eastern, or Orthodox, Churches to our day. This view is vividly illustrated by the portrayals of Christ which dominate the interiors of eastern churches and western churches influenced by the artistic expressions of Orthodox Christology. On the central domes, or on the half-domes above the altar areas, are representations of Christ–generally only his head and upper body–with his arms outstretched, signifying his divine dominion over the whole world. He is *Christos pantokrator*, Christ the all-powerful ruler. Before his frowning face one stands fearful, in dread of his awesome divinity and severe justice. The human being is seen as weak and lowly in the presence of the overwhelming force of this very divine Christ.

D. Christianity as the Imperial Religion

Surely the most formidable institution of the world in which the early Church lived was the Roman Empire. The initial Roman reaction to Christianity had been both confused and unfriendly. The refusal by Christians to worship the emperor worried Romans. For most people residing in the Roman Empire, burning incense before the statue of a Caesar thought to be godlike was the equivalent of a pledge of allegiance to the state. What Christians saw as a matter of conscience seemed to many Romans to threaten the unity of the state, especially since they saw Christians as both superstitious and atheistic. These strange Christians insisted on meeting in what seemed to be conspiratorial secrecy and sometimes refused to serve in the army.

From the time of Nero (54-68 A.D.) onward, Christians suffered from intermittent persecutions, most of them localized yet some severe. A particularly threatening persecution–threatening because widespread and extremely harsh–was initiated in 303 by the emperor Diocletian (284-305). Only ten years later, however, the emperor Constantine (306-337) proclaimed a policy of toleration for all religions of the Empire.

With the notable exception of Emperor Julian "the Apostate," who, during his brief reign, 361-363, abandoned Christianity in an attempt to introduce a reformed paganism, all the Roman emperors after Constantine were Christians. By the reign of Emperor Theodosius (379-395), the tide had turned completely. Edicts for the suppression of paganism were issued, many pagan temples were destroyed or converted into Christian churches, and the Roman state not only protected but fostered the Church. During the following century, most of the inhabitants of the Empire became at least nominal Christians.

Christianity had become the state religion. This brought both advantages and drawbacks. The Christian clergy were now freed from the burden of taxation, and the Church was permitted to receive legacies, which placed the institution on a firm financial footing. The education of the Christian clergy was accomplished, as we remember, through study of the liberal arts, a system long employed by the Roman state to train its administrators and judges. Armed with this training, bishops were given the authority and responsibility to try all civil cases in which one of the litigants was a Christian–by this time a nearly universal circumstance. Christian clergymen had become, in effect, agents of the state.

The price of this new status was an increasing threat to the Church's independence. Roman emperors, wary of diversity of opinion, attempted to control the Church in matters of both belief and practice. They often appointed bishops, and they treated the Church as if it were a branch of the government. Most early Christians were so grateful to that government for its support that they were willing to live with its control–and this relationship has continued to this day in the Orthodox Churches of Greece, Russia, and other eastern cultures and countries.

Two notable exceptions to this pattern of Church-state relations were Ambrose of Milan (c. 340-397) and Gelasius I, bishop of Rome from 492 to 496. Ambrose was bishop of Milan in the late fourth century, by which time that city had become the seat of imperial power in the West, and consequently its bishop was often in contact with–sometimes in conflict with–the emperors. Ambrose was forced to formulate and declare his position by a massacre ordered by Theodosius I, the same emperor who had made Christianity the religion of the Empire. Theodosius had heard reports of treasonable plots in Thessalonica. As the citizens of that northern Greek city were assembled in their hippodrome to cheer on their favorite charioteers, Theodosius' soldiers attacked them, and thousands were slain. Ambrose heard of this and forbad Theodosius entering the cathedral church at Milan. Ambrose knew that no state can tolerate treason and live, but he was convinced that Theodosius should have separated the innocent from the guilty before initiating wholesale executions. The killing of the innocent was murder, which was for Ambrose a moral as well as a political question. Ambrose declared: "The emperor is within the Church, not above it," that is, rulers are not free from restraint in moral questions. For Ambrose, the government must employ moral means to attain its ends, and it is the right and duty of churchmen to protest immoral behavior by state officials. As Ambrose put it, "palaces belong to the emperor, churches to the priesthood."

Gelasius I was bishop of Rome during a heated controversy between the churches of Alexandria, Constantinople, and Rome–a controversy over the relationship between the divinity and humanity of Jesus. In 482, the emperor Zeno sought to bring peace to his domains by issuing a statement of faith in the form of a creed, and this creed pleased no one. In 484, before his election as bishop, Gelasius wrote to the emperor: "The bishops of the Church, knowing that the empire has been conferred on you by the action of God, are, therefore, obedient to your laws dealing with material matters." On the other hand, said Gelasius, questions concerning the faith and discipline of the Christian Church are within the spiritual jurisdiction of the bishops, "so that, in such matters, you ought to depend on ecclesiastical judgment, instead of seeking to bend it to your own will."

Ever since the time of Gelasius, the insistence on a separation of ecclesiastical and temporal jurisdictions has been referred to as a reflection of the "Gelasian doctrine." The notion that the temporal authorities should control the Church and churchmen–a system for which the word Caesaropapism would be coined–lived on, however, and flourished. The conflict between adherents of these two theories would be one of the most important features of the Church's life in the world, of the relationship of Christianity to the cultures in which it was to exist.

E. The Cultures of Christian Monasticism

Virtually all the religious systems to which humans have adhered have featured, in some way or another, the institution of monasticism. Christian monasticism has assumed many forms and endured many permutations–largely as a result of the various cultures in which it has taken root.

From the beginning of their new religion, as we have seen, Christians suffered sporadic and sometimes intense persecution at the hands of the Roman state. The victims of this persecution, who openly declared their faith and refused to compromise their radically exclusive commitment to Christ, died as martyrs (witnesses). Their heroism elicited awed appreciation from their fellow Christians. Thus the lives of the martyrs became the ideal according to which a truly Christian life was measured–so much so that, at the end of the second century, Ignatius of Antioch would declare that one could only be a complete Christian by dying for Christ's sake. A martyr's exemplary life was that of a Christopher, a Christ-bearer, and the martyr's death led in a unique way to union with Christ.

In the course of the third and fourth centuries, as martyrdom became less likely, a new mode of Christian life emerged which called for the same total commitment as martyrdom. Monasticism became, for many, the truest, the most complete way of following Christ, prized as the most efficacious means to personal sanctification. Celibacy, viewed as an imitation of the life style of Jesus, became a widespread practice. Tertullian called these celibates brides of Christ.

The desire for total commitment to Christ took many forms in the early Church–forms heavily influenced by the geographic location and cultural orientation in which the monastic impulse flourished. Egyptian monasticism, for example, was largely a child of the desert. Although Egypt occupies much space on a modern map of Africa, its inhabitable area is largely limited to the five to fifteen mile wide alluvial plain on either side of the river Nile. When monks, both male and female, wished to embrace the Christian life intensely, they had to migrate but a few hundred yards from their village into the desert.

Many of these monks sought the solitary way of life of a hermit. They wished to live alone, though their reputation for sanctity often brought disciples to sit at their feet. Each day the monk would recite from memory all 150 psalms. Monks occupied their bodies in activities conducive to their prayer, often weaving mats which they traded to village women for food and their few necessities. These hermits were men and women of the desert. These were warrior monks and nuns who mastered their bodies through sleeplessness and fasting, who furiously battled the demons of their visions. These warriors, most of them ill-educated farmers, had no knowledge of, or use for, theological subtleties; they knew little of the saving role of Christ in their lives. Whether living alone as hermits, or in large, structured communities as "cenobites," theirs was a life of extreme asceticism, a life which became immensely popular in the eastern parts of the Roman Empire–in Egypt, Palestine, and Syria. That it did not succeed so well in the West–save for relatively few locations in Gaul–was due, at least in part, to its extreme asceticism. However, the Irish, newly converted in the fifth century, whose cattle-herding culture lacked both cities and commerce, embraced the harsh rigors of eastern monasticism with eager enthusiasm.

The urban and urbane sophistication of the Greek-speaking areas of the Roman Empire provided a radically different milieu for an equally flourishing form of monasticism. The central figures in the emergence of Greek monasticism were the so-called Cappadocian Fathers, highly-educated intellectuals who, in the fourth century, aimed at making Christianity accessible to a sophisticated Greek world. One of these Fathers, Basil, was to become the undisputed leader of the Roman East as bishop of Caesarea in Cappadocia–a Roman province on the southern shore of the Black Sea. Before Basil became bishop, he had retired deep into the countryside to live the life of a monk.

Indeed, Basil wrote a set of spiritual guidelines for monks which survived his death in 379, and which still today provides the guiding force in Eastern and Orthodox monasticism. Basil's "rule" reflects the culture of its Greek author. It contains relatively little on the structure and running of a monastery. Basil tells us much, however, about how to attain a deep relationship with God through growth in virtue. Basil's "rule" displays his profound insights into human psychology. That "rule" reflects a view of God, the universe, and human nature derived from the Platonism that also influenced Augustine.

The monastic rule which carried the day in the Roman West was written in the early sixth century by Benedict of Nursia. Although Benedict's *Rule* contains much of value to the spiritual life, it is primarily a straightforward statement of how to structure and run a monastery. In this it reflects the down-to-earth pragmatism of the Roman West, and the *Rule*'s practicality ensured its adoption and the subsequent success of monasticism among western Christians.

Benedict's *Rule* is characterized by moderation. The prayer life of his monks was structured around the recitation of the psalms, but, unlike the Egyptian practice, Benedict's monks prayed the 150 psalms in a week–not a day. Communal reading of the Bible and private meditation on the Scriptures occupied much of the day. Everyone in Benedict's monastery engaged in physical labor. This work sustained the monks economically, but it also reflected Benedict's view that God can be glorified through all human activities. Benedict took physical things seriously; he was no Platonist. Simple but ample food and drink provided the monastic fare. Seven hours of sleep were provided–and also naps when necessary. Benedict instructed his monks to treat their tools with the same reverence accorded the chalice on the altar.

Benedict's monastery was a Roman household. But it was a Roman household of God, a Roman attempt to lead a totally dedicated Christian life. Benedict's monks belonged to a family characterized by fraternal love. Their monastery was a school in which they learned through experience to live a life of virtue. The monks were fellow pilgrims on the path to perfection in God. It is no wonder that Benedict's *Rule* has provided the principle underpinning for western monasteries, both male and female, to this day.

Of course cultural forces would influence the forms western monasticism would take in the ages since Benedict's death in 547. Benedict's younger contemporary, Cassiodorus (c. 490-580), brought to monasticism a vigorous intellectual life based on classical culture. As we shall see, the successful mission of a monk, Augustine of Canterbury, to sixth-century England and the equally effective mission to eighth-century Germany of another monk, Boniface, turned many monasteries into centers for the conversion of the frontier folk of early medieval Europe. One of the results of this was that, by the year 800, most monks were priests, ordained to serve the spiritual needs of the people they had converted. Christianity was to inform the culture of non-Roman peoples; in turn the culture of those people would influence the way Christianity was lived–and not only in monasteries.

III. CREATING A NEW CHRISTIAN CULTURE

Some Useful Data

c. 55-117	Tacitus, Roman historian
481-511	Clovis, king of the Franks
c. 454-526	Theodoric, king of the Ostrogoths
527-565	reign of Justinian I, emperor
538-594	Gregory, bishop of Tours
590-604	reign of Gregory I, bishop of Rome
605	death of Augustine of Canterbury
673-735	Bede, monk and historian
c. 680-755	Boniface, apostle to the Germans
752-757	reign of Stephen II, bishop of Rome
741-768	reign of Pepin the Short, king of the Franks
735-804	Alcuin of York, monk and scholar
814	death of Charles the Great, king of the Franks from 768, emperor from 800
795-816	reign of Leo III, bishop of Rome
c. 770-840	Einhard, biographer of Charles the Great

A. A Clash of Cultures

The Christian-Roman culture of the first centuries lived on during and after the decline and eventual demise of Roman political rule. But, from the fourth century on, the Christian Church was increasingly faced with a new and radically different culture, that of the various Germanic peoples who, by the sixth century, had become the new rulers of western Europe.

As Germanic tribes migrated to the borders of the Roman Empire, and then entered it to form new kingdoms across the West, their culture was much modified by their contact with, and eager embrace of, Roman institutions and Christian values. To ascertain the details of pre-migration Germanic culture–the raw material, so to speak, of the early medieval cultural confrontation–is difficult, because that culture had no written language. Fortunately, about the year 100 A.D. the Roman historian Tacitus published a detailed account of what he knew about the Germans in a work called, appropriately enough, *Germania*.

One of the best keys to understanding the values of a culture is an examination of its leadership qualifications, for in every society leaders are expected to exhibit the virtues of that society to an exemplary degree. The Germanic leader exhibited superior strength and agility because his task was to lead men in the hunt and into battle, thereby providing nourishment and protection for his small society. Knowledge of weapons and their use was critical to both hunt and war, and this know-how was especially needed by the man who led these, the vigorous and virtually constant activities of the tribesmen. To be successful meant courageously confronting and overcoming a dangerously powerful opponent, whether human or wild animal.

The educational system that formed and fostered the development of these virtues was apprenticeship. Youths accompanied their fathers on the hunt or into battle, observed their fathers' techniques, and then were assigned increasingly demanding tasks through which to prepare for their eventual proficiency in full-scale battle or arduous hunt. Even after the warriors of medieval Europe no longer needed to procure their own food–for reasons which we shall address later–they spent much of the year in the hunt, which required the same skills and strength as those needed for battle.

Another means of developing strength and skill was involvement in intense and demanding games. "About these games," Tacitus wrote, "naked youths leap and dance among life-threatening swords and spears. Constant practice has endowed them with skill. Skill has conferred grace....The pleasure of the spectators is the sole reward for their reckless daring." One German pastime Tacitus considered a "bad practice." He complained: "They indulge in games of chance...with such disregard for winning or losing that, when everything else has been gambled away, they stake their very liberty on the last and decisive throw. The loser goes into voluntary slavery....This stubborn practice they call honor." What Tacitus failed to understand is that both battle and hunt require a heroic willingness to wager one's life for the welfare of the community.

Another early Germanic educational practice which was to live on in western culture was story-telling. After a long day of tracking, and perhaps killing prey, the men would gather around the camp fire–later the great fireplace in the lord's hall–to share stories of battles heroically won and heroes whose strength had overcome monsters, dragons, and giants. These stories have so stirred the western soul that some of them–the marvelously crafted Anglo-Saxon epic poem *Beowulf*, for example–have come down to us.

A society protected and fed has still other needs. Among them is a means of settling disputes, of seeking the peaceful ordering of society which we call justice. Lacking a public institution, a government, to provide police and judicial services, the Germanic family and its extension, the tribe, cared for its own and avenged wrongs done to them. A murder of a family member would bring down the equally murderous wrath of the victim's kinsmen on the perpetrator. But the slain murderer's family could–and often did–then seek to avenge the retributive killing of their kinsman. Pursued to its wrathful end, revenge could become feud. For the sake of peace and order, Germanic tribes instituted a simple but effective process. The family of the initially wronged man would bring the matter before the assembled tribe, which then judged the case and assigned a fine, the *wergild*, a payment that varied according to the economic value of the dead person to his family.

What did that family ask of its members in return for protection and justice? It required of the men, of course, warfare against enemies and the fruit of the hunt. Of women more was expected than child bearing and nurturing. They cultivated the small fields surrounding their village. They served as prophets and soothsayers. Women even had a role in battle, standing close at hand to urge on the warriors, to supply provisions, and to bind up wounds. Women, Tacitus related, served as the most sacred witnesses of a warrior's bravery; they were known to rally their men by baring their breasts to the enemies' weapons.

The bravery of these women and their men won from their families and tribes the highest reward, honor. Conversely, the harshest punishment which could be meted out by the tribe was not execution, but disgrace. "It is the greatest ignominy," Tacitus wrote, "to leave one's shield on the field. It is unlawful for a man so disgraced to be present at the sacred rites or enter the tribal assembly. So many who have run from battle have ended their shame with a noose."

These were the Germanic people who migrated from central and eastern Europe into the western Roman Empire in the fourth and the fifth centuries. Some of them, called Visigoths, marched into the Iberian peninsula and southern Gaul. Their relatives, the Ostrogoths, migrated into Italy and Provence. The Burgundians settled in the valley of the Rhone. Some Saxons and their kin sailed across the North Sea to England, and the Franks expanded from their homeland along the Rhine and Main rivers to inhabit what is now northern France and Belgium. All but the Franks and Saxons had been converted to Christianity, but to its Arian, anti-trinitarian form, and these Arians kept themselves aloof from their orthodox subjects. Over time, however, these peoples converted to trinitarian orthodoxy and eventually disappeared as a distinguishable people through intermarriage with the Roman populace that vastly outnumbered them. To the pagan Saxons we shall return, but the people who will occupy our attention now are the equally pagan Franks.

B. Clovis and His Franks: The Demise of Germanic Values

Unlike the other Germanic peoples, the Franks did not migrate. Rather, they expanded from the valleys of the Rhine and Main rivers into northern Gaul. From there they conquered the rest of the Roman province of Gaul by subduing the Visigoths in what is today southwestern France, the Ostrogoths in southeastern France, Alemanians in southwestern Germany, and Burgundians who ruled what is now east-central France.

Much of this conquest was accomplished under the leadership of Chlodovech, a war chieftain whom we call Clovis. The history of the Franks under Clovis and his immediate successors was written by Bishop Gregory of Tours, a native of Gaul, who lived from 538 to 594. Gregory tells us first of the Frankish conquest in 486 of the last Roman-ruled territory in the West, the area around Paris. Syagrius, the Roman governor, was executed and his province, including its churches, looted. Among the loot, Gregory tells us, was a "vase of wondrous size and beauty." The bishop of the despoiled church sent a message to Clovis begging for the return of the vase. Clovis' response to the bishop's messenger tells us much about early Frankish culture: "Follow us as far as Soissons, for all that has been taken will be divided there. If the lot awards me that vase, I shall do what the father asks." Before Clovis received his one share of the booty, a share whose contents he could not select, he asked his warriors to grant him the vase over and above his legitimate share. Whereupon one of the warriors "lifted his battle-ax and struck the vase, crying out in a loud voice: 'You will get nothing here but what the lot fairly bestows on you.'" Clearly, Clovis was a war leader, not the king Gregory calls him, for his power depended on the loyalty of his followers.

One year later, Clovis was conducting a review of his troops when he came upon the warrior who had struck the vase. Clovis verbally abused him: "No one has brought armor so carelessly kept as you. Neither your spear nor sword nor ax are in serviceable shape." Clovis seized the man's ax and threw it to the ground. When the warrior bent over to pick it up, Clovis "drove his own ax into the man's head." Gregory reports that Clovis then "ordered the rest to depart," and they did, "filled with great fear." Clearly, loyalty was no longer the basis of Clovis' power. Clearly too, honor, the most important Germanic virtue, was no longer necessary for leadership.

Gregory's story encapsulates the course of a revolutionary change that took a number of years to complete. The story graphically recounts a shift in the power base of Clovis, a chieftain become king. As a Germanic warrior the only people and things over which he had absolute control were those that belonged to him: his wife and his children, his sword, shield, spear, and battle-ax. Now he had acceded to the power and authority of a Roman governor, who had had jurisdiction, but, of course, not ownership over his province. Jurisdiction was an abstract concept beyond the ken of Clovis. Northern Gaul was his, he owned it, and he treated it like any other of his possessions—even dividing it among his sons at his death. Land was the new source of power. By distributing it among his followers he could now buy the loyalty he had previously had to earn.

As the power base of the Frankish ruler had changed, so too had traditional Germanic values. Gregory's *History* is replete with stories of treachery and betrayal, of murder and mayhem directed against members of one's own family. We learn, for example, that Gundobad, a Burgundian prince, "killed his brother Chilperic with a sword and threw his wife into a lake with a stone tied around her neck." Godegisel, another of Gundobad's brothers and his bitter enemy, approached Clovis with the promise of annual tribute in return for help against his brother, and Clovis "accepted this offer gladly." Gundobad was defeated by the allies, but, when Godegisel regained his power, he refused to pay the promised tribute. Gundobad then took up his brother's promise and won Clovis' support. Godegisel sought refuge in a cathedral, but to no avail. He was slaughtered there along with the bishop. Brother betraying brother, sons sometimes slaying fathers—all this shows that the old Germanic virtue of familial loyalty had all but disappeared. Honor had been the goal of early Germans; now their greatest ambition was power.

C. The Meeting of Christian and Germanic Cultures

Traditional Germanic values had been turned upside down. But what were the values and institutions of the Christian people in the land now ruled by the Franks? At first nothing changed, because the pagan Franks were ignorant of and indifferent to Christianity. Christian communities in Frankish Gaul continued to elect their leaders, the bishops, and those bishops were expected to display the traditional leadership qualifications of virtue and learning—learning, we remember, that was rooted in the liberal arts. For the moment, the now centuries-old fusion of Christian and classical values survived.

But that cultural fusion would not survive the conversion of Clovis. In 496, a war with the Alemanians (living in today's southwest Germany and Alsace) led to a battle nearly disastrous for Clovis: "There was much slaughter, and Clovis' army was in danger of destruction." Clovis' astute response was to appeal to the power of his wife's God:

> Jesus Christ, whom Clotilda asserts is the Son of the living God, you are said to give aid in distress and bestow victory on those who hope in

you. I beseech the glory of your aid, with the vow that, if you grant me victory,...I will believe in you and be baptized in your name.

The Alemanians were indeed defeated, and Clovis cheerfully lived up to his part of the bargain. Baptism he thought an unbelievably cheap price to pay for victory. And, we are told, 3000 of Clovis' loyal warriors followed him as bravely into baptism as they had into battle.

Baptism, however, had absolutely no effect on Clovis' behavior. He continued to betray his allies and kill off his kinfolk. Clovis' Christianity merely provided him an excuse for further conquest. Of the Visigoths who ruled southern Gaul, Clovis now declared: "I take it very hard that these Arian heretics hold part of Gaul. Let us go with God's help and conquer them." Christianity was for Clovis and his Franks an additional source of power, not a guide to ethical behavior, not a life-altering relationship.

It was the Church's wealth, not its moral code, which attracted the cupidity of Clovis and his successors. Over the centuries, churches had accumulated a great deal of land through donations by pious Christians. Land meant wealth and power to the Franks, and so they quickly stepped in to control the elections of new bishops. Traditional Christian leadership qualifications went out the window. The new breed of bishops were likely to be the bastard sons or old drinking buddies of local Frankish lords. Their virtues were prowess in battle, at the table, and, often, of sexual conquest. The meeting of Christian-Roman and Germanic cultures had virtually destroyed both.

D. Missionary Activity and Cultural Continuity

The mutation and near destruction of classical, Christian, and Germanic values did not affect all of Europe. In a great circle around Frankish Gaul–in Italy, in England, and in Germany–the leadership qualifications in the Church remained as they had been: virtue and learning.

Curiously enough, Italy's tumultuous history during the sixth century accounts for the stability of its Christian and classical values and institutions. The century began with the rule of Clovis' contemporary, Theodoric the Ostrogoth. The Ostrogoths were Arians and lived apart from their orthodox, trinitarian subjects, interfering little with their Church. The Ostrogoths were few in number and encouraged the continuation of the well-ordered apparatus of Roman administration. Theodoric saw to it that aqueducts were repaired and schools of law and rhetoric flourished. He fostered a revival of classical art as well, the coins of his reign, for example, showing a high degree of artistic taste and skill.

All this came to an end in the years following 535, in the wake of an invasion from the East, an invasion not by Germans but by Romans, Greek-speaking Romans whose ambitious emperor was Justinian (527-565) and whose capital city was Constantinople (today's Istanbul). Justinian had in his service the greatest general of the time, an astute warrior named Belisarius. The wars that Belisarius initiated, and that lasted until 552, caused more devastation than all the comings and going of Germanic peoples had in the past two centuries. But the Byzantines—as we call the peoples of the Eastern Roman Empire—were unable to defend the Italy they had at great cost largely won. In 568, another group of Germans, the Lombards, swarmed over the Alps and established a kingdom in northern Italy and two isolated duchies in the interior of the South. The Byzantines kept their tenuous hold on several strips of coastal lands that included a number of the larger cities, Rome among them. When the Lombards attacked these territories, resistance to the new Arian invaders usually devolved upon bishops, who, as a consequence, became civil and military leaders as well as spiritual shepherds. Thus protected and governed, the churches of Italy remained largely free to choose bishops with appropriate leadership qualifications, including virtue and learning. And so Christian and classical culture lived on in Italy.

From one of these churches, the Church of Rome, much of the remaining areas of pagan Europe, notably England, were christianized. The story of the mission to England and its conversion was told by a well-educated and highly sophisticated historian, an Anglo-Saxon monk named Bede, who lived from 673 to 735. Bede credited the christianization of England to Gregory I (often called "the Great"), a bishop of Rome who lived from 540 to 604, more than one hundred years before Bede.

Gregory was a man of great talent and wealth who entered public service and became prefect (governor) of the city of Rome under the nominal Byzantine rule. In 574, Gregory left this career behind, however, to establish a monastery on his family's lands near Rome. Gregory the monk and abbot was entrusted with many tasks by the bishop of Rome, including that of ambassador to Constantinople. In 590, the people of Rome saw fit to elect him bishop, and he took charge of both the spiritual and temporal affairs of the city. Gregory directed the defense of the city against Lombard incursions, reorganized the Roman Church's lands in southern Italy so that his people could be fed, and set up regional courts to provide order and justice.

Before Gregory became bishop, Bede tells us, he was wandering one day through the market-place of Rome where he came across some captives offered for sale. They were pagans who "had fair complexions, finely cut features, and handsome hair." Gregory inquired about their native land, and was told "the island of Britain." Gregory asked for the name of the lads' people, and the answer was "Angles." "Only right," said Gregory, "for they have the faces of angels and will be joint-heirs with the angels in heaven." Gregory resolved to set out on a mission to convert these pagan Anglo-Saxons whom he had called "angels," but his bishop could not spare the loss of his service.

But when Gregory assumed the see of Saint Peter, he sent a band of his monks, under the leadership of a reluctant Augustine, "to preach the word of God to the English nation." When the little band reached the English kingdom of Kent, they discovered that the king's wife was already a Christian. They were given a house, and "they began to emulate the life of the apostles," thus practicing what they preached. "Before long," Bede tells us, "a number of the heathen, admiring the simplicity of their lives and the comfort of their heavenly message, believed and were baptized."

This success brought the ever anxious Augustine perplexing problems, the answers to which he sought from Gregory. One question concerned pagan temples and their blood-stained altars. Gregory's response was that "the temples of the idols among that people should on no account be destroyed." Purified of pagan influence by the liberal sprinkling of holy water, the temples should be "dedicated to the service of the true God," and the new converts could thus "flock eagerly to their traditional places of worship." Gregory added that, "since they have had a custom of sacrificing oxen to their pagan gods, they should continue that practice on special Christian feast days." Surely, no such ox roast took place after the liturgy at Gregory's cathedral in Rome, the church of Saint John Lateran. Yet Gregory cheerfully condoned the pagan practices of the Germanic people of England. Gregory was quite comfortable with celebrating the Eucharist or Lord's Supper on altars once dedicated to animal and even human sacrifice.

E. Baptizing Germanic Culture

Gregory's letter articulates a position which was to transform both Church and culture. Gregory was a learned Roman and a devout Christian, the descendant of early Christian forbears who had synthesized classical culture and Christian beliefs and practices. In Gregory's time all Romans were Christians and all Christians were Romans–at least culturally. Was it possible for another culture to be a vehicle for Christianity?

A person's answer to this question is always a function of that person's anthropology, his or her view of human nature. If the human condition is depravity due to original sin, then the culture produced by such benighted souls must be evil, and Christianity must stand in opposition to the culture of the "world." Americans are bound to think here of fundamentalist prohibitions of dance and drink, of makeup and movies. Another Christian attitude toward culture–one characteristic of post-Reformation Germany–is based on the same premise of human depravity, but the response is to live with and suffer the effects of "worldly" culture, especially its expression in oppressive government. Another, and nearly universal tendency in responding to the problem of Christianity and culture, is to identify the two. This identification makes it possible for a person to believe that his or her way of doing or expressing Christianity is God's way. For example, many Roman Catholics might surmise that God understands only Latin because their Church addressed God only in that language–at least until the middle of the twentieth century. Some Eastern Orthodox believers, on the other hand, hold that the angels speak only Greek. If true, this must make for some celestial communication problems. Issues such as the ordination of women, the celibacy of clergy, even the way one recites the Lord's Prayer, are often "settled" by reference to the "divine" origin of the traditional practices of one group or another.

Gregory's view on the relationship between Christianity and culture rejects all these positions. Gregory rejected the notion that humans are depraved because of original sin. To him humans are both graced and good–even though they sometimes succumb to sin. Hence human culture–*all* human culture–is good. And thus all cultures are potentially potent vehicles for Christian life and understanding. Gregory's view would be embraced by medieval missionaries who then proceeded to baptize all sorts of native cultural expressions.

The Anglo-Saxon people of England, for example, celebrated a week-long festival at the end of winter in honor of the goddess Eostra. As a spring goddess, Eostra was also a fertility goddess–whose well-chosen symbols were eggs and rabbits. When missionary monks encountered this Germanic feast, they substituted their own great springtime celebration, the feast of the Resurrection. They now called the feast Easter–and they kept the rabbits and eggs. Germanic peoples also celebrated a feast at the winter solstice. To bring back the sun, a deep-seated longing among people north of the Alps, people would sacrifice animals and string the intestines on evergreen trees–the origin of our Christmas tree decorations.

The Germanic penchant for tales of heroism also found expression in powerful poems telling stories of Christ and his apostles turned warriors. One of these verse epics, the *Heliand* or healer, was written down in the Saxon tongue of the continent about the year 830. In it, the Germanic love for alliteration is employed to capture the hearts of the hearers. Thus the birth of the "Mightiest of Babes in Bethlehem-burg" is foretold by the prophets, "as the sages had spoken." The shepherd witnesses became "war-men on watch," and "the Child in the crib" becomes "the Master of men." The Last Supper is a banquet held in a hall at which "the [Power] Wielder did bless the wine and the bread." But "Fate is at hand,...the troth-breaker Judas," a "fiend" whom "Satan, a strong-sword foe, shall tempt in spirit." The Crucifixion is not mentioned–perhaps because it shows unheroic weakness–but Christ triumphs over "the folk-clans of the foe," who are the Romans.

Even the Crucifixion becomes a heroic scene in an Anglo-Saxon poem, *The Dream of the Rood*, composed, some scholars suppose, before the year 750. "Rood" is the Old English word for "cross," and it is the Cross which tells the tale:

> I saw the Lord of the world boldly
> > rushing to climb upon me....
> The young hero, God himself, threw
> > off his garments, determined and brave.
> Proud in the sight of men, he mounted
> > the meanest of gallows,
> > to make men's souls eternally free.

Jesus, seen as a Germanic leader, triumphs over evil through the cross: "He broke our bonds and gave us life–and a home in heaven."

Still earlier than the *Heliand* and the *Dream* is the *Boat Song* (c. 600) of the Irish missionary to Germany, Saint Columban. Columban's boat, constructed of timber "cut in the forests, sweeps down the two-horned Rhine; its keel, tight-caulked, now floats upon the sea." The *Song* admonishes its hearers:

> By virtues armed, defend yourselves with valor.
> Firm faith and holy ardor conquer all.
> The ancient fiend, defeated, breaks his arrows.
> The Source of Good and Being, the Highest Power,
> Offers the warrior and gives the victor prizes.
> Let your souls, men, remembering Christ, cry heigh-ho.

The young men of early medieval Europe, already aspiring to be great warriors, set out to emulate the greatest of warriors, Christ.

F. Rome and the Conversion of Germany

The missionaries who brought Christianity to Germany came not from neighboring Gaul, but from Ireland in the early seventh century and then, in the eighth century, from the still more successful English. Most of the Frankish bishops of Gaul were neither virtuous nor learned, and few seemed interested in pursuing an activity that would take them out of their comfortable residences to search out and convert unsympathetic tribes.

The "Apostle of the Germans" was an English monk by the name of Boniface (c. 680-755). His experience in converting the peoples east of the Rhine illustrates well why Frankish bishops did not embrace missionary efforts. One of Boniface's fellow monks, whose name was Willibald, tells us that Boniface once entered a German village and confronted the hostile inhabitants with an ax. With this tool he attacked the tree in the middle of the village; it was an oak tree sacred to the Germanic god Thor. The villagers "cursed him bitterly" but waited for Thor to destroy the desecrator. Instead, "the oak, with all its huge bulk, fell to the ground." The villagers "left off their cursing and, now believing, blessed God." Courageous as is this conversion technique, it is surely not without risk. And indeed, in 755, Boniface met his martyrdom at the hands of another group of less impressed and still more irate Germans.

Boniface had early on sought support in Rome for his mission, and, after making the long trip from England, he was there ordained bishop, in 722, by Gregory II. Boniface preached widely in the lands east of the Rhine and established numerous monasteries to serve as centers for continuing missionary activity. Designated by the bishop of Rome as archbishop for all the lands through which he had wandered, Boniface organized the churches he had established into eight dioceses stretching from Austria to northern Germany.

In 741, Boniface was sent by Bishop Zachary of Rome as his legate or ambassador to the Church in Gaul. Boniface strove mightily to reform the Frankish Church by reviving traditional leadership qualifications. His efforts at this would only bear fruit in the next generation, but Boniface's life reminds us that it was in the frontier lands of England and Germany that the values of virtue and learning were retained. The people of those lands, supported by the bishop of Rome, would bring those values back to the heartland of Europe in Gaul.

The role of the bishop of Rome in these many missions should not be underestimated. The English and German churches looked to Rome for leadership, and pilgrims from these Germanic lands flocked to visit the tombs of the apostles Peter and Paul in Rome. There was no doubt that, in the West, the bishop of Rome was becoming a leader who was more than an honorary first bishop of the Church.

G. Charles the Great and the New Synthesis

Boniface was also instrumental in the metamorphosis of Frankish Gaul from a fragmented domain of weak rulers to the overwhelmingly dominant power in Europe. This extraordinary sequence of events was initiated by the Lombard capture of the Byzantine capital of Italy, Ravenna, in 752. Rome was seriously threatened by this event, and the new bishop of Rome, Stephen II (752-757), sought help. Rome's nominal sovereign was the Roman emperor in Constantinople, but Stephen did not turn in that direction. The emperors of this period were iconoclasts opposed to the use of images in ecclesiastical art. Gregory the Great had enunciated the catholic position on this question already in the sixth century: "To adore a picture is wrong. To learn through a picture what should be adored is praiseworthy." Tension between Rome and Constantinople was high, and Stephen needed a military ally against the Lombards, not a theological discussion. He turned to a Frank, to Pepin the Short (741-768).

Pepin was the mayor of the palace, the chief officer of the king and the real ruler of the Frankish realm, and Pepin wished to rid his land of the last of Clovis' increasingly weak descendants. Stephen sanctioned Pepin's deposition of the last of Clovis' dynasty, King Childeric, and sent Boniface to solemnly anoint and crown Pepin king of the Franks. In return Pepin invaded Italy and, in 756, defeated the Lombards. He then ceded authority over the Byzantine lands in north central Italy to the bishop of Rome. This "Donation of Pepin" formed the nucleus of the territory later known as the Papal States, which endured as a political entity until 1870. Pepin was succeeded in 768 by his two sons Charles and Carloman. The latter died in 771, leaving his brother to create one of the central institutions and basic structures of European history, the reconstituted Roman Empire.

At the court of Charles the Great (or, in French, Charlemagne) lived a friend and biographer named Einhard. Einhard has left us a physical description of the king of the Franks who would become Roman emperor. Charles was a large and a strong man, well over six feet tall. Although stately and dignified in appearance, he was a robust and active man. "His neck," says Einhard, "was thick and his belly rather prominent, but the symmetry of the rest of his body concealed these defects." Charles' favorite activities–riding, hunting, and swimming–and his dress, which "differed little from that of common folk," show that he was as much Germanic chieftain as Roman emperor. Because the first business of a medieval ruler was to provide protection for his people, the Germanic virtues of physical strength, courage, and skill in arms continued to be crucial not only to Charles, but to kings and princes of the entire Middle Ages.

The education of the medieval ruler largely followed Charles' practice and program for his own sons, who, "as soon as their age permitted, had to learn to ride like true Franks and practice the arts of war and the chase." Charles and his medieval successors also followed another ancient Germanic educational practice, for "during meals there was either singing or a reader to whom he could listen. Histories and the great deeds of men of old were read." Indeed, he "had all these old, rough songs which celebrate the deeds and wars of ancient kings written out for transmission to posterity." Charles even "began a grammar of his native [Germanic] language."

Such aspirations to scholarship may seem strange in a Germanic warrior chief, but this was only the beginning of Charles' academic interests. Einhard relates that "the plan he adopted for his children's education was to have both boys and girls instructed in the liberal arts." In this his children were but following in their father's footsteps, for Charles "was such a master of Latin that he could speak it as well as his native tongue." He was less fluent in Greek, though he could understand it well. Charles would often employ his spare time to practice the writing of Greek, but the moments he could devote to that pursuit were too rare to let him win great success.

Charles brought to his court at Aachen the best scholars of England, Italy, and Germany. Thus the periphery of Europe would continue to supply the stuff of scholarship to the center. Charles relished his conversations with these scholars, held them "in great esteem, and conferred great honors on them." Most celebrated of this group was the English monk Alcuin of York, who entered Charles' service in 782 as director of the palace school. To him was entrusted the restoration of the text of the Bible that had been corrupted by copyists' errors over the centuries. Alcuin also undertook a revision of the lectionary, the readings from the Bible and the Church Fathers that graced the everyday church services in the Middle Ages. It is still used to this day in many Christian denominations. One of Alcuin's greatest contributions to scholarship was to popularize the clear style of script, the "Carolingian minuscule," which is the ancestor of the type face in which this book is set.

In initiating this renewal of classical scholarship, this "Carolingian Renaissance," Charles was motivated both by his appreciation of the knowledge of antiquity and by practical considerations. His empire and its tributaries, which included all of western and much of central Europe, required educated administrators. There was no other or better way to educate them than through the liberal arts curriculum that had been devised in ancient times for the express purpose of preparing public officials.

As we have seen, the Church had adopted classical studies, finding them indispensable for understanding and teaching the Christian religion and thus serving as the educational prerequisite to leadership positions in the Church. Charles was eager to raise the level of competence of both civil and ecclesiastical officials throughout his empire. Consequently he mandated that all cathedrals and monasteries should establish or reform their schools, so that talented lads–even from humble families–could prepare themselves for careers as counts, bishops, abbots, or scholars.

Charles considered himself first and foremost a Christian king. Einhard tells us that "he cherished with greatest fervor and devotion the Christian religion." We learn that "he was a constant worshiper, attending church each morning and evening, and even after nightfall–in addition to attending daily Mass." His children went with him whenever possible, thus imbibing both Christian doctrine and practice. In addition to the Germanic sagas which we have mentioned, Charles had selections from Scripture and the Church Fathers read at meals–his favorite source was the *City of God* of Augustine of Hippo.

The result of Charles' efforts was to produce a growing body of leaders who, like the emperor himself, exhibited or at least valued the best qualities of three cultures: Germanic, Christian, and classical. Like many other geniuses–Pericles the Athenian, the Roman Emperor Octavian Augustus, Saint Bernard of Clairvaux, and the reformer Martin Luther–Charles was not only a leader of society but also a sort of incarnation of the cultural forces that characterized his age. Charles exhibited in his life and thought the characteristics of something new: western European culture. That culture is a synthesis of Germanic, Christian, and classical components.

A synthesis is not merely a mixture of elements but a combination that produces something new. If we combine oxygen and hydrogen, the result is a simple mixture of gases. But if we throw a lighted match into that mixture, the result is not only an explosion, but also water–a compound quite different from the elements of which it is composed. Western culture was born in a strikingly similar way.

Nothing new, however, is born without labor pains. There are, indeed, tensions in the synthesis that is western culture, some of which were apparent even in Charles' time. A continuing problem in Christian culture is apparent from an examination of Charles' sex life. Einhard tells us, with some embarrassment, that his hero

> married a daughter of Desiderius, king of the Lombards, in response to his mother's bidding, but he repudiated her at the end of a year....He then married Hildegard, a woman of high birth...and fathered three sons by her–Charles, Pepin, and Louis–and as many daughters–Hruodrud and Bertha and Gisela. He had three other daughters besides these–Theoderada, Hiltrud, and Ruodhaid–two by his third wife Fastrada...and the third by a concubine whose name has escaped my memory. At the death of Fastrada he married Liutgard,...who bore him no children. After her death he had three concubines: Gersuinda,...by whom he had Adaltrud; Regina, who was the mother of Drogo and Hugo; and Ethelind, by whom he had Theodorich.

It does seem as if Charles kept a woman behind every curtain in the palace. And there is obviously some tension between this sort of behavior and traditional Christian morality. Yet Charles, all his embarrassed contemporaries admitted, was a sincere, even an exemplary Christian. This schizoid sort of behavior has not disappeared from our culture. We all know of people who attend church regularly on Sunday, but have no scruples about cheating their customers on Monday. Christianity delineates a rigorous standard of behavior which people, even those sincerely professing that religion, find it difficult to achieve or maintain.

Another persistent tension in western culture has been the relationship of Church and state. One of Charles' favorite books, as we have seen, was Augustine's *City of God*. It would be quite fair to say, I think, that Charles saw his empire as the realization of the City of God on earth and that he considered himself its mayor. After all, the bishop of Rome had anointed him Roman emperor on Christmas day in the year 800. He was thus surely God's agent on earth, chosen, like David of old, to rule God's people. And, indeed, Charles' nickname in the colloquies in his palace school was "David."

Charles appointed learned bishops, built churches, reformed monastic and cathedral schools, sponsored Christian missionaries, and sent alms to churches everywhere–notably those in Rome and the Holy Land. He also determined how church services were to be held and even made an unsuccessful stab at determining church doctrine by supporting a revival of a form of Arianism.

It is not that Charles denied the legitimate and traditional functions of the Church. It is simply that he thought himself the divinely-appointed head of the Church–at least of its temporal affairs. But what then was the Church's sphere of spiritual competence? In a letter of 796 to Bishop Leo III of Rome, Charles declared: "It is our part, with the help of divine holiness, to defend, by armed strength and everywhere, the holy Church of Christ from the outward onslaught of pagans and the ravages of infidels, to strengthen within the Church the knowledge of the catholic faith." What was left to the bishops? Prayer–and that prayer was to be for Charles and his armies.

The obvious difficulty with this sort of Church-state relationship is that religious goals can be ignored in the interest of the state. A good example is the forced baptism of Charles' enemies, the Saxons. He conquered them, lined them up at a river, and gave them the choice between emerging as Christians or not at all. Such forced conversions expressed Charles' self-defined role as leader of Christianity. Nevertheless, many contemporary churchmen were appalled; they knew it took more than submersion to make a Christian. They also realized that this sort of identification of Christianity with submission to a conqueror would make the Saxons hate both. Caesaropapism would continue to plague western culture, as we shall see.

IV. FEUDAL AND IMPERIAL CHRISTIANITY, CHURCH, AND CULTURE

Some Useful Data

814-840	reign of Louis the Pious, emperor
840-855	reign of Lothair I, emperor
850-875	reign of Louis the German, king of the East Franks
840-877	reign of Charles the Bald, king of the West Franks
881-887	reign of Charles III the Fat, emperor
955-964	reign of John XII, pope
973	death of Otto I, king of the Germans from 936, emperor from 962
973-983	reign of Otto II, emperor
997	death of Adalbert of Prague
983-1002	reign of Otto III, emperor
999-1003	reign of Sylvester II, pope
997-1038	reign of Stephen, king of Hungary

The splendid creation that was Charles the Great's empire—an empire he identified with the Roman Empire of antiquity—did not die with him in 814. But it was subject to such severe internal tensions and devastating invasions that, for all practical purposes, it had lost its effectiveness by the end of the ninth century. Out of the chaos that followed its collapse emerged powerful new political and economic institutions: a defense system based on land tenure and personal loyalty called feudalism, a system of local land management called manorialism, and a revivified Roman Empire that resembled Charles' empire far more than that of the ancient world. Although Christianity continued to supply the core values of Europeans, those values were immeasurably enriched by a new view of nature resulting from a world-shaking technological revolution. That new view, combined with a revival of classical education, would shape subsequent medieval thought and foreshadow the birth of the modern mind.

Charles was succeeded by his sole surviving legitimate son, Louis "the Pious" (814-840), who, for a time, continued the effective rule of his father. But, in the latter part of Louis' reign, his sons fought with each other and with their father over the territories they thought were due them. In 843, the surviving brothers agreed to divide the Empire into three parts. Charles the Bald took the West Frankish territory that is now the western two-thirds of France. Lothair was granted the imperial title and a long, narrow strip of land, including what is now the Netherlands, Belgium, and eastern France—as well as Italy. Louis received the Germanic lands to the East. In 870, Charles and Louis divided that part of the recently deceased Lothair's kingdom that lay between their lands, while Provence (now southeastern France) and Italy went their own tumultuous ways. These divisions of Charles' empire were potentially advantageous to the people who inhabited the various new kingdoms, for they placed rulers nearer the lands they were charged with protecting. And protection was desperately needed.

A. Invasion

The Germanic peoples of the fourth and fifth centuries had entered the Empire in search of new homes, better security, and the benefits of late Roman civilization. New barbarian invaders in the ninth century—the Vikings, Saracens, and Magyars—came to plunder, rape, enslave, and destroy. This wave of invasions would precipitate profound, indeed drastic, changes in the shape of western culture and civilization.

The annals of many a monastery allow us to reconstruct the terror and confusion caused by Viking raids from the North. Fierce Northmen sailed out each spring from their homes in Norway and Denmark, capturing much of England and Ireland, wreaking havoc in France, Spain, and Italy—and even reaching North America. These swashbuckling seafarers, ready to row and sail small, shallow-draft boats across the North Atlantic, were easily able to reach virtually all of Europe through its waterways. And, when the trip back home seemed too far or no longer appealing, they established winter camps on islands near the mouths of Europe's rivers. In one case, the Northmen simply settled a great section of West Frankland, which would come to be called Normandy. Swedish Vikings sailed East, established a state called Rus at Kiev, attacked the mighty walls of Constantinople, and exacted tribute from the eastern Roman Empire.

From the South, across the Mediterranean, sailed the Saracen warriors of North Africa. They were great seamen and notorious pirates, but soon piracy failed to satisfy them. They conquered Sardinia (809), Corsica (810), and finally Sicily (899), and they established bases on the Italian mainland from which to plunder and terrorize the whole peninsula. Nor did southern France escape their devastating raids.

From the East, somewhat later, came the Magyars. They swept out of central Asia, across the steppes of southern Russia and up the Danube, arriving in the German lands at the end of the ninth century. For over fifty years German people suffered from the surprise attacks of these fierce horsemen.

In this time of dire need, the people of western Europe naturally turned to their governments for protection. That help did not usually come. Charles the Great's grandsons and their successors recklessly spent their energy and resources in constant fraternal battles over territory and rarely came to the defense of their people. Even when willing to resist, these Carolingian rulers found it increasingly difficult to counter the highly mobile invaders. By the time an army could be assembled and ride to the relief of a city besieged by Vikings, the boats of the attackers had disappeared with loot and captives down the river up which they had come and were already heading up another river to plunder other towns and monasteries.

As a result of this inaction or incompetence, the people of Europe suffered. The fate of the people of Paris provides a good example. In 886, the Northmen attacked the city yet again. The bishop of Paris, Gauzelin, and the abbot of a nearby monastery were on the walls of the besieged city, leading its citizens' desperate attempt to shoot enough arrows, hurl enough rocks, and pour enough boiling water down on the Vikings to keep them at bay. Thus spiritual leaders became of necessity political leaders as well. Another Parisian who proved himself able and willing to lead the defense was the local count, Odo. A Carolingian count was simply a local administrator–rather like a combined sheriff and circuit judge–and was appointed and dismissed at the pleasure of the ruler. Now Odo, and almost all counts, defended their territories without waiting for orders or reenforcements. In 877, they won the right to make their positions hereditary and, therefore, virtually independent of the king.

Odo daringly slipped through the Viking forces besieging Paris and rode hard to the palace of Charles the Fat, great grandson of Charles the Great and ruler, from 881 to 887, of the recently and temporarily reunited Empire. At the approach of Charles and his army, the siege of Paris was finally lifted. The citizens of Paris, who by now had graduated from eating rats to consuming shoe leather, looked forward to witnessing a great revenge on the Vikings. Instead Charles paid the invaders 700 pounds of silver and gave them the lands to the North, around Sens, to plunder. His actions did little to inspire the citizens of Paris, still less of Sens, with confidence in the central government. They, and most of the people of France and Italy, by necessity looked to their local bishops, abbots, or counts for the protection and justice which they had expected from their emperor. In the event that no local leader provided the needed protective services, the people turned to whoever was willing and able to defend them. In this time of crisis, men could be humble blacksmiths one day and be saluted as counts the next. This is how feudalism came into being.

B. Feudalism and the Church

Feudalism was "do-it-yourself" government, born out of the bitter necessity of the time. The universal need for defense during the age of the Vikings, Magyars, and Saracens was the most important single factor in the development of feudal institutions. These institutions now provided, by private contract, the services that had been previously provided by public institutions. Bishops, abbots, or counts—or anyone able to supply military leadership—were looked to for protection, and governmental powers were either conferred on such persons or simply assumed by them.

Security was most frequently provided by building a fort or castle—in the ninth century often little more than a wooden stockade with an occasional tower. To this fortification inhabitants of a district could flee for safety in time of danger. Villages, and later towns, tended to cluster about these strongholds. The lords of these castles needed retainers to defend their walls and to carry the fight to the enemy. It was chiefly to provide a dependable means of support for these fighting men that an elaborate network of feudal contracts, conferring reciprocal rights and obligations on feudal lords and their vassals, was gradually introduced.

Since the primary function of feudal lords—both clerics and laymen—was to provide protection, military service bulked large among the services required of the vassals who entered into feudal contracts with them. These knights needed some way of paying for the expensive equipment of horse, lance, shield, and sword—and, as time went on, an increasingly elaborate suit of heavy armor. To respond to this need, each knight received from his lord a fief, a large farm or manor whose lands the inhabitants were to work, providing for their own sustenance as well as creating a surplus for the support of the knight.

Vassals also looked to their lord to administer justice. Since the law that governed feudal relationships was based on private contracts, the lord needed the presence of his vassals at his court to advise him about what the law was, how to proceed, and what decisions he should in justice hand down.

Vassals also undertook to discharge a number of lesser obligations. Feudal contracts were hereditary, and a sort of inheritance tax, called a "relief," was paid whenever the fief passed to an heir. Another contribution was due when a lay lord held an elaborate feast to celebrate the knighting of his eldest son or the marriage of his eldest daughter. Since the lord and his vassals were social equals–both being knights and thus belonging to the same military class–vassals were of course invited to all such feasts. Again, if the lord were captured and held prisoner by his enemies, his vassals were obliged to raise his ransom. The need for ransom was rare, because the lord–whether count or churchman–was a man with great military power and thus difficult to capture. Yet, if the need did arise, ransom, like everything else in the feudal relationship, was of mutual advantage: the lord was restored to freedom, and the vassal recovered his protector.

Feudalism was not an arbitrary, capricious, or autocratic approach to governance. Through a private contractual agreement, it provided those functions today performed by the state. As the contract was between equals who pledged loyalty to one another, it was no disgrace to be a vassal, and sometimes even kings were the vassals of others, while having vassals of their own. This knightly class of equals was the fighting and governing class, and their function was to provide protection and justice. Both were sorely lacking in the ninth and tenth centuries, and the society of the time rewarded the men who provided them with the status of nobility. This relationship of status to function is illustrated by the names we have given to the men of this class. The word for knight in the various European languages–*chevalier, caballero, cavaliere, Ritter*–all refer to the knight's military function. He was a horseman, a man who fought from horseback.

As we have seen, many of the great lords of feudal France and Italy were high churchmen: bishops and abbots. The lay lords of western and southern Europe soon discovered the advantages of having these prelates as their vassals. Since feudal contracts were hereditary, the sons of lay vassals owed their positions to their fathers; so their feudal lord could not always be sure of their loyalty. Bishops or abbots, on the other hand, had no sons–at least none to speak of–and their lords could fill their posts with men loyal to them. Although the traditional election of bishops by clergy and people–and of abbots by their monks–was most often observed, it was a mere formality; lay lords universally appointed these prelates.

The effects of this practice on the Church were what might be expected. If the lay lord were a sincere Christian, he would likely appoint loyal prelates who also possessed the traditional qualifications of virtue and learning. Even then, however, the feudal bishop or abbot would need to divide his time and energy between his governmental and ecclesiastical functions. His temporal duties as a political leader were often performed at the expense of his spiritual obligations as pastor.

If the bishop or abbot's lay lord were indifferent to Christian values–or defiant of them–the results could be often be catastrophic. Many of the prelates appointed by lords like this were men for whom success was measured in terms of the hunt, the table, and the couch, and whose social utility was purely political and military rather than spiritual. Lay lords sometimes sold church offices to the highest bidder or reserved them for their own offspring, legitimate or illegitimate. Where the leadership of the Church was in the hands of men of this sort, the effect on the lower clergy and the rank and file of Christians was bound to be deleterious.

C. Reviving the Roman Empire

Feudalism proved an effective solution to the problem posed by invasions of the ninth century. Despite the threat posed by the invaders, feudalism did not then come to Germany except along its western frontier. Instead Germany served as the center of a new revival of the Roman Empire–sometimes called, incorrectly, the Holy Roman Empire. The reasons for this are several. For one thing, Germany was spared the attacks of the Saracens who found the Alps too formidable an obstacle to cross. And, while the Vikings did sail up German rivers to plunder and destroy, Germany did not suffer extensively at their hands, partly because most of Germany had not been part of the Roman Empire in antiquity and did not have the legacy of a long-flourishing civilization to tempt the Vikings. The Northmen found it much more profitable to raid the wealth of France than the less affluent areas east of the Rhine. Another reason is closely related to the first. The society of Gaul or France was relatively specialized at the time of the invasions. French farmers had long since ceased to be able to fight; that was the function of the government and its army. When this government failed to defend them, people were relatively helpless. This was not the case in Germany, where the society was still largely tribal and where every man and boy was trained in the use of arms. The Vikings met with a most discouraging reception when they leapt ashore in Germany.

This relative freedom from Viking invasion was not the sole reason why there was no feudalism in by far the largest part of Germany. Against the Magyars German warriors fought with little success. The German farmer had remained an infantryman. He could not stand alone against the tactics of a mounted adversary who appeared suddenly from nowhere, struck swiftly, and used his arrows to deadly effect. To meet this threat, German kings constructed a series of frontier forts as places of refuge against attack. Then they used heavy cavalry–well-armored men riding heavy horses–against the lighter horses of the lightly armored Asiatic invaders. The tactic worked well. The Germans crushed the invaders decisively at the battle of the Lechfeld in 955.

The king who defeated the Magyars at the Lechfeld was Otto I (936-973). He was the duke, the tribal leader, of Saxony and had been elected king by the other dukes and great lords of Germany. His military prowess, however, was not alone sufficient to make him an effective ruler. Germany was not one state or one people. The Saxons, Franks, Frisians, Swabians, and Bavarians each looked for leadership primarily to their tribal leader, their duke, and not to the king. To rule the vast German lands–territories in which transportation was often primitive–Otto needed local administrators. But dukes and counts were most often unwilling to serve any but local interests. Otto attempted to overcome their opposition by installing members of his family as dukes, but even they quickly identified themselves with local interests.

Otto's solution to this problem was a stroke of genius, and it saved Germany from reduction to a collection of small, independent, warring territories characteristic of contemporary France and Italy. Otto reduced the power of the great lay lords by granting independent political jurisdiction over large territories to the higher clergy, the abbots and bishops. This reduced the territorial power base of the lay lords, leaving them less capable of effective rebellion. It also provided each area with clerical watchdogs to see to it that the lay aristocracy continued to serve the interest of the king. Furthermore, the king could command the loyalty of the bishops and abbots far more easily than he could that of the lay lords. When a duke or count died, his son took over his office. That son owed his position to his birth, not to the king, and was likely to adopt an independent attitude. A bishop or abbot could leave no legitimate heirs, and the king could appoint a successor loyal to him. This system worked well for a century and a half. It made Germany the most effective state on the continent until the twelfth century, and the kings of Germany, beginning with Otto I in 962, assumed the title of Roman Emperor. Otto was anointed and crowned by John XII (955-964), perhaps one of the least saintly men who has ever held the Roman papacy.

The bishop of Rome–by now commonly called the pope–was by far the most powerful feudal lord in central Italy. The feudal vassals of the pope coveted the papal office and its political power, with the result that intrigue, treachery, and murder had come to surround the see of Peter. From 896 to 904, there was, on the average, one pope a year. The tenth century saw worse: for several decades Rome was controlled by an infamous "lady Senator," Marozia, who appointed her son to the papal office and aided her lover in storming a later pope's refuge, the Castel Sant'Angelo.

In the tenth and eleventh centuries, the German kings often rescued the bishops and people of Rome from domination by the local nobility. These kings controlled the Church in their lands, lands that had come to include northern and central Italy. Pope John XII invited Otto I to come down across the Alps to Italy in 960 and offered him the imperial crown as a reward for introducing peace and order into that chaotic land. In Italy, as in Germany, the emperors ruled through their bishops and abbots, and this included the bishop of Rome, who thus became an imperial appointee like the others. Since the emperors of the tenth and eleventh century were sincerely interested in the welfare of the Church, they appointed generally well-qualified men as popes. But when the emperor was too busy in Germany to exercise adequate control in Italy, the Roman nobles reasserted their control of the papacy and resumed their family rivalry for the power to name the pope. They were never secure in this control, however, for time and time again the emperors crossed the Alps to restore order and appoint virtuous and learned men as bishops in Rome and the rest of Italy.

The interest which the German emperors from Otto I to Henry III (died 1056) took in the welfare of the Church meant that they insisted on restoring the traditional qualifications for high office in that Church. This reform necessitated a revival of the classical education that often had been disregarded in the confused times that accompanied the breakup of the Carolingian Empire. If a classical education were necessary to provide the sort of clergymen the emperors wanted, they had to patronize and encourage schools. And this was indeed done by Otto and his successors. This "Ottonian Renaissance" also fostered the education of women. Around the year 1000, in the convent at Gandersheim in Saxony, we find the nun Hroswitha writing Christian plays in the style of the Roman dramatist Terence.

Most of the best schools of the times were in German monasteries like Fulda and Saint Gall. German monasteries not only provided educated men for high church posts; they also sent out missionaries to the Scandinavians, Hungarians, and Slavs, doubling the area of Europe which adhered to Latin Christianity.

D. A Vision of Christendom

This great expansion of Latin Christianity was the result of the heroic endeavors displayed by missionaries like Adalbert of Prague. Born into a noble family of Bohemia (now the Czech Republic), Adalbert entered a monastery in Rome. There he became a friend of the emperor Otto III. This close relationship continued even after Adalbert left Rome to bring or restore Christianity to the Bohemians, Hungarians, and Poles. He met his death at the hands of the pagan Prussians in 997.

In the winter of 999-1000, Otto III set out on a pilgrimage to Poland, to the tomb of his friend Adalbert. Otto's entrance into the lands of Duke Boleslaus of Poland could have been taken as a threat to that ruler's independence. But Otto brought with him a papal decree issued by another of his friends, Pope Sylvester II. This decree gave Poland an archbishopric independent of ecclesiastical or political control from the emperor. Otto also presented Boleslaus with a replica of what was thought to be the lance that had pierced the side of Jesus. Otto then named Boleslaus a "brother and fellow servant of the Empire." Otto's vision of Empire did not demand political submission from the Polish people but their fraternal cooperation in a federation of Christian states.

The vision of this federation, of "Christendom," which Otto and Sylvester shared was extended to areas other than Poland. In 1000 or 1001, Sylvester established an independent Hungarian church and sent the Hungarian ruler, Stephen, a crown symbolizing his status as an independent king. Otto and Sylvester sent missionaries to lands as far away as Russia, in hopes of bringing the Slavs of that farthermost outpost of Europe into a federation that recognized local political and ecclesiastical autonomy within one Church and one Christendom.

In the remarkable life of Sylvester II we can see how politics, religion, and culture were tightly interwoven in the days surrounding the millennial year 1000. Sylvester had been given the name Gerbert at time of his birth in 940. The son of a farmer, Gerbert was recognized as a boy of exceptional talent by the monks of the nearby monastery of Aurillac, who took him in and gave him an education. Gerbert's mastery of mathematics was so impressive that he attained the post of director of the cathedral school in the northern French city of Reims. His mastery of all the disciplines of the liberal arts caught the attention of Emperor Otto II, who was known for his interest in intellectual matters. So, in 982, Otto made Gerbert abbot of an old and by this time disreputable Italian monastery, Bobbio–in hopes that he could reform it. Despite Gerbert's noble attempt, in the end he failed and returned to Reims.

In 991, Gerbert was elected archbishop of Reims, but the election was disputed and so Gerbert left Reims for Rome in 997, and there became the fast friend of Otto III. Otto saw to it that Gerbert was elected archbishop of Ravenna in 998, and, in the following year, Otto arranged his election as bishop of Rome. Gerbert's choice of a papal name was no accident. The first Sylvester had been bishop of Rome at the time of the Christian refashioning of the Roman Empire by the fourth-century emperor Constantine. Otto and Gerbert saw themselves establishing a new Christian empire, becoming the new Constantine and the second Sylvester.

E. A Technological and Cultural Revolution

The warrior and clerical classes of Europe–from kings to simple knights, from bishops to parish priests–probably never included more than five percent of the people who lived in the ninth through eleventh centuries. The other ninety-five percent, whose culture we shall now consider, supported themselves, their governors and protectors, and their spiritual guides through their agricultural labor.

Medieval farmers lived on manors–large, virtually self-sufficient farms on which some thirty or forty families lived in a village, a collection of modest dwellings centering on a church and including a house for the manorial lord. Manorial lords and farmers lived in a symbiotic relationship. The lord, a knight granted the manor by his feudal lord, provided protection, justice, and land. The farmers, in return, provided the lord with a portion of the manor's produce and worked his share of the land–thus freeing him for the exercise of his military duties.

The farmers found it efficient to work the land together. Plowing, harrowing, fertilizing, weeding, and harvesting together made community decisions mandatory. The village council gradually evolved from this, taking on almost all the functions of local government. Each season and each major farming activity was marked on the manor with appropriate festivals celebrated by the entire community. The villagers were deeply involved in one another's concerns and cares and accepted collective responsibility for each other's health and welfare. However, hard work and the vagaries of weather made the lives of early medieval farmers no idyllic existence.

During the tenth century the peace, law, and order provided by the twin institutions of feudalism and empire made farming life more secure and less burdensome. Still more important for this progress was a series of inventions that brought about a true agricultural revolution and not only changed Europe's way of farming but stimulated a new way of thinking in the West.

The first of these technological innovations was the introduction of a new sort of plow. This heavy, wheeled plow–the ancestor of the plows still used by farmers–turned the soil over, thus aerating and enriching it. With this new machine it was possible for the first time to exploit the soil of the rich river valleys of western and central Europe.

To pull this heavy plow medieval farmers replaced the ox with the far more efficient horse. This innovation was made possible by two other brilliant inventions. The first was the horse-shoe, which protected horses' hooves from injury. The horse-shoe was vital in the moist climates north of the Alps, for wet soil causes hooves to soften, to rot, and to break when a horse steps on stones. It was, however, the invention of the horse collar that made the horse an effective farm animal. Ancient horse harnesses consisted of straps around the animal's neck, which reduced the horse's intake of air and blood supply to the brain when the animal was employed to pull heavy loads. With the invention of the horse collar, the animal could push with its whole strength against a pad resting on its shoulders–a pad that would not interfere with either its breathing or its circulation.

Properly shod and harnessed, the horse was able to exert about fifty percent more pulling power than the ox, and the horse's greater endurance made it possible to work an additional hour or two each day. The gain in efficiency was clearly substantial, resulting in a corresponding increase in production. Since horses move much more swiftly than oxen, the benefits in terms of cheaper and more rapid transportation by road were also significant. Furthermore, the horse's greater speed made it possible for farmers to live in larger villages farther away from their fields. The ensuing benefits included greater security and easier access to the amenities of community life.

Another of the important agricultural innovations of the Middle Ages was the widespread adoption of the three-field system. Ancient farmers had most often used a two-field system that had meant that only half the land was producing crops at a given time. This system was necessary because land had to lie fallow if it were not to become exhausted. The new system divided the same amount of land into three fields, two of which were planted. This increased the productive portion to two-thirds of the available acreage. Thus, with the same number of plowmen and draft animals, a larger total amount of land could be kept under cultivation. We can see the tangible results of this great gain in labor productivity in the eleventh and twelfth centuries when the extra manpower was devoted to the clearing of forests, the draining of swamps and marshes, the building of dikes, and the reclamation of land by using windmills (another medieval invention) to operate pumps. Nor were these the only benefits of the three-field system, for by making possible a better rotation of crops it helped maintain the fertility of the soil when nitrogen-adding legumes like peas, lentils, or beans were planted as an early crop. These legumes added valuable proteins to the average family's diet, and this benefit was reflected in greater capacity to work, increased resistance to illness and disease, and longer life-expectancy. All these factors, as well as a warming of the climate, contributed to the steady growth in Europe's population that began shortly before 1000.

Even before the ninth- and tenth-century innovations we have been discussing, the technological advances of medieval Europe over the slave based (and inefficient) agricultural economy of antiquity had already dramatically increased the capacity of the environment to support human beings. The new inventions made it possible to exploit the rich, heavy–and often virgin–soils of western and central Europe. Thus occurred a shift northward in the cultural center of gravity. It was in Europe north of the Alps that some of the most distinctive features of the modern world developed.

The indirect effects of the medieval agricultural revolution were no less momentous. The expanded production of Europe's farmers made possible the accumulation of economic surpluses that were necessary not only to support a larger population but also to encourage the increasing specialization of functions necessary for the process of urbanization. Freeing some workers from fields meant that new towns could come into being by drawing food and raw materials from the surrounding countryside. Villagers were now rich enough not only to spare some of their output but also to purchase the manufactured goods and the professional services of townsfolk. Surpluses, too, were and are absolutely necessary to provide talented people with the leisure that is the basis of art, science, and all other forms of high culture.

Perhaps most important, this agricultural revolution helped change the European's attitude toward nature. Once humans had considered themselves part of nature. Now they were able to think of themselves as nature's masters and exploiters. Modern western civilization would not have been possible without this radical change in attitude.

Medieval people were spared the ecological consequences of their eager exploitation of nature. The population of Europe, although it was expanding rapidly, did not yet put an undue strain on the environment. Although new sorts of machines were being invented at a prodigious rate during the Middle Ages, those machines did not produce carbon monoxide exhaust which polluted the land and seas. Medieval people did indeed think of themselves as masters of creation, assigned that role by God in the persons of their first parents. But the men and women of the medieval centuries also saw Adam and Eve, and thus themselves, charged with responsibility for the well-being of that creation.

In the ninth, tenth, and eleventh centuries, new ways of expressing traditional Christian values were generated by a new cultural environment. More fundamentally, perhaps, revolutionary technological changes influenced the emergence of radically new ways of thought. Thus, the culture of a maturing western civilization profoundly affected Christianity.

V. THE MEDIEVAL REFORMATION

Some Useful Data

910	William of Aquitaine founds Cluny
994-1048	Odilo, abbot of Cluny
1002-1024	reign of Henry II, emperor
1039-1056	reign of Henry III, emperor
1059-1061	reign of Nicolas II, pope
1073-1085	reign of Gregory VII, pope
1088-1099	reign of Urban II, pope
1056-1106	reign of Henry IV, emperor
1099-1118	reign of Paschal II, pope
1119-1124	reign of Calixtus II, pope
1106-1125	reign of Henry V, emperor
c. 1090-1153	Bernard, abbot of Clairvaux
1198-1216	reign of Innocent III, pope

One of the most often recurring and enduring cultural expressions of Christianity is the idea of reform and the consequent efforts at reformation. The Middle Ages were no exception. The period from about 1000 to roughly 1300 was an age–ordinarily called the High Middle Ages–in which the dominant cultural force was reform. That three-century period saw the flourishing of all forms of culture and the development of institutions that have profoundly influenced our own world.

The medieval reformation–like all reform movements–aimed at restoring the life of the Church to the pristine purity of the apostolic age, as described in the biblical book of Acts. The apostolic community, the earliest expression of Christian living, was regarded by medieval people as the one in which the faith and organization of their Church most perfectly reflected the ideals and purposes of its founder. The medieval reform movement thus consciously looked back to an idealized past. But to achieve its goal it ultimately became a revolutionary force aspiring to a radical transformation of the society of the time.

The revolutionary aspect of this reformation was first apparent in its profound effect on what had become the traditional relationship between Church and state. We have already discussed much that helps us understand this Church-state conflict. Late Roman caesaropapism, the reaction of Ambrose of Milan and Gelasius of Rome, and the control of the Church by the Byzantine Emperors are all important elements in the background of this conflict. We have seen to what degree the Church had become subject to the state in Merovingian Gaul, how narrowly Charles the Great had defined the function of the Church and how widely he had extended the jurisdiction of the state. Whatever was in any way temporal had been subject to his jurisdiction, including church buildings, the order of worship, the education of clergymen, and the appointment of bishops and abbots. The Church regained its independence briefly in the ninth century when the Carolingian Empire collapsed under the pressure of invasion. Both feudalism and the German emperors put an end to this freedom. Once more bishops and other churchmen were appointed and dismissed at the pleasure of the temporal ruler. The moral condition of the Church thus depended on whether the lay authorities appointed pious or impious men as shepherds of the Christian flock.

A. The Cluniac Reform

Almost as soon as the Church in western Europe was subjected to the control of feudal lords, a largely successful counter movement began. One of the greatest centers of this independence movement was the French monastery of Cluny. When William the Pious, duke of Aquitaine, founded Cluny in the year 910, he specifically forbade any temporal lord, including his own son, to exercise feudal control over it or to appoint its abbot. This permitted a return to the practice of early monasticism, in which the monks themselves had elected the head of their monastic family. To keep Cluny out of the hands of any feudal lord and thus ensure that the reform would live on, Duke William gave the monks of Cluny only allodial land–that is, land that had never been feudalized and was, therefore, owned outright. On such land Cluny flourished spiritually and became an example to all those wishing for reform.

The success of the reform at Cluny led many pious noblemen to donate land to Cluny or to ask that Cluny send some of its members to reform the monasteries subject to them. The monks of Cluny agreed only when the allodial status of the land, and thus the independence of the new or newly reformed monastery, were assured. Several hundred (eventually some 2000) monasteries joined in a federation under the abbot of Cluny and presented a solid front against powerful lords who might seek to subvert their independence.

Cluny was so successful in preserving the integrity of the reform movement that feudal lords who sympathized with its program began to use it as a source of virtuous and learned bishops. Thus what began as a monastic reform became an attempt to restore the entire Church to its original spiritual autonomy and purity.

The Cluniac movement also received the support of the manufacturers, merchants, and farmers of high medieval Europe, largely because of the reformers' attempts to reduce the number and frequency of private feudal wars from which both farmers and middle class people suffered grievously. Abbot Odilo of Cluny (994-1048) succeeded in introducing a "Truce of God" into France, and from there it spread throughout Europe. Beginning in 1040, councils of reform-minded bishops and abbots forbade armed conflict from Wednesday evening until Monday morning and during the whole week for some four months a year. A more positive, and more successful, approach was the "Peace of God"–also initiated in the eleventh century. This attempt to christianize feudalism called on knights to swear to use their arms only in righteous causes and to defend women and other non-combatant members of society. This was enforced by spiritual sanctions of the Church, like excommunication, and by the armed force of knightly neighbors. As we shall see, the transformation of feudalism that resulted led to the code of chivalry which is the ancestor of the modern notion of the lady and the gentleman.

The German emperors of the tenth and eleventh centuries supported the reform movement by appointing capable and pious abbots and bishops–including bishops of Rome whenever German armies controlled that city. Perhaps the extent of the reform movement's influence on the German rulers of the revived Roman Empire is best exemplified by the reign of Henry II (1002-1024). So important was the spirit of monastic reform to Henry and his wife Cunigunda that they lived a celibate life together, apparently oblivious to the effects of their choice on the succession to the throne. Henry's commitment to the reform movement led to his appointing only learned and virtuous men to the highest posts in the imperial Church.

Henry's bishops–including, notably, the bishop of Rome–not only accepted his control of the Church, but offered a theoretical basis for his supremacy. Henry's coronation in Rome featured his ordination as a clergyman by the pope.

Henry had previously been dressed in ecclesiastical vestments by attending bishops. Henry did indeed receive a crown from the pope, but–more significant to their contemporaries–the pope anointed him with holy oil, as the Old Testament prophet Samuel had anointed King David. These were the symbols of Imperial Theocracy, the view that the ruler was chosen by God to lead his people to justice in this world and from there to celestial happiness. Henry took this exalted role seriously, appointing as his agents bishops who were often monks and who were committed to continuing reform.

B. The Reform Captures Rome

The emperor Henry III (1039-1056), though chosen from a different family than Henry II, shared his predecessor's enthusiastic support for the reform movement. To accomplish that end, he too maintained virtually complete control over the Church. A striking example occurred in 1046: three men in Rome each claimed to be its bishop. Henry marched his army across the Alps to Italy, and, at the Council of Sutri, deposed all three. He then appointed one of his own reform bishops as pope. The reform movement was once again established in Rome. Yet the danger continued that an emperor or a Roman noble not so reform-minded as Henry would come along and appoint an unworthy man.

To prevent this, the reformers tried to improve the method by which the papal office was filled. In the year 1059, a Roman reform council under the leadership of Pope Nicholas II issued a Papal Election Decree that amounted to a declaration of independence of the Roman Church from the empire. According to this decree, succession to the bishopric of Rome was henceforth to be regulated in accordance with the practice of the early Church: election by the clergy and people of the diocese. As representatives of the clergy, the decree designated seven bishops from the Roman suburbs, twenty-eight pastors of the most important parishes in Rome, and the eighteen deacons who assisted the pope in the administration of the Roman church. These chief or "cardinal" clergy were to name the bishop of Rome and then seek the assent of the rest of the clergy and people of Rome. Nicholas II appointed reformers as cardinals who then elected another member of the reforming party after his death. This pope in turn appointed more reformers as cardinals. This system for maintaining the reformers' control of the papacy worked well until the late thirteenth century.

Two circumstances aided the reformers in maintaining their control of the papacy. First, Henry IV (1056-1106) had only recently succeeded his father. He was a boy of only six and unable to control the political situation in Germany, much less travel to Italy to quash the challenge to imperial domination of the Church. Secondly, some Norman adventurers had by this time conquered most of southern Italy. The bishops of Rome took advantage of their proximity to form an alliance with these Norman kings, and this provided the popes with allies as well as a secure place of refuge in the event of another German expedition.

C. The Gregorian Reform

The reformers, having gained control of Rome, now pursued a policy of securing independence from lay control for the rest of the Church. This phase of the reform was to find its champion in the person of the monk Hildebrand, who was elected pope in 1073 as Gregory VII. Like many of his reforming predecessors, he had been a Cluniac monk, and his chief aim was to complete the reform by freeing the clergy entirely from appointment by lay lords. To accomplish this, Gregory sent out legates, papal representatives who encouraged local and regional councils to attack abuses and install only men of virtue and learning as clergymen. Reform councils held in Rome under Gregory also repeated earlier prohibitions against simony, the buying and selling of church offices.

Simony, however, was just what Henry IV, now an adult, was practicing. Henry not only appointed bishops, he raised money by selling the appointments. After appointing a bishop, he followed the contemporary practice in bestowing the symbols of the bishop's office on the candidate. These symbols were a ring (symbolizing the marriage of the bishop with his church) and the crosier (a shepherd's crook which symbolized his function as pastor). The new breed of Church reformers, who saw reform possible only through independence, declared that lay investiture, the bestowing of these symbols by a layman, was also simony.

Henry had no intention of complying with this decree. He continued to associate with his bishop-administrators who had been excommunicated by the reformers for having bought their office. In a letter of December 1075, Gregory reproached Henry for frustrating Church reform. Henry's response was a masterpiece of indignation, embodying a view of the Church that had become traditional. Henry claimed that his office derived its authority from God–something that none of his contemporaries, including Gregory, would have denied. But he also claimed much more: that he could not be judged by anyone except God for his actions. This was a reassertion of Byzantine and Carolingian caesaropapism with which Gregory could not agree. In his letter, Henry addressed the pope as "Hildebrand" not as "Gregory," implying Henry's refusal to accept a pope whom he, as God's agent on earth, had not appointed. Henry also called Gregory a "false monk," a still more revealing title. Gregory had been a monk, but had come out of his monastery in an effort to reform the Church. For Henry this was a task for the rulers, not for monks, and thus Gregory had been false to his vocation. Gregory's usurpation of a reforming role–and still more his criticism of Henry's control of the Church–earned him this scathing rebuke: "You who do not fear God, dishonor in me his anointed one." The appropriate punishment for such sacrilege was more than deposition. Henry wrote: "You have been damned by the judgment of all our bishops and by our own....Descend, descend, to be damned throughout the ages!"

Henry's view reminds us of the definition of the roles of Church and state long before promulgated by Charles the Great: the state is to serve society in all ways physical, including the organization of the Church; the clergy are subject to the state in all matters save the one function proper to them–prayer for the world. This position had centuries of custom on its side. Even many reformers were skeptical of Gregory's claim that kings should not control bishops. They remembered the gains that had been made under imperial control from Otto I to Henry III.

There was, of course, a practical reason why Henry resisted the attempt of Gregory to eliminate lay investitute. What meant freedom for the Church to Gregory and his successors meant the destruction of the empire to Henry and his successors. The German imperial constitution was at stake, because, as we have seen, the emperor governed largely through his bishops and abbots. If Henry gave up appointing the higher clergy, he could not be assured of the loyalty of many of his chief administrators.

For Pope Gregory, however, the freedom of the Church transcended all material considerations. In February of 1076, Gregory issued a decree that declared Henry excommunicate, released his subjects from their oaths of allegiance, and also declared him deposed. The great lords of Germany, eager to rid themselves of an emperor who threatened their power, then rose up against Henry, and, at the Diet (the imperial assembly) of Tribur in October 1076, they resolved to depose Henry and elect a new king if he stayed at odds with the Church for more than a year. Expecting Henry to remain obdurate, they invited Gregory to act as their adviser in the imperial election to be held at Augsburg in 1077.

Gregory did not claim the right to choose whomever he wished as emperor; that, he thought, was the political function of the German princes. Gregory's own function was to rule on what was for him–and for most of his contemporaries–the moral question of whether or not the king was providing justice. The conflict between Henry and Gregory was rooted not in determining whether the pope or the emperor was to rule the world, but in determining the extent and limits of the temporal and religious jurisdictions of Church and state. According to the promoters of the second, or Gregorian, phase of reform, the clergy could judge the ruler only in moral questions. Such a question surely arose when the king interfered with the spiritual welfare of others, as Gregory thought Henry had done by appointing unqualified bishops and by selling church offices. Gregory's position was to prevail in the centuries down to the fourteenth, but only at the cost of continuing struggle.

In the short run, Henry scored a diplomatic victory over Gregory and the German rebellion. In 1077, he evaded his rebellious subjects and crossed the Alps to Italy where the pope was wintering at the castle of Canossa. Henry stood barefoot in the snow and cold outside the castle for three days, all the while protesting his repentance and desire for absolution. Suspicious but mindful of his role as priest, Gregory was obliged to absolve him.

Henry's reinstatement gave him the upper hand in battling the German opposition that had now lost the moral justification for its rebellion. Once Henry was victorious, he returned to his practice of simony and lay investiture. When Gregory sent word of a second excommunication, Henry led an army into Italy and installed his own appointee as an anti-pope. Given refuge in Sicily by his Norman allies, Gregory died. His last words were a sad rephrasing of a verse from Psalm 44: "I have loved justice and hated iniquity–and so I die in exile." Despite the setback, however, the work of the reform went on.

In 1106, Henry V succeeded his father on the German throne. He followed his father's practice of investing bishops, even going so far as to capture Pope Paschal II in 1111 and forcing his recognition of the emperor's right of investiture. The reformers were furious with Paschal, and reform councils all over Europe condemned the pope's submission. From these events, one obtains an interesting insight into the medieval conviction that with authority goes responsibility. The man considered by his contemporaries to be the vicar of Saint Peter not only admitted his error and repudiated his capitulation to Henry, but caused himself to be scourged publicly as penance for his weakness.

D. Compromise and Continued Reform

Paschal's second successor, Calixtus II (1119-1124), ushered in a new phase in the relationship between Church and state. Theologians and experts on church law like Ivo of Chartres offered a theoretical basis for a practical solution to the controversy. The difficulty, they said, was with the dual function of the bishops and abbots as spiritual shepherds and as imperial administrators. Both Church and state had a legitimate interest in the choice of prelates. In investiture it was necessary that a church official bestow the ring and crozier as symbols of the spiritual function of the prelate. Investiture with a scepter–the symbol of temporal power–could properly come from the temporal ruler. These principles were to serve as the basis for settlement of the disputes between Church and state in England and France.

Pressure from his subjects also forced the Emperor Henry V to accept these principles. The result was a compromise, the Concordat of Worms of 1122. This agreement provided for two methods of selecting a bishop in the empire. North of the Alps there was to be a free election of the candidate by representatives of the clergy and people (the goal of the reformers). This election was to be held in the presence of the emperor or of his representative (a concession to the rights of the temporal ruler). The ruler was to then bestow on the bishop-elect a scepter, the symbol of his office as an imperial administrator. Only then was the archbishop of the area to consecrate the new bishop and invest him with the ring and crozier. Thus in Germany the emperor could not appoint bishops, but he could veto the election of a man whom he was loathe to have as an imperial administrator.

South of the Alps, a free election was to be held, without the presence of an imperial representative. The bishop was then consecrated, and within six months the emperor was to give him the symbol of his temporal office. The lack of an imperial veto meant that the bishops and abbots of Italy, although nominally still agents of the emperor, were, for all practical purposes, independent. Since the government of the empire was based on the use of bishops and abbots as agents of the crown, Italy became to all intents and purposes independent. The principal Italian cities quickly threw off the temporal–though not the spiritual–authority of their bishops and seized hold of the freedom to follow their own commercial policies. Italy was already prospering, but the twelfth and thirteenth centuries saw the Italians assume the leading position in international trade and finance. The great wealth they amassed provided the economic basis for a flourishing culture that reached its climax in what many call the Italian Renaissance.

The compromise at Worms freed reformers to redouble their efforts. A leader in this new phase in the reform of Church and society was Pope Innocent III (1198-1216), surely the best known and perhaps the most able of medieval pontiffs. Innocent was only thirty-seven when elected bishop of Rome. He had studied law at Bologna and theology at Paris, the finest of the new universities instituted by the reform Church to provide itself with educated leadership. His spiritual treatises *The Disdain of Worldliness* and *The Holy Mystery of the Altar* seem to contrast sharply with his active career as pope, but are essential in understanding him. For Innocent, his action in the world was necessary, but its purpose was the spiritual welfare of Christians, and its success could be measured only by reference to the next world.

Though Innocent's ambitions were otherworldly, he shared the conviction of the reformers that the Church must not merely serve the people of this world through prayer, preaching, and administering the sacraments. His goal was to completely reform society, to make it truly Christian. Injustice was not merely to be deplored; the Church was to take an active role in bringing about social justice. The reformers aimed at nothing short of a perfect Christian society, and it is little wonder that they failed. Indeed, they themselves did not expect to establish heaven on earth, for they believed that human weakness and tendency toward sin would necessitate ever-recurring personal and institutional reformations. Innocent's efforts to secure Christian justice in the world led him to assume a quasi-political role. His relations with the Empire, with France, and with England are important in understanding that role.

During Innocent's reign, for example, the Empire was torn by dissension as there were three claimants to the throne. One was Philip of Hohenstaufen, the brother of the late Henry VI. Another claimant was Otto of Braunschweig, the inheritor of his family's long-standing leadership of the German opposition party. And finally there was the child Frederick, son of Henry VI, who was now the ward of the pope. Philip and Otto both submitted their claims to Innocent for arbitration. Innocent accepted this role because the bishop of Rome was charged with the function of anointing and crowning the emperor and thus had to decide who had been validly elected.

Innocent's decision is a fine example of the so-called scholastic method of weighing evidence, balancing authorities pro and con, and finally resolving the argument by an appeal to logic. According to Innocent, authority is given the ruler so that he can provide justice; Frederick was thus eliminated because, as a mere lad, he was not able to provide it. In Phillip's favor was the fact that he had been the choice of the majority of the electors. But, still more important, he was "so strong in wealth and supporters" that he was able to fulfill the functions of a ruler. Innocent, however, ruled Philip out: though able he had not proved himself willing to provide justice. The case against Otto was his relatively weaker position and the smaller number of electors who supported him. Innocent decided for Otto, since he had been "elected by as many or more of those princes that have the best right to elect the emperor and because he is much more fit to rule than Philip." For Innocent, then, the function of the office, providing justice, established the basis for the choice. For Innocent the decision was a moral one.

The reform Church, of which Innocent was the acknowledged leader, thus provided the people of Europe with a standard of personal virtue. But it also offered a standard of justice, the basis for a re-formation, a re-newal, of European society and culture.

E. The Crusades

Innocent III's insistence on justice seems to ring hollow when we consider that he was but one of a series of spiritual leaders who urged Europeans to wage war on the people of the Mideast. That the leaders of a culture dedicated to the realization of justice should sponsor a movement, the Crusades, which gave rise to monstrous injustices seems, at the least, inconsistent. That a religion, Christianity, whose founder, Christ, was a man of peace, should promote cruel warfare on a grand scale seems, at best, hypocritical. And the fact that atrocities were committed by both sides in the crusading conflicts excuses neither side. Understanding the crusading movement, while not excusing its aberrations, requires an inquiry into the motivations of the crusade preachers.

The primary goal of the popes, bishops, and other religious leaders who preached the crusades was to free Palestine from hostile occupation. In the eleventh century, the relatively tolerant Arabs, who had allowed Christian pilgrimages to the Holy Land, were elbowed aside by the Seljuk Turks, an Asiatic people of great military prowess who swept into the lands of the Mideast. The Seljuks had only recently embraced Islam, and they were filled with the intolerance so often found among the newly converted. Besides violently disrupting the path of Christian pilgrims, these Turks were threatening the Greek Christians of the Byzantine Empire. Following the crushing defeat of the Byzantine army at the battle of Manzikert in 1071, and the subsequent loss of all of Asia Minor to the Turks, the emperors at Constantinople appealed to the West for aid. Pope Urban II, in his 1095 response to this appeal, hoped that, if western Christians came to the aid of the Eastern Roman Empire, the schism or split between the Latin and Greek Churches, which dated back to 1054, would be healed.

Bernard of Clairvaux (c. 1090-1153), who almost singlehandedly roused Europe to the expedition known as the Second Crusade, insisted vehemently that the fact that the rampaging Turks were Muslims was no reason to resist them. Bernard, however, saw no option other than combating these Muslims, because they threatened peace and justice in the Holy Land. For Bernard, the crusade was, so to speak, the foreign policy of a reform Church dedicated to justice in all lands.

If Bernard preached the crusade in the cause of Palestinian peace, he also saw the crusades promoting the peace and tranquility of a Europe bursting with the militant energies of all-too-often undiscriminating and badly motivated warriors. Bernard sent them off to the East in a cause he considered just, and, by that action, he hoped unjust warfare in the West would be diminished.

What of the motives of the men who set off on the perilous journey to the East, a trek often lasting years? There is no doubt that many of them ignored the distinction between the Turks as unjust invaders and the mideastern people whose religion offended them. We call to mind the frightful massacre of the people of Jerusalem after its fall, in 1099, to the knights of the First Crusade. We less often recall the benign governance of all peoples in the Crusader states that were established after that fall. Courts under Palestinian judges provided for the needs of the native population of Muslims, Jews, and Christians. Muslim sources tell us that the people of Palestine and Syria learned to live peacefully with Europeans who had grown tolerant of the Muslim religion and who understood the ways of the East. The rough wool garments of the European knights were soon shed for flowing Arab garments more suited to the climate of the Mideast. And Muslim and Jewish physicians were welcomed into the houses of crusaders whose children were ill.

Many crusaders settled in the states created in the Mideast. These were often men whose status as younger sons denied them lands in the feudal society back home. Most–perhaps ninety percent–of the crusading host returned home after fulfilling their solemn vow to free Jerusalem. The vast majority of those warriors who "took the cross"–who sewed a red cross on the front of their surcoats as a symbol of their vow–placed that cross on their backs and returned home to Europe once they had reached their goal. We suspect from this evidence–and know from their letters to their wives–that they were confident that their hardships in travel and battle had enriched their religious life by making reparation for past sins.

Religion was not the only motive which led crusaders to the East, as we learn, for example, from the Fourth Crusade. In 1204, Innocent III, concerned about the weakness of the Christian position in the Mideast, launched a new crusade. The crusaders gathered at Venice, where they were unable to pay the staggering sum demanded for their sea passage. The Venetians proposed that, in partial payment, the crusaders might help to conquer the town of Zara, a Christian rival of Venice on the Adriatic Sea, and the leaders of the crusade secretly agreed to the bargain. When word of the attack reached Pope Innocent III, he was so indignant that he excommunicated the Venetians. Though some of the crusaders objected to the Venetians' next proposal, which was to conquer Constantinople, many had no such scruples and proceeded to ravage and loot the capital city of their allies. This brutal sack of Constantinople resulted in a short-lived Latin kingdom on the Bosporus, but more lasting was the commercial hegemony of Venice established by the Fourth Crusade in the eastern Mediterranean. The Crusade was a debacle which did not even reach the Holy Land.

The Crusades did not succeed in realizing their religious purpose or their political aims: the Christian kingdom of Jerusalem lasted less than a century. The schism between the eastern and the western Churches was temporarily healed by the First Crusade, but the Fourth Crusade left the Greeks with an implacable hatred of the Latins as barbarous invaders. What had been merely a hierarchical and administrative division between the eastern and western Churches became an unbridgeable gulf of popular antagonism. The Churches were formally reunited on two occasions after 1204, it is true, but real trust could never again be re-established, and, years later, when Greek prelates announced a proposed reunion with Rome to the people of Constantinople and the East, their words were greeted with stones and derision.

As a safety-valve for the excess energy of European society, the Crusades were far more successful. A direct consequence was to reduce the destructiveness of feudal warfare. Every bellicose warrior who left his bones to bleach along the way to or from Palestine was one less warrior riding across the fields of France, England, or Germany. In addition, the rising cities of northern Europe benefited from the need that lords about to go on crusades had for ready money, both to finance their expedition and, on their return, to purchase the eastern luxuries for which they acquired a taste during their travels. To raise cash these lords often sold rights of self-government and exemptions from feudal jurisdiction to the citizens of wealthy towns. Farmers benefited as well, for at this time many manorial obligations were commuted from labor or produce sharing into money payments, and many semi-free peasants were thus able to become free tenant farmers. But the Italian cities, particularly Venice, reaped the greatest benefits: the Mediterranean was converted from a Moslem into an Italian lake, and the immense profits of the now rapidly expanding eastern trade found their way chiefly into Italian pockets.

Perhaps the most impressive of all the features of the crusading movement was the tremendous response of people all over Europe to the call to action by the reformers. Perhaps nothing shows more clearly than the Crusades the strength of Europe's Christian convictions or the effectiveness of the reform Church's leadership in the culture of the High Middle Ages.

VI. HIGH MEDIEVAL CULTURE AND SOCIETY I: THE REGULARS

Some Useful Data

1129	death of Rupert, abbot of Deutz
1080-1139	Norbert of Xanten, archbishop of Madeburg
c. 1090-1153	Bernard, abbot of Clairvaux
1145-1153	reign of Eugenius III, pope
1158	death of Anselm, bishop of Havelberg
c. 1110-1167	Aelred, abbot of Rievaulx
1170-1221	Dominic Guzmán, founder of the Order of Preachers
1182-1226	Francis of Assisi, founder of the Order of Friars Minor
c. 1182-1253	Clare of Assisi, founder of the Order of Poor Clares
1225-1274	Thomas Aquinas, Dominican scholar

Medieval society was complex. Medieval people embraced several distinct ways of life. And within these, there were innumerable subdivisions–to say nothing of the variations within each derived from the sex of its members. The expectations society had of the lord of a castle, for example, were quite different from those of his lady, though she often was more influential in society than he.

Even though the society of the Middle Ages was complex, it is more easily understood than many because it was informed by a culture based on a unified world-view, the core of which was a commitment to Christianity. This is not to suggest that medieval people behaved in a more Christian fashion than those of other ages; people of all ages seem to behave in strikingly similar ways. It is rather that almost all medieval people agreed how they *should* behave–and this is rare in the history of culture. The story is told–a medieval story–of a knight who had divorced his wife and taken another. He demanded absolution from his bishop, and, since the knight had no intention of restoring his first wife to her place, he approached the bishop sword in hand. The bishop replied to the knight's demand for absolution by stretching out his neck and said only: "Strike!" The knight was taken aback and, after some hesitation, retreated, saying: "I hate you too much to send you straight to heaven." For all his refusal to behave according to medieval Christian standards, that knight believed in those standards. In short, although medieval people often behaved outrageously, they called their behavior sin and not social maladjustment.

Because medieval people were unique not in their behavior, but in their ideals, and because those ideals have been extremely influential in the subsequent history of western civilization, we shall discuss their society primarily in terms of those ideals and the institutions created to realize them. In one area of society, however, not only ideals but practice as well have influenced us mightily: the medieval approach to dissident elements in society has greatly affected our social norms and behavior. Thus the heretic and the Jew must be discussed along with monks, nuns, and popes, with kings, queens, and knights, with townsfolk and farmers.

Our discussion will begin with an examination of the spiritual basis of medieval society, of the values that virtually all the people of the time shared. Then we shall consider the ideas and ideals that informed each individual group in society and the institutions that medieval people created to bring those ideals to life. Lastly, we shall examine the effects, sometimes revolutionary, that followed from each groups' efforts to realize their aspirations and longings.

"Medieval society" will thus involve for us both ideas and institutions, goals and consequences–considerations which go far beyond what is ordinarily meant by social history. To put it another way, we shall try to see holistically as much of medieval life and thought as possible within the scope and purpose of this book. Our consideration of culture and society–as thus broadly defined–embraces a very large package indeed. So we shall divide that consideration into two categories: "regular" and "secular"–terms themselves products of the time. "Regular" in this context does not mean ordinary. Indeed, the members of medieval society who were called "regular" were relatively few in number. "Regular" comes from the Latin word *regula*, which means "rule." Thus those men and women who lived according to a rule were "regulars." This group included monks and nuns, canons and canonesses, friars and the cloistered women who supported the friars by their prayer.

"Secular" comes from the Latin word *saecula* which means "world." Medieval people, most of whom were "seculars," did not think of themselves as "worldly" when they used the word. It meant for them that they lived out in the world and not cloistered in monasteries. The "secular" folk included secular clergy–bishops, priests and other clergymen living in the world and serving as pastors, as shepherds to their flocks. The lay people called "secular" were members of those flocks. This group included the warrior and governmental class of knights and noblemen; the "middle" class of artisans and craft people, of manufacturers and merchants; and, of course, the most important group of all, the farmers. These "seculars" we shall consider in the chapter that follows this one. In this chapter we shall discuss the "regular" members of society–but only after we examine the spiritual basis on which this whole social structure was built.

A. The Saintly Ideal: Bernard of Clairvaux

Because a commitment to Christianity was the enduring basis of medieval society, it is necessary to explore the view of Christian life reflected in the lives and works of those who shaped and led society. Few people have ever had such a great influence on their age as did Bernard of Clairvaux, who lived from 1090 to 1153. Bernard's powerful personality and magnificent rhetoric made such an impact on his own generation and on people of later generations–such as Martin Luther and John Calvin–that his descriptions of the path to God have greatly influenced all subsequent Christian thinking.

Bernard was a monk, a man dedicated to a life of prayer, meditation on Scripture, and manual labor. Yet he was also the active leader of Christendom in the twelfth century in so many aspects of the life of the time that it would be difficult to find a parallel in any other similar period. Perhaps more than any other single event in his life, Bernard's role in settling the papal schism of 1130 reveals the extent of his influence. Bernard played a powerful part in deciding who was to be pope, and, through his letters and preaching, he converted the most powerful persons in Europe to his point of view. In an age in which religion is as important as it surely was in the twelfth century, the person instrumental in the choice of the leader of the institutional expression of that religion is a person of great power. And from 1136 to his death in 1153, Bernard did not cease to play a role of primary significance in the affairs of his world.

Bernard's role in preaching the Second Crusade was critical to the launching of that expedition. His influence aroused the European conscience to the point that he could write to Pope Eugenius III:

You have commanded, and I have obeyed. And the authority of your command has made my obedience fruitful. Since "I have announced and have spoken, [the soldiers of the Cross] have increased beyond number [Psalm 39:6]." Cities and castles are emptied, and now seven women can hardly find one man to hold [Isaiah 4:1]–so much so that everywhere there are widows whose husbands are still alive.

In the course of launching the crusade, Bernard enrolled, at Vézelay in March 1146, the army of a willing–indeed eager–King Louis VII of France. At Speyer, in December of that same year, Bernard enlisted the army of a hesitant emperor-elect Conrad III. Conrad was understandably reluctant, since the tensions in Germany between his family and the supporters of Conrad's old enemy, Duke Welf IV, were approaching a state of civil war. Bernard's influence won Welf to the same cause as his ruler and thus enabled both sides to join in the crusading pilgrimage. Largely because of Bernard's efforts, a vast army of men took the cross and set out for the Holy Land.

Bernard had a strong voice in the direction of the society of his time. Many of the over five hundred letters of his which have come down to us are addressed to clergymen, exhorting them to fulfill their ministry according to the pattern of Christian virtue. Bernard admonished and praised scores of lay leaders as well. He was truly a tutor to popes and the conscience of kings. The administration of early twelfth-century society was thus subject to Bernard's surveillance. But that was not all.

Bernard also powerfully influenced the intellectual and spiritual life of Europe. His own contribution to theology was great, and his influence on the development of this discipline was strong. Bernard also affected the politics of his time by insisting that lay rulers have the same goal as spiritual leaders: to promote the peace and order that allows the growth of love among their people. Bernard brought his weight to bear on economic and social theory not only by his voluminous writings, but also by his energetic action in these spheres. In short, Bernard was a leader in so many aspects of early twelfth-century culture that it is impossible to study his age without studying him.

Bernard's leadership makes us wonder how a monk could play so significant a role in society. How a man dedicated to withdrawal from the world could have so much influence on the world? My conviction is that Bernard could lead Europe to a crusade, powerfully influence who Europe's leaders were to be and how they were to act, and help shape the spiritual life of Europe's inhabitants because his life and teaching embodied so many ideals of his age, some of which had not yet crystallized until his coming. The ideals of twelfth-century Europeans centered on spiritual values. Since so many thought monks exemplified these ideals most perfectly, it was possible for Bernard to articulate the values and aspirations of his age. Because of his genius, Bernard was able to explicate convincingly the ideals and values implicit in his society's choice of him as leader.

B. The Spiritual Foundation of Society

Bernard and a number of his contemporaries—most of whom were also monks—introduced a revolutionary view of Christian life to twelfth-century Europe. We recall that the universe envisioned by early Christian spiritual writers, notably Augustine of Hippo, was a Neo-platonic cosmos. That universe was structured and arranged hierarchically: God, who was Pure Spirit, was at the pinnacle of a host of descending ranks of spiritual entities. Human beings were seen as vastly inferior to all this army of assorted angels, for the spiritual component of humans, their souls, was imprisoned in material bodies. The rest of the universe, made of mere matter, was still more inferior and literally next to nothing.

The twelfth century saw the introduction of a radically new view of the universe and of the humans who inhabit it. The path to happiness trod by most people in the High Middle Ages had been but dimly seen and hesitantly explored before this time. Their understanding of Christ and of the Church they believed he had founded was also startlingly new.

The universe in which Bernard lived was energized, he was sure, by the creative and redeeming force of love, the love of a Creator God who is Love. All of creation, both matter and spirit, thus reflects the overwhelming goodness and indwelling love of God. Bernard and his friends were convinced that human beings, though often flawed by prideful self-centeredness, are basically good because God created them good. They are capable of the happiness for which they long and God destined them. These revolutionary thinkers did not see the human body as a prison for the soul. For them the body is so essential to human nature and its perfection that they thought we cannot fully enjoy the beatitude of paradise until the resurrection of our bodies at the end of time.

Twelfth-century spiritual leaders like Bernard followed Augustine of Hippo's analysis of the soul's faculties to know (the intellect), to choose (the will), and to recollect (the memory). But to this triad they added another faculty, the *affectus*, that functions in human attachment, emotion, feeling, and passion. Passion was not viewed as evil, and Augustine's aversion to sex they rejected out of hand. Indeed, Bernard spent some eighteen years offering to his monks sermons on the Old Testament book, the Song of Songs. In his talks, Bernard lyrically portrayed the sexual union between husband and wife as a convincing symbol of Christ's passionate love for each and every human soul.

The teaching of Augustine on the Church Bernard rejected as well. The Neo-platonic hierarchy of monk, cleric, and lay person was replaced by the conviction that people with all sorts of vocations are on the path to perfection, that all cross the sea of life with every prospect of success.

An image of Jesus as a remote and all-powerful divine being was shared by ancient Christian thinkers—and by medieval and modern Orthodox theologians as well. Bernard, and most other twelfth- and thirteenth-century thinkers, celebrated Jesus' human nature. They learned from their reading of Scripture that Jesus had a body, that he got hungry, thirsty, and at times sad and angry, that he wept, slept, and sometimes was exhausted. They thought of him as a babe at his mother's breast, as a boy debating the sages in the Temple at Jerusalem, and as a man suffering pain and experiencing death.

In the early thirteenth century, Francis of Assisi (1182-1226) created the first Christmas crib scene. And, in the years between Bernard and Francis–and after–the representations of Jesus on the cross showed less and less the triumphant God and more and more the suffering man. If Jesus were really a man, these people believed, human potential seemed, with God's aid, to be limitless. The world became less a place to be feared and shunned than a splendid stage on which humans could play a glorious part.

The drama in which humans act was also viewed as a pilgrimage, one that leads from humility, the perfection of the intellect in self-knowledge, to love, the perfection of the will. For Bernard and the other intellectual leaders of the High Middle Ages, human happiness is attained through true love–love for self, love for neighbor, and love for God. And for them, the human capacity for emotion and attachment is perfected in friendship, the most natural and holiest of human relationships, which is a ladder by which to ascend to friendship with Christ and thus to union with him.

In a universe animated, indeed inundated, by God's love, all creatures have a need for relationship. To this rule, Bernard believed, humans are no exception. One of Bernard's friends, Aelred of Rievaulx, wrote of this basic human need:

> When God created [the first] human, in order to commend the goodness of society he said: "It is not good for the man to be alone; let us make for him a helper like himself" [Genesis 2:18]. It was from no merely similar stuff, nor even from the same sort of matter, that the divine power formed this helper. But rather, as a most impressive incentive to love and friendship, he brought forth the woman from the very substance of the man.

Thus, from the very beginning of human existence, the social nature of the human species was affirmed. Aelred's admiration for God's plan is clear:

> How beautiful it is that the second human being was taken from the side of the first [Genesis 2:21-22], so that nature might teach that all [human beings] are equal–side by side, so to speak–and that there should be no superior or inferior in human affairs....Thus, from the very beginning, nature imprinted in the human heart the desire for friendship and love....

Aelred and Bernard and their friends believed that human nature demands the society of others. It is understandable, therefore, that they thought the human quest for happiness could be pursued only in a social context. And that context was, for them, the people of God, the Church.

C. Society as Church

For Bernard and his contemporaries, Church and society were two sides of the same coin. They saw each person and each social group having a place and a role in a process very much like a pilgrimage. That pilgrimage has individual and corporate perfection as its goal. Bernard was sure that that society, that Church, is called to union with God, and thus that all individuals within Church and society are so called. The Church is not simply an institution or a corporation. She is the sum total of all those following, however feebly, the path to perfection.

The many images of the Church that Bernard employed show his conviction that communal and individual happiness are intimately associated. Perhaps the most enduring image of Church that Bernard put forth is that of a bride, for "the Bridegroom of the Church [is] Jesus Christ, our Lord." Christ's bride is thus the entire community of those made righteous by God. Each become a bride of Christ within the one bride who is the Church.

This intimate relationship of individual and community is evident in Bernard's images of Church as a mother who feeds her nurslings "from the breasts of wisdom," as a vineyard "planted by the Lord, bought with his blood, fertilized by grace, and made fruitful by his Spirit." The Church is a city "because she is an assembly of souls, a bride because beloved, a sheep because gentle."

Bernard's still more dynamic image of the Church is a sea crossed by three sorts of wayfarers: monks, clergy, and laity. Whatever group in society we belong to or whatever spiritual way of life we find most compatible with our own individual nature or personal inclinations, God's love will provide for our needs. Different people receive different gifts. The very diversity in our paths to God was for Bernard a sign of unity, "a unity that consists in one love." Bernard was confident that a loving response to God's love will lead each person to happiness, no matter what path he or she follows. For "there is not just one path to follow," and "whatever path one follows,...no one will be left outside the Father's house."

D. Cistercian Monks and the Third Wave of Reform

The Cluniac Reform of the Church was successful, as we have seen, in restoring monastic life and in serving as a recruiting ground for reform-minded bishops. The Cluniac movement also encouraged movements–such as the Peace and Truce of God–devoted to peace and justice for all of society. But what happens so frequently in history also happened to the Cluniac Reform. Reforms–like other ideas–must be translated into institutions to be effective. And what happens to those institutions–invariably, I think–is that they become more important than the idea which the institution was created to realize. As a result, a new idea, a new reform must take its place. Cluniac monasticism was not corrupt, but by the twelfth century it had become comfortable. As is true for all times, young people who wished to devote themselves completely to God were not attracted to the merely comfortable.

The second wave of reform, the Gregorian, was directed primarily at institutional change in the Church at large. As we have seen, the laborers in the vineyard of this reform aimed at freeing the institutional Church from control by contemporary governments. This movement, begun in the eleventh century, had largely succeeded by the twelfth. In almost all the churches of Europe, local bodies that represented the clergy and people of their dioceses elected bishops. This success led to a shift in focus of the whole notion of reform: from institutional reform toward personal re-formation aimed at attaining a deeper spiritual life.

And it was this longing for a more complete and fulfilling form of Christian life that led, in the late eleventh century, to a wide variety of individual and institutional responses that together constituted a third wave of reform. Men who chose the solitary life often wandered from place to place preaching the good news of the gospel to groups small and large. Followers of Bruno of Cologne retreated to the isolated valley of La Grande Chartreuse, in the French Alps, and there spent their lives in meditation and prayer for the world outside. But by far the most popular new institution of the time was the order of Cîteaux, founded in 1098 in Burgundy.

There, and in the hundreds of monasteries soon founded from Cîteaux, the monks called Cistercian sought to live according to the *Rule* of Saint Benedict in all its original purity. Thus, they were reformers, looking back to what they saw as a golden moment in the history of monasticism. But, to capture that moment, the Cistercian founders introduced or popularized some revolutionary institutions. At a time of expanding population, the lands donated to Cistercians by lesser feudal and imperial lords were generally not as extensive as the lands once ceded to Cluny and similar houses by the great lords of the less densely populated tenth and eleventh centuries. As a result, Cistercian land was often scattered throughout the countryside at some distance from the monastery. To farm these lands Cistercian houses sent out *conversi* (sometimes erroneously called "lay brothers") who lived on these isolated farms called granges. The *conversi* most often came from farming families–though some were the offspring of noble families–and they usually did not know the Latin that would enable them to pray the entire communal office of the choir monks. But, through the institution of the *conversus*, uneducated men could once more lead a monastic life–though their public prayer was both shortened and simplified.

Another revolutionary institution adopted by the Cistercians was a system of filiation by which the abbot of a "mother" house would visit annually each of its "daughter" foundations to offer encouragement. An annual meeting of all Cistercian abbots, the Chapter General, also supported each house in maintaining a vigorously committed life of personal and institutional reformation.

By these means Cistercians aimed at the sustained pursuit of an intensely Christian life of love. Cistercian monks spent between three and four hours a day in communal prayer, singing hymns, chanting psalms, and hearing readings from the

Bible and from early Christian writers. There was also much time for private prayer and meditation on Scripture. Their life was simple and free of visual and noise distractions. Manual labor was a central part of the Cistercian day–for choir monks as well as *conversi*. This was a conscious rejection of the usual monastic practice of Cluniac and other Benedictine monasteries of the time. These non-Cistercian monasteries lived from the labor of the farmers who worked their vast estates. Cistercians, on the other hand, refused to "live off the sweat of other men's brows."

The Cistercian commitment to live permanently in a specific monastic family aimed at enhancing the love that monks and nuns were to have for their brothers or sisters. And this love was extended to all of society through a flood of letters and spiritual writings. Some Cistercians, like Bernard, would travel outside their monasteries when the pressing needs of society required that loving response.

Twelfth-century Cistercian life proved intensely appealing to thousands of young people of all classes. At the time of Bernard's death in 1153, there were 350 Cistercian monasteries all over Europe, from Ireland to Poland, and Bernard himself had founded sixty-six of them. The spiritual leadership that Cistercians offered to society led scores of church communities to elect Cistercian monks as bishops, thus bringing deeply spiritual values to an increasingly wide sector of society. One of Bernard's monks was elected bishop of Rome in 1145 and served in that leadership position as Pope Eugenius III.

E. Regular Canons and the Philosophy of History

Another twelfth-century reform movement was initiated by Bernard's friend Norbert of Xanten (1080-1139), who attempted–largely successfully–to do for regular canons what Bernard and the Cistercians had done for monasticism. A canon was a priest attached to a church whose spiritual needs were served by several clergymen. As an indication of his commitment to this church, a priest inscribed his name on the clergy list (or canon) of that church and thus was himself called a canon. As a part of the reform movements of the eleventh and twelfth centuries, many groups or chapters of canons adopted what they called the "apostolic life." This was a conscious attempt to live the life of early Christians, as recorded in the biblical book, the Acts of the Apostles. The canons prayed together, shared a common purse, and supported each other's pastoral and educational ministry. These canons sought to institutionalize their "apostolic life" by adopting a rule, and were thus called "regular" canons. Most chapters of canons adopted the *Rule* of Saint Augustine that was based on that fifth-century bishop's spiritual instructions to a community of women.

Norbert founded a new house of regular canons at Prémontré near Laon, and the life there attracted so many men that new foundations were required, many of them in Germany and central Europe. These houses were, like the Cistercians, linked through the legislation of a Chapter General. The Praemonstratensians–so-called from the Latin word for Prémontré–lived a prayerful life in monasteries, from which they went out to serve the spiritual needs of the surrounding communities. Praemonstratensian communal prayer was open to all and thus designed to serve the canons' essential purpose: serving as an example to others of the joys of living the Christian life.

These reform movements of the twelfth century, notably the Cistercian and Praemonstratensian reforms, went beyond the institutional framework of traditional monasticism or canonical life. All this was symbolized by the simple, undyed clothing which they adopted–white instead of the traditional black. Traditionalists found these changes and, above all, the more rigorous life-style of the new reformers to be unnecessary, impudent, and downright insulting. One such traditionalist, Rupert, a monk of the monastery of Deutz, asked of the innovators:

> Why should there be so many novelties in the Church of God? Why all these new orders? What is the point in having so many sorts of clerics and monks? Who would not be scandalized by such diversity? Is not a religion contemptible that is continually agitated by so many new laws, new customs, new rules, and what-not? How can a wise man consider anything so changeable and variable worth imitating?

Anselm of Havelberg was admirably suited to answer these charges. He was a disciple of Norbert of Xanten and, like his mentor, became a bishop in Germany (1129) and an advisor to emperors. Anselm also had to defend himself against the charge of novelty when he undertook missions to Constantinople, in 1135-1136, for the emperor Lothar and again in 1153, this time for the Cistercian pope Eugenius III. At the capital of the Eastern Roman Empire, Anselm engaged in friendly debate with theologians of the Greek Church who found the western positions on the Holy Spirit, the use of unleavened bread in the Lord's Supper, and the primacy of the bishop of Rome to be unacceptable innovations. In response to the charges of traditionalists abroad and at home, Anselm undertook to show, in a book called the *Dialogues*, that the history of humankind is an evolutionary process. This process calls for continual change in the institutional expression of truth (for example, new orders) and in how people understand and express their Christian beliefs. In this way the Church is constantly renewed and perennially youthful. The faith remains essentially the same, but each age must understand it in ways applicable to that age. Because people are not stirred by the familiar and comfortable, variety and new developments in theology and religious life are necessary.

Anselm elaborated a theory of history in which the unifying thread was a continual, progressive movement of reform in the Church. Most ancient thinkers were concerned with the logic of things as they are at a given moment, not as they become over the course of time. By and large, thinkers of the Early and High Middle Ages adopted this ancient analytical approach, but they added a concern with development in time that enabled them, as they thought, to use the past to see the present and the future more clearly. As Bernard of Chartres said in the early twelfth century, "We are like pygmies who stand on the shoulders of giants [the ancient writers], and we are therefore able to see much farther than they." Medieval thinkers acknowledged their debt to antiquity, but saw their own, their "modern," world as still better.

F. The Friars: A New Reform Idea and Institution

By the early thirteenth century, the Cistercians and Praemonstratensians had become successful, both in numbers of monasteries and in the economic security of the individual houses. Neither order was corrupt, but with institutional middle age came a measure of relaxation in the commitment that many young women and men sought. And so the thirteenth century saw a new movement of reform, a movement based on a new idea of how the Christian life could be led, a movement which produced a new element in medieval society, the friar (from *frater*, the Latin word for "brother"). The friar was a member of the regular clergy like the monk and the regular canon, for like them he followed a rule. But friars were unequivocally committed to a life of apostolic service in the world. Friars went wherever they were needed to preach, teach, and minister to the spiritual needs of Christians. They even took the message of Christianity outside Europe: the thirteenth century saw them preaching to the Muslims of North Africa and the Middle East and traveling across Asia to take their message to China. The friars felt a special call to minister to the needs of the growing and increasingly prosperous middle class in medieval cities. They hoped by the example of the poverty in which they lived to lead people away from an undue preoccupation with material things.

Franciscan friars are named for a remarkable figure, Francis of Assisi (1182-1226). Francis was the son of a wealthy merchant who left his carefree ways for a life of prayer and penance. One day in church he heard the priest read the gospel "describing how the Lord sent out his disciples to preach." We are told that "when the Mass was over, Francis humbly begged the priest to explain the gospel to him." From the priest

> Francis heard that the followers of Christ must not possess gold or silver, no money or purse or wallet–not even bread. They were not to carry a staff on their way. Nor were they to wear shoes or possess more than one tunic. But they were to preach the kingdom of God and a life of repentance for sin. Then Francis was so filled with joy in the Holy Spirit that he declared: "This is what I wish; this is what I seek; this is what I long for from the bottom of my heart."

And so Francis set out to follow the path pointed to by Jesus. Since Jesus had had "no place where he could lay his head," Francis had none. He wandered from place to place, earning his keep by the most menial of tasks, and taking shelter wherever it was given.

Francis' simple, straightforward, and literal reading of the Christian message was enthusiastically received by thousands who heard it. And those folk delighted in repeating stories about how Francis preached to birds and how he protected the people in the town of Gubbio by reasoning with a predatory wolf. There is no doubt that Francis did think the natural world is infused with God's love. Francis embraced that world and saw it as a mirror of the Divine. His intimate relationship to nature is reflected well in his splendid *Canticle of Brother Sun*:

> Praised be you, my Lord, with all your creatures,
>   especially Sir Brother Sun
> Who is the day and through whom you give us light.
> And he is beautiful and radiant with great splendor,
>   and bears a likeness of you....
> Praised be you my Lord, through Sister Water,
>   who is very useful and humble and precious and chaste....

Just before his death in 1226, the now blind and seriously ill Francis added these lines to his hymn:

> Praised be you, my Lord, through our Sister Bodily Death,
>   from whom no living person can escape....
> Blessed are those whom death will find in your most holy will....
> Praise and bless my Lord and give him thanks
>   and serve him with great humility.

Francis' openness to God and the world, his generous attempts to follow Jesus, no matter what the cost, won him disciples from the first days of his ministry. Soon a flood of followers embraced his life. Francis' approach to life was simple and sincere, but the ragged preacher of Assisi made no provision for the hundreds of young men and old who embraced his ideals. Some of those initiates needed an education to become effective preachers; some of the friars who were seriously ill or nearing death needed care. If they were not to become social parasites, they needed fixed shelter for their bodies and churches from which to serve their flocks. Francis' magnificent vision was unclouded by any awareness of these practical needs. The attempts of his followers to create institutions to meet those needs were understood by Francis as attacks on his idea of absolute poverty. Francis abdicated the leadership of what had rapidly become a structured order and retired to a mountain retreat. There he experienced pain like that of crucifixion, the marks of which, it was believed, he carried to his death.

The friars who followed Dominic Guzmán (1170-1221) faced no such ideological or institutional crises. The official name of these Dominicans, the Order of Preachers, expresses these friars' single-minded approach. They sought to serve their neighbors through their preaching–preaching by word and example. Whatever institutions they saw might serve them in their ministry they eagerly embraced. The Order possessed churches and houses, though the individual friars remained without personal possessions. Their houses were not only residences but schools for continuing education in theology. In each house resided a lecturer in theology and a director of studies. As preachers and missionaries, the Dominicans had to be well educated, and so very early they began to establish regional schools of theology. They attended the newly emerging universities of the time too, and some, notably Thomas Aquinas (1225-1274), became professors at Paris and other universities.

Only slowly and painfully did the Franciscans follow the Dominicans in all these institutional developments. Their ideal was a life style, that of Francis, rather than being task oriented, as was the aim of the Dominicans. Indeed, there was always a group of Franciscans who resisted institutionalization by insisting on a radical, absolute poverty. We shall meet these "Spiritual" Franciscans again.

G. Women of the Cloister

The twelfth and thirteenth centuries saw women play a significant role in the Christian society of the world. This was equally true of the life of women who embraced Christianity by separating themselves from the traditional female roles of mother, homemaker, and helpmate–though they did not reject those callings. There were nuns, regular canonesses, and women who embraced the ideals, if not the activities, of Francis and Dominic. There were also women who adopted new ways of living a dedicated life–ways which had no male equivalent and were inspired by their own inventiveness. Many women, especially in England, chose a solitary life. They lived in simple dwellings attached to their parish churches, supporting themselves by their own labor. These women lived lives of prayer and scriptural meditation, and they offered spiritual guidance to the men and women of their village or town.

The founders of the Cistercian reform did not provide for women within their organization. This left women who felt attracted to Cistercian life free to found their own monasteries and within them to follow Cistercian customs. Consequently, hundreds of houses of Cistercian women were founded all over Europe. Eventually Cistercian men accepted some of these monasteries for women within their order. Indeed, in the thirteenth century, women followed the life of the earliest Cistercians more faithfully than did Cistercian men, and several of these Cistercian women gained widespread recognition of their holiness, prompting frequent requests by lay folk for spiritual guidance.

Norbert of Xanten intended that all Praemonstratensian houses be double monasteries, housing both men and women who would support by prayer the teaching and preaching work of Praemonstratensian canons. By 1190, this plan was abandoned, which allowed the now autonomous nuns to settle in the neighborhood of the canons' houses and call on them only to serve as chaplains. Hundreds of houses of regular canonesses–not all of them Praemonstratensian–dotted the medieval countryside. Within those houses the canonesses lived very much the same life as Cistercian nuns–a life of prayer and meditation that promoted love for each other and for their neighbors in the world.

Perhaps the most influential of monasteries of women in the twelfth century was the abbey of Fontevrault. This house of nuns was led by an abbess who also was the superior of a group of priests who, in addition to their own separate liturgical life, served as chaplains to the nuns. There was also a contingent of *conversi* living at Fontevrault, and these men helped the nuns with the most demanding physical tasks of farm life. That a woman should be the spiritual leader of a group of men no one considered shocking in the twelfth century. As we shall see, women of that century were a major force in society.

Both the Dominicans and Franciscans quickly established or recognized communities of women associated with their orders. The Dominican houses for women were initially a result of the friars' success in converting heretics in southern France and Italy. The women who had lived an extremely austere life in the esoteric sects of those areas–sects of which we shall later speak–sought a new outlet for their spiritual longings. As a result, the friars supported the foundation of houses for Dominican nuns, who, in turn, supported the friars by their prayers.

Franciscan women are often called Poor Clares, a name derived from their founder, Clare of Assisi (c. 1182-1253). Clare met Francis sometime about 1210, and embraced his ideal of poverty with total abandon. Francis arranged to house her and her nuns next to San Damiano, the first of the churches that he had earlier repaired. There Clare lived for some forty-two years until her death. Like Francis, Clare faced problems of institutionalization. It was difficult to reconcile her reckless embrace of absolute poverty with the necessity of housing and feeding the women who flocked to her.

The increasing insistence by the thirteenth-century institutional church that preaching should be a task confined to men meant that Franciscan women lived the cloistered life of the nun. The fact that monasteries of Poor Clares were usually in towns or near them led their papally appointed protector, a cardinal of the Roman church, to insist on a strict enclosure of the nuns, isolated by walls and grills from the outside world. In the fourteenth century, this draconian solution to a practical problem was associated with, perhaps replaced by, a growing misogyny that led to the strict enclosure of nuns of all orders. Misogyny, the devaluation of women, would become an attitude limiting the lives of all women, regular and secular, in the Late Middle Ages, the period from 1300 to 1600. Indeed, misogyny would continue, as we well know, to be rife in the western world down to our very own day.

VII. HIGH MEDIEVAL CULTURE AND SOCIETY II: THE SECULARS

Some Useful Data

1030	death of Adalberon, bishop of Laon
c. 1103	death of Manegold of Lautenbach, political theorist
c. 1090-1153	Bernard, abbot of Clairvaux
c. 1110-1167	Aelred, abbot of Rievaulx
c. 1120-1180	John of Salisbury, bishop of Chartres
1198-1216	reign of Innocent III, pope
1227-1241	reign of Gregory IX, pope
1225-1274	Thomas Aquinas, Dominican scholar
1235-1315	Ramon Lull, Franciscan scholar
1265-1321	Dante Alighieri, Italian poet
c. 1340-1400	Geoffrey Chaucer, English poet

One of the images Bernard of Clairvaux employed in describing the human quest for happiness is the crossing of a sea–the sea of life. For Bernard the means of crossing that sea varies from person to person. "This extensive sea," he wrote, "is traversed by three classes of people, each crossing safely in its own way." Bernard saw these classes typified by three biblical figures. Daniel, "a man of longings," crosses the sea with his eyes fixed on God by means of the bridge of monasticism. Noah, who signifies the secular clergy, keeps one eye on the goal and the other on his passengers. He crosses the sea by ship, and, indeed, captains the "ark" of the Church, so that it does not "perish in the flood." Job, who wades across a ford and is adept at "dispensing the goods of the world in the married state, signifies the faithful laity." We have spoken of Daniel, so we shall now speak of Noah and Job.

A. The Secular Clergy

The secular clergy lived in the world (*saecula*) and served its people and God as bishops, priests, and deacons. Their functions were to preach and teach Christianity and to minister to the needs of their people–to serve as pastors, that is, shepherds, of their flocks.

The basic unit of organization for the secular or pastoral clergy in early and medieval Christianity was the diocese–also called a bishopric or see. In those regions of Europe that had formerly been part of the old Roman Empire, this unit was the rather small area of one city and its environs. In northern Europe a bishopric was originally a missionary area and was much larger. Over a diocese presided a bishop who was its spiritual shepherd and whose symbols of office were, as we have seen, a crosier, or shepherd's crook, and a ring that symbolized his marriage to his Church. The pastoral work of the various bishops was coordinated by an archbishop, usually the bishop of the most important city in a region. The activities of all the archbishops and bishops of the western Church were similarly coordinated by the bishop of Rome, the pope.

About the year 590, Gregory the Great wrote a book entitled *Pastoral Care* that was to serve the medieval clergyman as a manual for the conduct of his office. It instructed him that

> it is necessary that in thought he should be pure, in action firm, discreet in keeping silence, profitable in speech. He should be a close neighbor to everyone through his empathy, brought near to God through meditation. He should be a humble and familiar friend to those who live well but unbending against the vices of evil-doers–out of zeal for their righteousness. He should not relax his concern for the inward life because of his occupation with outward things, but he should not neglect to provide for outward things in his anxiety over what is inward.

Bishops were assisted in the pastoral ministry of their dioceses by priests and deacons. From the eighth century onwards, dioceses were divided into parishes under the care of priests who ministered to the religious needs of local communities. The ideal life of a parish priest was sketched by the English poet, Geoffrey Chaucer (c. 1340-1400), in his *Canterbury Tales*:

> There was a good man of the priest's vocation,
> A poor town parson with true consecration,
> But he was rich in holy thought and work.
> Learned he was, in the truest sense a clerk,
> Who truly knew Christ's gospel
> And would preach it devoutly to his parishioners.
> He was a kind man, wonderfully diligent,
> And patient when adversity was sent....
> Wide was his parish, with houses far asunder,
> Yet he neglected not in rain or thunder,
> In sickness or in grief, to pay a call
> On the remotest, whether great or small.

Chaucer capped his praise of the priest's pastoral ministry to the pious and to the sinful by remarking: "I think there never was a better priest." He then concluded: "Christ and his twelve apostles and their love he taught, but followed it himself before."

Chaucer knew–as do we–that not all priests lived up to this high standard, this ideal of the Cluniac, Gregorian, and Bernardine reforms. But Chaucer also knew that priests who betrayed their ministry were in danger of reprimand or removal by their bishops. And bishops who were unfaithful to their Church and people were subject to condemnation by their fellow bishops who met in regional church councils.

B. The Lay Leaders of Society

The world, like the Church in the world, was a union of three components. Toward the end of the tenth century, Adalberon, the bishop of Laon, wrote:

> The city of God which is believed to be one is divided into three: some pray, others fight, and the others work. These three groups live together and could not endure separation. The services of each one of them allows the work of the other two. Each, by turn, lends its support to all.

If Adalberon's characterization of medieval society is overly simple, as it is when applied to the High Middle Ages, the eleventh through thirteenth centuries, his brief description of the upper class of that society was cherished by clergymen throughout the whole Middle Ages: "The nobles are the warriors and the protectors of the Churches. They defend all the people, great and small, and, incidentally, protect themselves." We have already seen how this feudal structure developed out of urgent necessity, but the feudal code was to serve as a standard of behavior for the upper classes even after feudalism ceased to be the only way of governing Europe.

In addition to protecting all the members of their society, the nobility were to govern the people, and govern them justly. Power is a necessary prerequisite to the task of governance, and the eleventh-century political theorist Manegold of Lautenbach placed the source of that power in the people. The ruler must "exercise the power committed to him with...equity. For the people do not...concede to the ruler an unlimited power of tyrannizing over them, but rather of defending them against the tyranny and wickedness of others." In Manegold's view, the people provide the ruler with power; the ruler's part in this social contract is to use that power to provide justice. Manegold added:

> If the ruler breaks the contract by which he was elected, and ruins and confounds what he was established to order correctly, reason justly considers that he has absolved the people from their duty of submission to him. This is because the ruler first broke the bond of mutual fidelity by which he was bound to them and they to him.

Manegold's assertion of the right of revolution would eventually be reflected in the American Declaration of Independence. And George III was not the first ruler to feel its effects. Several medieval rulers, including the emperor Henry IV and George's predecessor on the English throne, King John, found themselves deposed or threatened with deposition as a result of the near universal acceptance of Manegold's principle. If the unjust ruler resisted deposition, the result could be disastrous. As John of Salisbury, an early twelfth-century political commentator, put it:

> To kill a tyrant is not only licit but fair and just....Tyranny is not only a public crime, but, if this were possible, more than a public crime. For, if the crime of treason admits all people as prosecutors, how much more the crime committed against the laws which ought to have empire over emperors themselves.

C. Chivalry

To fulfill the functions assigned him by society, the ideal medieval ruler, whether great nobleman or simple knight, had to possess certain virtues. Foremost among these was, of course, military prowess. His role demanded not only great physical strength and skill. In addition he was expected to exhibit courage and steadfastness, integrity, loyalty, generosity, and humility–that is, moral qualities of a high order. In the thirteenth century, Ramon Lull (1235-1315) wrote a popular treatise on chivalry that sets forth some of the ideal requirements for an aspirant to knighthood:

> Inquires should...be made of the squire who is a candidate for knighthood, asking if he were ever guilty of the falseness or treachery which are contrary to the order of chivalry. If a squire be vainglorious of that which he does, he is not worthy to be a knight. For vainglory is a vice which destroys the merits and blessings that flow from the benefits of chivalry. A squire who flatters brings discord to the order of chivalry. For a man who is a flatterer corrupts good intentions, and the nobility which pertains to the courage of the knight is thereby destroyed. A squire who is proud, ill taught, full of wicked words, of base courage, avaricious, a liar, untruthful, slothful, a glutton, perjured, or who is afflicted with any similar vice is not acceptable to chivalry.

The medieval knight was rewarded for the exercise of chivalric virtues with the honor accorded him by society. That knight felt an obligation to maintain those virtues or risk disgrace. This catalogue of knightly virtues allows us to see clearly that chivalry was a christianization of the feudal ethic that was itself the descendent of the old Germanic warrior code.

As an aid in inculcating the virtues of chivalry, the candidate for knighthood went through an elaborate ceremony, partly dictated by feudal usage, but with a strong Christian element added by clergymen. Ramon Lull advised:

> Before a squire enters the order of chivalry, it is necessary that he confess the sins which he has committed against God, and that he be determined to serve God, who is glorious, in the same manner as chivalry. After he is cleansed of his sins, he should receive his Savior [in Communion]....The squire should fast on the vigil of his knighting,...and he should go to church and pray to God. He ought to remain awake during the night and be in his prayers, and hear about the word of God and the responsibilities of chivalry....

After attending Mass and swearing fealty to his feudal lord, "the squire should lift up his eyes to God and his hands to heaven. His sponsoring knight should gird him with a sword, a sign of chastity, of justice, and of love." Ramon Lull recommended that "the new knight ride through the town and show himself to the people, for the awareness that people know him as a knight will lead him to concern lest he sin against the order of chivalry."

The newly knighted lad entered an order just as surely as a novice enters a monastery. Even his weapons had a religious significance. The whole process of becoming a knight was calculated to instill in the knight the idea that he was to be a servant of society. The idea of *noblesse oblige*, the notion that noble status imposes serious obligations, was a natural outgrowth of the knightly ideal.

The literature of the governing class reflected all these values. The ideals of the Christian warrior were reflected in the excitement of the *chansons de geste*, songs of heroic daring. These tales of war and adventure were filled with edifying examples of heroism. This was masculine literature, and the hero of the most famous of them all, the *Song of Roland* (written about 1100), embodied a military ideal:

> Then Durendel Roland bares, his saber good,
> Spurs on his horse, is gone to strike Chernuble,
> The helmet breaks, where bright carbuncles grew,
> Slices the cap and shears the locks in two,
> Slices also the eyes and features,
> The hauberk white, whose mail was close of woof,
> Down to the groin cuts all his body through
> To the saddle, with beaten gold 'twas tooled.
> Upon the horse that sword a moment stood,
> Then sliced its spine, no join there any knew,
> Dead in the field among thick grass them threw.

D. Courtly Love

In the twelfth century, this masculine literature was complemented by a new, "courtly" literature. The courtly tradition emphasized women's role in the ennoblement of men. Young men traditionally received training in warfare from men. The lord of the castle where the young man lived–often his maternal uncle and godfather–usually took on this responsibility. The lady of the castle was in charge of his religious and social education. To please his lady, the young man needed not only military virtues, but good manners and social graces, the ability to compose poetry and to sing it. The songs the ladies liked to hear–either from the young men at their court or from wandering minstrels–was not at all the "blood and guts" epic poetry their husbands preferred. They wanted lyrics, most often love lyrics, and they got them. Women–already influential because they controlled the education of the future leaders of society–now were praised and exalted as the most noble of creatures for whom men should long. From the pen of the thirteenth-century knight and poet Walter von der Vogelweide came this verse:

> But when a lady, chaste and fair,
>   Noble and clad in rich attire,
> Walks through the throng with gracious air,
>   As sun that bids the stars retire,
> Then where are all thy boastings, month of May?
> What hast thou beautiful and gay
> Compared with that supreme delight?
> We leave thy loveliest flowers and watch that lady bright.

The people of antiquity had seen marriage primarily as a convenience; romantic love was a medieval invention. Yet, since diplomatic considerations governed most marriages in the upper class and since most love poetry was composed by men whose rank was inferior or whose age junior to the lady's, the poet or troubadour often complained of the hopelessness of his passion. It sometimes happened that courtly love degenerated from a harmless social game into an extramarital affair. By the twelfth and thirteenth centuries courtly love had moved in the opposite direction. Romantic love between husband and wife became the ideal. The manly virtues which attracted the lady became christianized. Sometimes the lady herself was spiritualized, so that men dedicated their actions to Notre Dame, the Lady in Heaven, and Francis of Assisi could speak of himself as the troubadour of Lady Poverty.

The poetry of Dante Alighieri (1265-1321) is generally regarded as the highest point in the medieval idealization of love. As a young man, Dante fell in love with a Florentine girl named Beatrice, who had an immense moral and spiritual influence on him: "She went along crowned and clothed with humility, showing no whit of pride in all that she heard and saw." Indeed, Dante thought it was his love for Beatrice that led him to the love of God, who is Love itself. Dante relates in his *La vità nuova* (New Life) how he once saw Beatrice following her handmaid Joan:

> I, Lady Joan and Lady Beatrice see,
> > Unto the place approaching where I was;
> > One marvel following the other came.
> And, as my mind reporteth unto me,
> > Love said, "This one is Spring, and this, because
> She so resembleth me, hath Love for name."

There is more symbol than narrative in this poem. There is a play in the original Italian on the words *primavera* (spring) and *prima verrà* (she shall come first). Joan (the feminine form of John) precedes Beatrice ("the Blessed One") as John the Baptist came before Christ. Joan is called "Spring." Dante saw love as the redeeming force in the world; Beatrice is called "Love" and thus symbolizes Christ, the loving redeemer. Dante thus used the form of a love lyric to express profound philosophical and theological ideas. Dante's poetry marks the culmination of the literature of courtly love, originally an expression of aristocratic culture, though Dante was himself a member of the middle class.

E. The Middle Class

If Dante's ideal was perhaps too refined to appeal to most of the solid citizens of his native Florence, there was an ideal to which most men of the medieval middle classes did aspire. The members of this group were primarily manufacturers and distributors of those goods necessary to the maintenance of medieval life and the enrichment of it. The agricultural revolution of the Early Middle Ages had produced an ever increasing food surplus that made it possible to provide nutrition to ever larger numbers of these manufacturers and merchants and thus support the towns in which they lived.

Within those towns, most citizens were grouped into guilds. The guild was an economic and social organization that included all those working in a particular trade or industry: the goldsmiths, the bakers, the fine cloth makers, the shoe makers, for example. The guild protected its members and their customers by guaranteeing fair prices and high standards of workmanship. Members could compete with one another only by increasing the quality of their product. Fines, imprisonment, or exclusion from the guild punished those who sold articles defective in either quality or quantity.

Training in the guild's craft was given through an apprenticeship system. For two to five years a boy served a master craftsman without pay. In return, the master took the boy into his home and cared for his professional, social, and religious education. After completing the apprenticeship, the young man would become a journeyman, now paid by the day (French: *jour*). He often wandered from place to place working and learning the techniques of masters in other cities and countries. There was no social gap between the master and the journeyman, between employer and employee. Wages were set at a level which permitted a reasonable standard of living, hours of work were limited, and there was no work on Saturday afternoons, Sundays, and many holidays. To qualify as a master, the journeyman presented his guild with a special piece of work to demonstrate his skill. If the work met the standards of the guild, it was acknowledged a "masterpiece," and the young man became a full member of the guild.

The guild was not merely an association of craftsmen. Its members provided for the religious and social needs of one another. If a member were sick, some of the others sat with him; if he were disabled, a guild fund supported him; if he died, his widow and orphans were supported. Their guildhall often included a chapel with its own chaplain. The guild frequently contributed windows for the town's cathedral or principal church and sponsored scenes for the religious plays that the city presented on the great feast days. The guild also provided dances and banquets to enrich the lives of its members. In short, the guild members not only served society, they took care of their own.

For most members of the medieval middle class, there was a higher goal in life than either enlightened self-interest or altruism. Most medieval merchants and craftsmen saw their service to society and to one another as a means to union with God. For this reason, members of the middle class often looked to theologians for practical guidance in their business behavior. Thomas Aquinas (1225-1274) was one of those who addressed himself to their problems. Some excerpts from his *Summa theologiae* illustrate the kind of advice churchmen gave to businessmen:

> If either the price exceed the quality of a thing's worth or, conversely, the thing exceed the price, there is no longer the equality of justice. Consequently, to sell a thing for more than it is worth or to buy it for less than it is worth is in itself unjust and unlawful. If one person derives a great advantage by becoming possessed of another person's

property and the seller be not at a loss through being without that thing, the latter ought not to raise the price, because the advantage accruing to the buyer is not due to the seller, but to a circumstance affecting the buyer. Now no person should sell what is not his or hers. On the other hand, the buyer may of his own accord pay the seller something additional. If defects be hidden and the seller does not make them known, the sale will be illicit and fraudulent, and the seller will be bound to give compensation for the loss incurred.

These are high standards that were sometimes ignored. But even when violated they remained powerful influences on behavior throughout the Middle Ages. Sometimes theologians like Thomas did not fully understand the problems of finance, and then their advice was little heeded. This was particularly true in the taking of interest on loans. Interest of any kind theologians initially regarded as usury, and they condemned it as an example of the deadly sin of avarice or greed. But gradually theologians came to redefine usury, recognizing a difference between interest justly earned and unjust, excessive interest.

F. Farmers and the Value of Labor

Justice was also the standard which ideally–if sometimes not in actuality–governed the life of the lower class of medieval Europe. The members of this class were the farmers who provided the most necessary commodity of all for their society, its food. If the farmers' occupation was not romanticized, it was nonetheless regarded as essential. John of Salisbury, comparing the state to the human body, referred to farmers as

> ...the feet of the commonwealth who discharge the humbler offices and by their services the members of the whole commonwealth walk upon solid earth. Among these are to be counted the farmers, who always cleave to the soil, busied about their plough-lands or vineyards or pastures or gardens....All of which occupations, while they do not pertain to the authority of the governing power, are yet in the highest degree useful and profitable to the corporate whole of the commonwealth.

This rather equivocal tribute to the dignity of labor at least emphasizes the social utility of the farmer.

The monastic *Rule* of Benedict of Nursia had confidently proclaimed that "work *is* prayer." A twelfth-century monk who followed that *Rule*, Aelred of Rievaulx, tells us that, in addition to practicing an essential occupation, the vast majority of farmers possess a honest dignity and an openhanded generosity which derives, perhaps, from their closeness to the soil. Spiritual power can be found among the simplest of rustics, as Aelred saw it. Geoffrey Chaucer included in his *Canterbury Tales* a description of a farmer that supports Aelred's view:

> There was a plowman with him there, the parson's brother.
> Many a load of dung one time or other
> He must have carted through the morning dew.
> He was an honest worker, good and true,
> Living in peace and perfect charity,
> And as the gospel bade him, so did he,
> Loving God best with all his heart and mind
> And then his neighbor as himself, repined
> At no misfortune, slacked for no content;
> For steadily about his work he went
> To thrash his corn, to dig, or to manure
> Or make a ditch; and he would help the poor
> For love of Christ and never take a penny
> If he could help it, and, as prompt as any,
> He paid his tithes in full when they were due
> On what he owned and on his earnings too.

From the medieval point of view, the farmer in his plowing, reaping, and tending of livestock was giving as much glory to God as the priest in his pulpit or the monk in his choir. Medieval theologians taught that people of all classes could attain happiness in this world and the next by doing their job in the best way they knew how, that is, by doing whatever they were called to do as Jesus would have done it.

Medieval thinkers–like John of Salisbury–often conceived of their society as an organism or functionally interrelated whole, with each class or part performing an essential role in keeping the whole alive and well. But each cell in that body was not a mere servant of the whole. The body social existed for the sake the well-being of each of its individual members.

G. The Dissidents

There were some inhabitants of the high medieval world who did not fit easily into the view of society shared by most Europeans. These were Jews and Muslims, who did not share the common faith, and schismatics and heretics, who in some way repudiated it. But most medieval thinkers, Bernard of Clairvaux for example, did not exclude them from the possibility of salvation.

The schism that affected the Church of Bernard's time was the split that divided the western, Latin Church from the eastern (now referred to as Orthodox) Church. Bernard believed that responsibility for the rending of the seamless cloak of Christ could be laid at the feet of both sides. Although Bernard believed "God is indeed angry with the [eastern] schismatics," he found God "no more pleased with Catholics." Bernard's response to the schism was concern and care for the welfare of the Churches of the East–even to launching a crusade on their behalf.

As we have seen, Bernard did not preach that crusade against Muslims. He advocated only a war of self-defense against the "evil men" who were threatening peace and security in the Middle East. The fact that the invaders were Muslims was not Bernard's concern. Had they remained peaceful, then Bernard thought they should be treated with fraternal toleration.

In 1146, in the course of Bernard's preaching of the Second Crusade, he heard disturbing reports that a renegade monk named Rudolf was going about preaching the crusade in the lower Rhineland, in the area around Cologne. Rudolf asserted that the extirpation of the infidel in the Holy Land might suitably be preceded by the slaughter of infidels closer to hand. The results for the Jews of the area were severe persecutions–until Bernard came to their rescue.

Bernard was a confident adherent of the position stated by Saint Paul in his letter to the Romans (11:25-26): that all Israel will be saved. This is why Bernard could thunder that "Jews must not be persecuted, slain, or cast out." Persecution, he continued, is "the foulest heresy, a sacrilegious prostitution, impregnated by the spirit of lies. It is conceived in sorrow and gives birth to injustice." Bernard even forbade attempts to convert Jews to Christianity, for Jews, he thought, attain salvation by living up to the Covenant which God made with them in and through the Old Testament Law.

Bernard's friend Aelred of Rievaulx shared his conviction that Jews must not be persecuted and his confidence that they will surely be saved. But Aelred went still further. He envisioned a great banquet at the end of time, held in the Holy Land and thus hosted by the Jewish people. Christians will flock to this feast, where they will aid their hosts by preparing and serving the food. At this banquet the Jewish hosts will embrace gentiles "with arms of love." And this love feast will serve as the introduction of all people into the heavenly life of everlasting love.

Slowly but surely, inexorably, Europe's sphere of tolerance narrowed in the thirteenth century. Innocent III was convinced that "salvation is from the Jews," and yet the Fourth Lateran Council, over which he presided, decreed that, for the protection of Christians, Jews and Muslims were to wear some sort of distinctive clothing. Jews, who were forbidden to own land and had turned to money lending to support themselves, were to cease charging "immoderate usuries." Not much later, one of Innocent's successors, Gregory IX (1227-1241), forbade Jews and Christians from engaging in theological discussions with one another.

H. Heresy and Heretics

Perhaps the first reference in Christian literature to the problem of dissidents occurs in the gospel of Luke (9:54-56). When the people of a Samaritan city refused to receive Jesus, the apostles James and John asked indignantly: "Lord, do you want us to call down fire from heaven to consume them?" To which Jesus replied: "The Son of Man came not to destroy souls, but to save them."

Early Christians were convinced that they had the responsibility of faithfully transmitting the truths of their faith. Their method of correcting persistent dissidents was not to employ physical punishment but simply to exclude them from their church assemblies. Most early Christian theologians vehemently rejected compulsion. The Christian theologian Lactantius wrote in the year 308: "Religion being a matter of the will, it cannot be forced on anyone. In this matter it is better to employ words than blows....It is true that nothing is so important as religion and that one must defend it at any cost....It must indeed be protected, but by dying for it, not by killing others."

With the advent of Roman toleration of Christians in 313 A.D., and still more so after Christianity became the official religion of Rome in 380, the emperors considered it their duty as head of the Church to protect Christianity. Because they identified the state with the Christian Church, these emperors considered doctrines defined as false, or heretical, by Church councils they themselves had convened, were tantamount to treason. The punishment for heresy–as for treason–then became death. Contemporary churchmen were generally opposed to state imposition of the death penalty for heretics, but they accepted the aid of the government in preventing the preaching of what they considered false doctrine. Early Christian thinkers had made what they considered an important distinction: between the consciences of heretics–which must be respected–and the danger which their errors might pose to the salvation of others. This view formed the basis of the medieval attitude toward dissenters from generally accepted Christian teachings.

In the eleventh century, a new religion appeared in western Europe. Mistaken for a Christian heresy, it was to bring about a crisis in the medieval attitude toward dissidents. This religion was a revival of Manicheanism, an ancient Persian religion, brought to the West by Byzantine believers called Bogomils. The adherents of the new religion called themselves *cathari* (the purified ones) and were often called Albigensians, a name taken from Albi, a town in southern France that was one of their centers.

Apparently, the Albigensians believed in the existence of two gods, one that had created matter and whom they identified with the Old Testament Yahweh. The other, the New Testament God, created spirit. Matter was evil and spirit good, and these two principles were eternally at war. It followed that the greatest act of perfection for an Albigensian was suicide, freeing the spirit from the prison of the body. This liberation was accomplished by a prolonged fast or by requesting suffocation at the hands of other Albigensians. Private possessions, being material, were considered evil, and, since the state existed for the ordering of material things, they denied that governments held any authority over them. Hence they refused to take oaths in a society held together by oaths of allegiance. Since the state was evil, the Albigensians refused to pay taxes, a position sure to gain attention, and some went so far as to allow stealing since this act merely relieved the victim of evil material things.

Albigensians also considered sex evil, since sexual union produces children whose souls are thus imprisoned. Consequently, marriage was considered worse than incest or fornication since it aimed at permanent union and the partners felt no shame in it. Practicing Albigensian men would fast on bread and water for three days if so much as touched by a woman. They thought a pregnant woman was possessed by an evil spirit. If the woman died in this state, she was doomed, and hence abortion became a virtue. The products of sexual union, such as meat, eggs, and milk, were forbidden to practicing Albigensians.

It would seem that a group such as this would die out before they became much of a problem to their neighbors, but such was not the case. There were two classes of Albigensians, the "believers" and the "perfect ones," and only the latter were required to observe their exacting code. The "believers" received a sort of sacrament, called the *consolamentum*, that made them "perfect ones," thus ensuring their salvation, that is, escape from reincarnation. In serious illnesses, "believers" received this sacrament. If, however, they recovered, they were obliged to observe the exacting code, and it was at this point that suicide was sometimes the solution. Fatal fasting or suffocation was the practice among children as well as among adults.

The reaction to the Albigensians by ordinary people in the Middle Ages was often mob action. The alleged destruction of churches and suffocation of children by the Albigensians angered the common folk to the point that many Albigensians claimed sanctuary in Christian churches to escape the fury of a lynch mob. The response by most medieval governments was equally strong–if more legal. To government officials, the Albigensians were tax delinquents, murderers, in contempt of court, and implicated in high treason. The results were violent: as early as 1022, King Robert of France had thirteen Albigensians executed.

The reaction of churchmen varied, but Bernard of Clairvaux held what was at first the prevailing opinion. Bernard recognized that the appeal of the Albigensians was strongest where the Christian clergy were laxest in their own lives and in their care for their flocks. He advised that the first step in dealing with dissidence should be reform. Since Bernard believed people could be won to the faith only by persuasion, not by violence, he advocated intensive missionary activity among the Albigensians. The goal, he said, was the salvation of the dissident's soul, not bloodshed.

The Albigensians, however, had won the protection of the powerful count of Toulouse and Christian missionaries were being ignored and sometimes murdered. Soon, therefore, Pope Innocent III conceived the idea of a crusade against the Albigensians. An army was assembled, made up chiefly of men from northern France under the leadership of Count Simon de Montfort. The crusade quickly took on the character of an invasion, and, in defense, the Christians of southern France fought alongside the Albigensians. But after long bloody struggles the invaders were successful. Large numbers of "heretics" were killed, often with extreme cruelty, and the lands of the local nobility who had supported them became the possessions of northerners, ultimately passing into the hands of the king of France. The original intent of the crusade had been largely ignored, and, in the end, the Albigensians who survived went underground.

In 1231, Pope Gregory IX approved a new approach to heresy, an inquiry in which the judge acted as accuser, that we call the Inquisition. Though new to the Church, the inquest was a common legal procedure widely used in secular law, notably in England, and has survived to our day in the coroner's inquest. Despite the negative connotations which the word now carries, the Inquisition, as originally conceived, was an attempt to replace lynch law by due process. The pope appointed judges to seek out and reconcile the remaining Albigensians. The judges were often Franciscans or Dominicans since the popes believed these friars unlikely to be influenced by worldly motives. This confidence was sometimes misplaced, as in the case of the Dominican Conrad of Marburg, the Inquisitor for Germany, whose severity led to his assassination, with the subsequent approval of the pope. Gregory IX warned that the wicked were not to be punished in a way that also hurt the innocent.

The procedure of the Inquisition was as follows. The judges would come to town and preach a sermon on the basic doctrines of Christianity. They would then urge the Albigensians to come forward and be reconciled. If any did so, they were given a mild spiritual penance and accepted back into the fold. If the evidence were strong that a person was an Albigensian, but he or she refused to admit it, the judges would empanel a jury of local clergy and laymen who would examine the witnesses, determine whether they were telling the truth, and decide whether the suspect was guilty or innocent. The accused possessed certain protective safeguards: they could reject judges whom they considered prejudiced, and they could appeal the case if convicted. Defendants, however, were not allowed to confront witnesses, though they could draw up a list of known enemies, who were then disqualified from testifying. From a modern point of view, the greatest evil connected with the Inquisition was its use of torture–even though in theory this was carefully regulated–as a means of eliciting information. The irony of the Inquisition's use of torture is that it was adopted from the newly revived Roman law of antiquity. Torture had no precedents in patristic or medieval church law.

The punishments meted out to the guilty were graded according to the offense: a repentant heretic was given a relatively mild penance. Those who feigned renunciation were imprisoned–if later convicted of perjury–so that they would not corrupt others. Those who abjured their errors but then returned to their old beliefs and actions were turned over to the state, often to be executed.

Murder, treason, and contempt of court have been punished in all societies. But what is significant about the Inquisition is that the fear the Albigensians aroused in the late twelfth- and early thirteenth-century was increasingly directed toward all dissident elements in medieval society. The Albigensians were not Christian heretics; they were devotees of a quite different religion. But they were thought to be heretics, and the measures directed against the Albigensians were increasingly applied to Christian dissidents.

The Waldensians provide a typical example. One of many medieval anti-sacerdotalist groups–groups that rejected the clergy on the grounds that they were sinful–they set out to preach a "pure" gospel. This was clearly at variance with the generally accepted position that even sinful clergy were empowered by God to administer the sacraments. But is equally clear that the Waldensians were not the threat to medieval society that the Albigensians were. Yet they were sought out and punished by the Inquisition in the thirteenth and fourteenth centuries until they, like the Albigensians, were reduced to insignificant numbers. This shift in the medieval outlook was a harbinger of the end of medieval culture.

VIII. THE MIND OF THE HIGH MIDDLE AGES

Some Useful Data

c. 1033-1109	Anselm, archbishop of Canterbury
c. 1079-1142	Peter Abelard, abbot and scholar
c. 1140	Gratian's *Concord of Discordant Canons*
c. 1090-1153	Bernard, abbot of Clairvaux
1145-1153	reign of Eugenius III, pope
c. 1095-1160	Peter Lombard, theologian and bishop of Paris
1159-1181	reign of Alexander III, pope
1227-1241	reign of Gregory IX, pope
1175-1253	Robert Grosseteste, bishop of Lincoln
1217-1274	Bonaventure, Franciscan Minister-General and cardinal
1225-1274	Thomas Aquinas, Dominican scholar

The great flowering of medieval thought came between the middle of the eleventh and the end of the thirteenth centuries. These years witnessed an outburst of intellectual and artistic vitality so remarkable that historians have often called the period the Twelfth-Century Renaissance. This name is misleading, however, because the movement was well under way by the year 1100, its climax was probably not reached until around the year 1250, and this period of important cultural achievement continued well into the fourteenth century.

Universities and cathedrals, while the best known, were only the most conspicuous results of this new cultural explosion. Taking all their varied achievements together, we may say that the twelfth and thirteenth centuries produced one of the richest and most harmonious fusions of religious and cultural life that the western world has ever known. The High Middle Ages saw the flowering of that synthesis of Christian, classical, and Germanic elements that we have seen taking form between 500 and 1000 A.D. During the twelfth and thirteenth centuries, the Church was led by a series of increasingly strong reforming popes. And throughout Europe the clergy, both regular and secular, furnished the trained minds and much of the moral impetus needed for cultural change. Christian monasticism, in particular, was periodically renewed by internal reforms, generating the learning and zeal which were indispensable to the movement. Aiming at the reinstatement of traditional Christian values, especially piety and learning, these reform movements heightened the power and sense of mission of the entire Church.

A. The Revival of Learning

As important as these religious factors were, we must not overlook other major influences. Foremost among these was the development of independent or semi-independent urban communities. The renewal of town life forced people to turn their attention to problems unknown to an earlier agrarian society living on self-sufficient manors. For the relatively wealthy city-dwellers of the twelfth century, the treatment of disease assumed far greater importance than for their less affluent rural ancestors. One of the pressing needs of the age, therefore, was for a specialized medical profession, and, in response to this need, there rapidly arose a demand for the medical textbooks of antiquity and for new schools to educate physicians and surgeons. The medical school at Salerno in Italy was important as early as the tenth century. The works of the ancient Greek physicians Hippocrates and Galen circulated widely, and the medical lore of Greece and Rome was further augmented by Moslem medical knowledge. In this way the traditions of early medieval folk medicine were enriched and extended and the way was opened for new research in anatomy, physiology, botany, chemistry, and astronomy.

Similarly, the merchants and craftsmen who lived in the growing towns needed a legal system better suited to their needs than either feudal or church law, the former stressing military and landholding relationships and the latter devoted largely to ecclesiastical or moral problems. The townspeople therefore took the lead in reviving the study of Roman law, a law that presupposed and reflected the structure and problems of an ancient city-state. Roman law was also popular with ambitious kings who appreciated its emphasis on the absolute power of the head of the state.

The crusades gave indirect support to this revival of antiquity–especially in the field of canon or church law. The feudal lords who went off on crusades left their lands, families, and manorial dependents largely unprotected. The Church undertook to solve this problem. Churchmen reasoned that, since the feudal lords were off fighting in the cause of Christianity, the institutional expression of Christianity, the Church, should see that their lands were protected against unscrupulous neighbors. The means were generally church courts and spiritual sanctions (like excommunication) by local bishops, but sometimes regional armies were organized under the guidance of a bishop to protect the crusaders' interests. And since the Church was now making good on its claim to be independent in spiritual matters, the administrative and judicial machinery of the Church had to be expanded drastically to meet the needs of the time. This was well-received since one could ordinarily get much better justice from a reform bishop than from a feudal lord. Hence, cases that even remotely concerned spiritual questions were often taken to church courts rather than to their lay equivalents. By the early twelfth century, the courts of the pope and the bishops had to cope with a flood of business. To administer and judge the spiritual affairs of Christendom, the Church needed educated men.

This in turn led to a revival and adaptation of material bequeathed by the ancient world. Roman law provided a model for the construction of a rational system of church (or canon) law. The logic of Aristotle, Porphyry, and Boëthius were necessary to introduce order into the mass of conciliar decisions, papal pronouncements, and often conflicting precedents of canon law.

The religious and spiritual tasks of the Church similarly demanded intensive study of the intellectual disciplines and educational methods of antiquity. Christian theologians recognized the utility of Greek philosophy in discerning a deep and subtle understanding of religious doctrines. The meaning of the Scriptures was not always completely clear, and the explanations given by the writers of the early Christian period, such as Augustine, Tertullian, and Ambrose, were not always in agreement. To achieve a consistent doctrinal position and to explain its meaning for a new age, twelfth-century theologians found it useful to apply the logical and dialectical tools of ancient thinkers, particularly the methods of Aristotle, "the master of those who know." To explain the theologians' conclusions to an increasingly sophisticated laity, churchmen also found it useful to master the persuasive techniques of ancient orators and teachers of rhetoric like Cicero and Quintilian.

B. Education and the Universities

Given the Church's growing need for an educated clergy, it was natural for its leaders to become the chief patrons of education and scholarship. Reformers had insisted from the beginning that all children, regardless of sex or social position, should be given some formal education, and on the primary and secondary levels this education was to be provided without charge. All parish priests were exhorted–not always successfully–to conduct primary schools for the children of their parishes, and every bishop was constrained to establish a secondary school at his cathedral. Out of some of these cathedral schools evolved the first universities. Teachers and students who migrated from the older institutions when teaching or living conditions did not satisfy them founded other universities.

Nowhere do we find more striking evidence of the amazing medieval ability to improvise new institutions to meet novel needs than in the creation of the university. The medieval university was truly a unique and original invention. In the modern descendants of these "communities of scholars" we see one of the most lasting contributions made by medieval civilization to our own. The name itself is revealing: it comes from the Latin *universitas*, which was one of the common terms for a medieval guild–and the university of the Middle ages was in fact a guild either of students or of teachers, organized in conscious imitation of other guilds such as those of the carpenters, merchants, or physicians. Instead of becoming a master of some craft or trade, the aspiring young scholar became a "Master of Arts." This came after a period of study and apprenticeship, and it was conferred only on completion of a "masterwork"–a learned thesis or dissertation. The degree carried with it the right to practice the scholar's profession, that is, to teach.

A university was considered a valuable asset for a city to possess. Not only did it confer prestige, but the students and faculty brought money into the community. To attract a colony of scholars, therefore, city fathers frequently offered valuable privileges. The university, consisting only of people and a few books at the start, could often improve its position by moving or threatening to move to another place if local authorities proved too niggardly or too oppressive. Reform popes in particular lavished privileges on the universities, including grants of immunity from the authority of local bishops who were apt to be troublesome. Sometimes, for example, the bishop's educational supervisor, the chancellor, would impose fees for the awarding of degrees; the popes forbade this practice by bringing it under the general prohibition of "simony," the sale of spiritual powers or offices. Pope Alexander III (1159-1181) issued instructions that every qualified person must be granted a degree. Then, to determine who was qualified, a regular system of examinations was introduced. The general effect of papal patronage was to free the universities from outside control–episcopal and civil–and to make them independent, self-governing institutions.

Instruction in a medieval university was given in four "faculties," what we would call colleges. In the Faculty of Arts the instruction roughly paralleled, and is the ancestor of, the liberal arts education of today. There all students began their study of grammar, rhetoric, and dialectic (the *trivium*), and mathematics, geometry, music, and astronomy (the *quadrivium*). In the twelfth century, the emphasis was on grammar and rhetoric and, as a result, the renaissance in the twelfth century was characterized by humanism. Humanism–as applied to the twelfth century–is the exploration of the meaning of human life as reflected in great literary works–what we would study today in many courses in literature and history. For a humanist, beauty of expression can lead to a deeper sensitivity to the human predicament and possibilities–not merely to a knowledge of truth, but to an understanding of reality.

In late twelfth- and thirteenth-century instruction, there was an increasing emphasis on dialectic or logic. The study of literature was largely replaced with more intensive philosophical studies. Now precision in language became more important than beauty of expression, a development later deplored by the humanists of the fourteenth and fifteenth centuries.

Rigorous examinations ended the student's work in the Faculty of Arts. If he passed, he received the degree of Master of Arts, a teacher's certificate that also entitled him to undertake graduate study leading to a doctoral degree in one of the other three faculties. The surest road to promotion in Church or state was to study law–civil law, canon law, or both. Medicine was another graduate faculty, and theology was the third. In the graduate faculty of theology the student would spend several years studying the Bible and then proceed to an analytical study of the doctrines of Christianity. To graduate as a Doctor of Theology, the student had to be at least thirty-six years old, and this often meant that he had been engaged in university studies for about twenty-two years.

Life at a medieval university was much like life at a modern university except that it was a good deal more informal and in many ways freer. The medieval university aimed at academic excellence, not at providing a home away from home or facilities for courtship and recreation. There were no dormitories or cafeterias, no administrators or counsellors. All students fended for themselves, since even the youngest of them were treated as adults. In the earlier stages of university development, there were often no classroom buildings; the professor simply rented a hall or gave his lectures at a local tavern. This lack of administration and regulation meant that attending a university was far less expensive and far less hedged about with bureaucratic formalities in the Middle Ages than it is today. This did not mean that the student's lot was an easy one; books were scarce and therefore expensive, and the examinations were all oral–sometimes lasting an entire day.

Medieval universities filled pressing religious and social needs. They also renewed the earnest cultivation of the humanities and sciences for their own sake. In these fields Christian Europe had to begin by filling the gaps in its knowledge of what the ancients and their Islamic successors had thought and done. The quantity and quality of Greek learning which had survived the barbarian invasions in the West was far inferior to what had been salvaged in the East.

When the Arabs conquered most of the Near East in the first half of the seventh century and swept across North Africa and through Spain, they engulfed a vigorous intellectual community that not only possessed the complete texts of Aristotle and other Greek classics, but was busily engaged in adding to this learning by commentary and by further investigation. The next three centuries witnessed the translation of nearly the whole body of Greek science and Aristotelian philosophy into Arabic at great cultural centers like Baghdad, with lesser schools flourishing in Syria, Egypt, and Spain. This gigantic task of translation was to be duplicated for the benefit of western Christians in the twelfth and thirteenth centuries when the same body of learning, augmented in the meantime by the works of Arab and Jewish scholars, was turned from Arabic and Greek into Latin and passed on to the West, particularly by way of Spain, Italy, Sicily, and Constantinople, the principal points of contact between the Muslim East and the Christian West.

The recovery of these intellectual riches lent additional impetus to the cultural revival which was already in progress. European scholars and churchmen felt an excitement that is difficult for us even to imagine when they were able at last to read the complete works of Aristotle on logic and metaphysics—works they had known existed but had not been able to study. Not only did the enormous prestige of Aristotle's name attract interest and inspire respect, the refinement of logical methods displayed in his work served as a guide to, and example for, a deeper study of philosophy and theology.

C. Scholasticism

One of most brilliant of the European thinkers who gained fame in the early twelfth century was Peter Abelard (1079-1142), a handsome and eloquent–though also arrogant and erratic–scholar who taught at the newly emerging university at Paris. Abelard greatly enhanced the methodological underpinnings of theology with his work *Sic et non* ("Pro and Con"). In this treatise Abelard collected and presented divergent opinions on all the major theological questions of his day. His citations were drawn from the Bible, the early Christian Fathers, and later Christian commentators. Abelard refrained from drawing any conclusions and left it to readers to resolve the contradictions he had set forth. This monumental task was to be undertaken by generations of theologians during the twelfth and thirteenth centuries. The method these theologians eagerly adopted to reconcile their different and apparently contradictory sources was a sophisticated use of the logic of Aristotle. This method was adopted by all the disciplines in the medieval universities, so that we can speak of scholastic philosophy, scholastic law, scholastic medicine–as well as scholastic theology. Scholasticism is simply the method employed by the scholars who taught in a medieval school (*schola*). The answers given by those scholars often disagreed, but their common method enabled them to communicate their disagreement with a minimum of misunderstanding.

By the year 1200, almost all of the writings of Aristotle had been made available to Latin-speaking scholars. The study of Greek logic in cathedral schools and in early university centers led quickly to the development of the scholastic method. The remarkable power of this method to analyze, resolve, and synthesize ideas was eagerly seized on. At the same time, the scientific and speculative thought of the Graeco-Arabic tradition provided texts on which Christian scholars found it necessary to comment because these new ideas were not always fully consistent with the accepted teachings of Christianity. For example, some Aristotelians thought that there had never been a divine creation, that the world had existed from all eternity. Some also taught that the soul was not immortal. The christianization of ancient philosophy became a crucial activity of leading university teachers in the thirteenth century, and the new orders of Dominicans and Franciscans provided well-trained scholars to address these issues.

One of the Dominicans was Thomas Aquinas (1225-1274). Born in south-central Italy of noble parentage, he joined the Order of Preachers and was a pupil of its most celebrated teacher, Albert the Great, a man of encyclopedic interests that included natural history. Thomas received his doctorate in theology at Paris and taught there and at Rome for much of his career. His lectures were eagerly attended by young men from all over Europe because of the power and lucidity of his thought. He had achieved complete mastery of Aristotle's logical tools, and he used them with originality and vigor. In his consideration of the physical world he was an Aristotelian, while his theory of knowledge, his understanding of fundamental reality, and his psychological doctrines bear the imprint of Plato as well. The influence of Aristotle is especially evident in Thomas's basic view that human knowledge (apart from divine revelation) comes initially by way of the senses and arises finally out of the abstractions that are made by the mind from sensory data.

Thomas took part in several important controversies. One of these was with the European followers of the Moslem Aristotelian philosopher Averroës. Thomas asserted that the Averroists had gone astray because they had misconstrued the proper relation between faith and reason. His analysis of this crucial question was of fundamental significance for his age as well as for subsequent western thought. He held that both reason and revelation (which is taken on faith) can lead us humans to truth, but that there are some truths about God which, in his words, "surpass the capability of human reason." There are other revealed truths which can be confirmed by reason and thus demonstrated philosophically to a person who is open only to logical persuasion. One such truth, he thought, was the existence of God, for which Thomas devised demonstrations addressed solely to "natural reason." Thomas was convinced that reason and faith can never conflict. The truth is one, though it can sometimes be reached by more than one path. Here Thomas opposed the Averroist view that in some matters there may be "two truths" on the same question, one according to reason and one according to faith.

Thomas used the scholastic method in a powerful and fruitful way, constructing a vast synthesis of pagan and Christian philosophy which he called his *Summa theologiae* (Theological Summation). This book followed the same format as Thomas' university lectures, beginning with a preliminary statement of a question in dispute, followed by an exposition of all actual or conceivable arguments against his own position. Then Thomas stated his own conclusion in which the truth was determined in the light of revelation, the authority of past tradition, reason, and experience. Finally, Thomas answered in detail all the arguments against his position. In the hands of Thomas this method produced a clarity and coherence in Christian doctrine that stimulated much fertile thinking.

Aquinas was not the only intellectual to win a wide following in his time. A leading Franciscan intellectual, Bonaventure (1217-1274), was a professor of theology at Paris at the same time that Aquinas taught there. Though friendly, the two disagreed about nearly everything. Aquinas embraced Aristotle; Bonaventure reluctantly adopted as few as possible of Aristotle's insights. Thomas accepted Aristotle's reliance on sense data as the foundation of knowledge; Bonaventure was a Platonist whose search for truth began with contemplation of the ideas or forms that existed eternally in the mind of God. Thomas was confident that God endows humans with an intellect which can know much about the world through its natural powers; Bonaventure believed that God's constant activity was essential to every act of knowing. Thomas' view of humankind was optimistic: humans are fundamentally good, even though they sometimes sin through selfishness. Bonaventure saw humans as fundamentally flawed through original sin. Bonaventure's pessimism would prevail in the later Middle Ages and become enshrined in the theology of both Protestants and Catholics. But Aquinas' optimism would surface again and again in subsequent thought, both within and outside of Christianity.

D. Faith, Science, and Philosophy

For medieval thinkers theology was the "Queen of the Sciences," of all fields of knowledge. But this did not mean that natural science was ignored. Our modern scientific method owes much to the Middle Ages: until the early thirteenth century what we call "science" was not clearly differentiated from philosophy.

The man of that age who did most to develop the scientific method was Robert Grosseteste (1175-1253), bishop of Lincoln from 1235 to his death. According to Robert, mathematics and experiment were the keys to science. The first step in science is analysis, the breaking up of composite sense data into basic elements. The next step is synthesis, the recombination of the elements in theoretical form (called today the hypothesis or model). Finally, the scientist tests the conclusions based on observation and discards theories proven false by this experimentation. The work of Robert Grosseteste and his medieval successors is essential in understanding the rise of modern science. Indeed, Galileo and Newton were later to make use of Robert's vocabulary in describing the scientific method.

The path to knowledge most often associated with the leading thinkers of the Middle Ages was the path that begins with faith. Almost all medieval people were certain that God could and did reveal something of the truth, of the nature of reality. The typical medieval reaction was to accept that divine revelation. If there should appear to be a conflict between the revelation accepted on faith and the conclusions of philosophy or science, Thomas Aquinas and his contemporaries would have maintained that faith, science, and philosophy all give us true knowledge of reality. If properly used, they could not contradict one another. All of them should indeed be used, according to Thomas, because of the vast dimensions of reality.

E. Nature and History

Medieval thought on the universe was a new synthesis of older cosmologies. Most ancient peoples had explained the universe in terms of myth, a poetic explanation of how the universe came to be the way it is. This mythological approach does not treat the world as a product of historical change: nature follows her unvarying cycle from year to year and even the gods are subject to nature's laws or to Fate.

The Jewish understanding of the world greatly influenced medieval Christian thought. Although there are ahistorical or mythological elements in the Old Testament, the Jewish religion was based on what Jews considered to be an actual historical event, the Exodus, the escape of God's Chosen People from their captivity in Egypt. Nature is God's creation, and God is not a part of it. The God of the Jews acts in history, however, changing the course of nature and humans' relationship to him. In the book of Exodus, for example, before giving the law to Moses on Mount Sinai, God established his authority to demand obedience from Jews by reference to what Jews regarded as the history's central event: "I am the Lord, your God, who brought you out of the land of Egypt, out of the house of bondage. You shall not have strange gods before me...."

Early Christians likewise saw man's relationship to God as based on an event viewed as historical. This was the Incarnation, God's becoming human in the person of Jesus of Nazareth. Both Jews and Christians saw nature as the working out of God's will.

In contrast to the Hebrew concept, the universe of the Greek philosophers operated according to natural causes comprehensible to human reason, not by divine will. Things operated according to a regular pattern, and even history was viewed as an endless recurrence of the same events. It was a cyclical view of history as opposed to the linear view of Judaism and Christianity, both of which saw historical direction and purpose. For the Jew, time would bring the Messiah; for the Christian, time would bring the Second Coming of Jesus and the Last Judgment.

The view of nature and history that prevailed in the High Middle Ages was a synthesis of the Jewish and Greek ideas. The universe operated according to God's will, but God was Reason (the Word or *Logos* of John's gospel). God's will, therefore, had a rational basis; it followed that God willed the existence of a nature governed by the law of reason.

F. New Developments in Theology

From its earliest days in Christian antiquity, the liberal arts curriculum, specifically the discipline of dialectic, had included the logical works of Aristotle. But, as we have seen, not all those works had been translated into Latin until the early twelfth century. The impact of Aristotle's "New Logic" on scholasticism was immense. The scholars of Western Europe embraced the new Aristotle with an intoxicated enthusiasm. From about 1150, all the intellectual disciplines were enthusiastically recast into rigorously logical, scholastic forms.

This was especially true of theology. Down to the middle of the twelfth century, most theological works had the form of commentaries on some book or books of Scripture. Occasionally a treatise was written on a theological topic like the relationship between grace and free will. But both commentaries and treatises were based on prayerful mediation on the contents of the biblical books. In the late eleventh century, the monk and later archbishop, Anselm of Canterbury, had attempted to demonstrate the existence of God, employing rational consideration of an extremely sophisticated sort. But even Anselm's proofs, which have to this day challenged philosophers of all sorts, were cast in the form of a prayer.

From about 1150 on, the theology taught in the schools–scholastic theology–found its fundamental form not in scriptural commentaries but in logical arrangement according to topics. For example, the massive *Summa theologiae* of Thomas Aquinas has three books arranged in logical sequence–the first dealing with God, the second with humans, and the third with Christ, both God and human. The basic source that Thomas mined to construct his theological synthesis was, of course, Scripture. But Thomas took pains to demonstrate his conclusions whenever possible on the basis of reason applied to sense data, that is, philosophy. Although Thomas' mid-thirteenth-century, scholastic approach to theology was far different from Bernard's early-twelfth-century biblical commentaries, the intent of both was the same. Down to the sixteenth century, the goal of theology was to describe to Christians the path to God and, therefore, happiness. After the Reformation, as we shall see, the focus of theology, both Protestant and Catholic, was defensive and argumentative.

The scholastic method led scholars to some developments in religious thinking that would later spark much controversy among theologians. For example, it was not until the Parisian scholar Peter Lombard's *Book of Sentences* (1150) that a sacrament was defined. Peter opined that it was an "outward sign of an invisible grace." Peter's book became the classic text on which all university theologians were to comment. By the end of the twelfth century, those theologians had added to Peter's definition the phrase "established by Christ" and had numbered the sacraments as seven. But the choice of which "outward signs," even those established by Christ, were to be included among the seven was a source of controversy. Had Jesus established matrimony as a sacrament? There was no scriptural evidence for this. On the other hand, it was clear from the gospel narrative that Jesus had washed the feet of his disciples at the meal held on the eve of his death. Had this not conferred grace? And should not the washing of the feet, liturgically reenacted on the Thursday before Easter, be counted as a sacrament? By the thirteenth century, scholastic theologians had accepted that the sacraments were indeed seven and consisted of baptism, confirmation, matrimony, the last anointing, penance, the eucharist (sometimes called the Lord's Supper or, alternatively, Communion), and ordination.

Another theological development of the High Middle Ages–a development which was to stir up furious controversy in the sixteenth century–was the newly developed doctrine of purgatory. From the beginning, Christians shared with their Jewish brethren the practice of prayer for the dead. Catacomb inscriptions from the second century included the phrase "pray for me." Since, as we have seen, the second half of the twelfth century displayed a prevalent impetus toward the rational structuring of all thought, the theologians of the time began to question the reason for the long tradition and practice of praying for the dead.

The rationale then offered became part of Catholic doctrine in the Late Middle Ages. It was held that, when a sinner sincerely repented, God could and did forgive the sin. However, the sinners were required to make "reparation" for their sin by doing some good work that would make up for the evil result of their sin. As this doctrine was developed more fully, theologians began to speak of the "temporal punishment due to sin." If sinners died without paying this penalty, they were placed in Purgatory until their debt had been paid and they could move on to Heaven. This was a rational explanation of an old practice. The practice had, arguably, a scriptural basis, but the doctrine devised to explain it surely did not.

G. Canon Law and the Growth of Papal Monarchy

We have often discussed the developing role of the bishop of Rome. By the fourth century, the bishops of the early Church had assigned to Rome a leadership role in the deliberations that led to their joint, conciliar declarations on Christian doctrine. But the role of "first bishop" was granted to the Roman see only in matters of Church teaching, not in the governance of the Church, which remained in the hands of the many individual bishops.

In the Early Middle Ages, the bishop of Rome became the central coordinator of the missionary efforts to the Germanic peoples of western Europe. That leadership role was vastly enhanced when the church reformers of the eleventh century gained control of the papacy and used it as the center for the successive reformations of the western Church. By the early twelfth century, in the time of Bernard of Clairvaux, the popes had assumed a role roughly analogous to that of the United States Supreme Court. People of all walks of life who were dissatisfied with the judgment of their bishop on matters spiritual–often matrimonial–could appeal to the pope's judgment. Bernard approved of this, but complained to his fellow Cistercian, newly elected pope as Eugenius III, that the immense volume of these appeals bred inefficiency and even corruption in the papal court.

In the later years of the twelfth century, the spiritual leadership of the popes increasingly developed into papal control. This was due in large part to the development of canon (or church) law as a rigorous discipline. Professors of canon law at the developing universities devoted themselves to collecting and organizing the many past conciliar decisions and papal pronouncements on matters of church practice and structure. The leader in this development of law was a professor at the nascent university at Bologna named Gratian. About the year 1140, Gratian produced a massive collection of legal texts, the goal of which is expressed in its title *The Concord of Discordant Canons*. This work became the basis for the teaching of canon law in all universities.

Lawyers–medieval lawyers among them–have a thirst for order, structure, and uniformity. And the sources employed in Gratian's textbook were chosen out of the conviction that a consistent law was best ensured by a powerful papacy. Popes like Alexander III (1159-1181) had themselves studied canon law from Gratian's texts. Alexander, facing an increase in appeals to Rome–an increase that he encouraged–appointed "judges delegate" to hear and decide cases in their own countries on papal authority. Alexander and his corps of canon lawyers in the papal court standardized church law by issuing numerous letters designed to guide judges delegate in difficult cases. These "decretals" were periodically collected, systematically organized, and incorporated into the teaching of canon law in the universities. An authoritative legal collection issued by Pope Gregory IX (1227-1241) became the sequel to Gratian's textbook and the new standard for the teaching of canon law. The previous papal role as appellate judge had been transformed into that of being the sole source of church legislation. During the late thirteenth and early fourteenth centuries, the popes would attempt to parley this legislative and judicial power into a position of unique executive authority. This attempt to create a papal monarchy in the Church–and the fate of that attempt–we shall discuss in the chapter that follows.

IX. A CHRISTIAN CULTURE COMING APART: LATE MEDIEVAL CHURCH, STATE, AND SOCIETY

Some Useful Data

1214-1250	reign of Frederick II, emperor
1226-1270	reign of Louis IX, king of France
1294	reign of Celestine V, pope
1294-1303	reign of Boniface VIII, pope
1272-1307	reign of Edward I, king of England
1285-1314	reign of Philip IV, the Fair, king of France
1305-1314	reign of Clement V, pope
1347	onset of the Black Death
1328-1350	reign of Philip VI, king of France
1370-1378	reign of Gregory XI, pope
1347-1380	Catherine of Siena, spiritual teacher and peacemaker
c. 1330-1384	John Wyclif, English theologian
1378-1389	reign of Urban VI, pope at Rome
1378-1394	reign of Clement VII, pope at Avignon
1409-1410	reign of Alexander V, Pisan pope
1370-1415	John Hus, Bohemian reformer
1410-1415	reign of John XXIII, Pisan pope
1417-1431	reign of Martin V, pope
1485-1509	reign of Henry VII, king of England

During the night of the seventh of September in the year 1303, a force of 600 cavalry and 1,500 infantry attacked the sleepy little central Italian town of Agnani. The town gates had been opened by treachery. Swarming in, the attacking force set fire to the cathedral and began to pillage and loot the city. The leaders of the expedition, however, made their way to the papal residence, for Pope Boniface VIII was staying at his ancestral home in Agnani.

Two men led the break-in to the papal apartments. One was Guillaume de Nogaret, the right-hand man of King Philip the Fair of France. Guillaume's partner was Sciarra Colonna, representing the most powerful of the Roman families–a family violently opposed to Boniface's 1294 election to the papacy. Guillaume and Sciarra planned to kidnap Boniface and bring him back to France and King Philip. Sciarra struck the aged pope's face, and with that blow, the cultural synthesis of the High Middle Ages was symbolically attacked as well. Boniface was quickly rescued, and the French incursion was beaten off. But the shock was too much for the octogenarian pope, and he died three weeks later. The result of the confrontation at Agnani was ultimately a decisive victory for Philip of France, and, from that time on, throughout the Late Middle Ages, the pope's influence on the secular world–and also in the Church–would weaken radically.

The early fourteenth century–the time during which Philip and Boniface lived and died–marks the beginning of a period sometimes called the "autumn of the Middle Ages." And indeed the two centuries from about 1300 to about 1500 did see both a rich harvest–in literature, architecture, and painting, for example–but also many signs of decay. The territorial expansion of medieval Europe came to a standstill, and in eastern Europe a process of contraction set in. Intellectually and psychologically western culture began to turn in on itself, and its social and cultural life became ever more rigid and closed. Ecological and economic changes began to make European life more difficult. The climate grew colder, and in large areas that had once produced abundant grain and grapes the land now lay untended. Trade and manufacturing declined over wide areas, population growth was checked, and millions went hungry and died in the successive outbreaks of pestilence that swept over Europe. The relative peace and order of the twelfth and thirteenth centuries was replaced by widespread warfare. A "Hundred Years' War" between France and England, filled with bloody atrocities and accompanied by famine and epidemics, dragged on for much of the period. Unrest and social conflict were widespread.

A. The Failure of the Institutional Church

In the Late Middle Ages, the spirit of reform which had been central to the synthesis which had been high medieval culture no longer drove the Church. After Innocent III's death in 1215, all the popes of the thirteenth century were canon lawyers–save one who reigned for less than a year. Each claimed universal jurisdiction over the Church as its administrative, judicial, and legislative head. But the considerable power of the Roman popes was largely squandered in securing the limited goal of political expansion of the Papal States and influence in the Italian peninsula. Popes preached crusades against their political enemies. They deposed monarchs and saw to it that their heirs were killed off. At one point, a pope even offered the crown of Sicily to the highest bidder. To many contemporaries, including the saintly king of France, Louis IX (ruled 1226-1270), the popes' use of spiritual authority to achieve political power seemed a gross abuse. As the thirteenth century went on, more and more people saw the popes as much more concerned with worldly power than spiritual ministry, and the result was a loss to the moral prestige of the papacy.

1. Boniface VIII

All these tendencies were apparent in the career of Benedetto Gaetani, who advanced from papal bureaucrat to pope as Boniface VIII, and whose precipitous fall we have already observed. Benedetto completed his studies in both canon and civil (Roman) law at the university at Bologna, and he immediately entered the service of the papal curia, the administrative and judicial court of the pope. Benedetto gained valuable experience on the staff of two cardinals, one the legate (or ambassador) to France, the other to England. In 1276, Benedetto supervised the collection of the crusader tax in France. As the name suggests, the tax had originally been assessed to support the crusades, but the revenues had long been diverted to the papal treasury for other purposes. Benedetto was made cardinal in 1290, and elevated to the Roman see as Boniface VIII in 1294.

The circumstances of that elevation are instructive. Boniface's predecessor, Celestine V, was that sole exception to the rule that thirteenth-century popes be trained in canon law. Celestine had been a saintly hermit before his election to the papacy. Nine of the eleven cardinals who elected him had been in the pay of Celestine's temporal ruler, King Charles II of Naples. Charles had hoped–vainly as it turned out–to advance his political agenda by installing his man in the papal office. Celestine's cardinals soon discovered that saintliness was an inadequate preparation for the administrative role demanded by the now thoroughly politicized papacy. Celestine resigned, being urged, if not forced, to this action by the most aggressive of his cardinals, Benedetto Gaetani, who then took his place as Boniface VIII. As pope, Boniface proved himself an able administrator, a forceful defender of papal prerogatives, and a generous patron of his family's fortunes. In the process he made enemies.

The outcome of a protracted quarrel between Boniface and the French king Philip the Fair we have already seen. That dispute had arisen out of a war Philip was waging against the English over political rights in southwestern France, and also over commercial rivalries. Philip's treasury was empty, and he sought to replenish it by taxing the French clergy. The French bishops did not protest, but the lower clergy appealed to the pope for relief. In 1296, Boniface responded by issuing a famous decree, *Clericis laicos*, that protested the tax. Behind this decree was the traditional view that the king had a right to tax the clergy–usually exempt–only for just purposes. In Philip's case, Boniface was convinced, the purpose of the conflict was a war of aggression and therefore was unjust. Consequently, logically, the tax was not permissible. Philip retaliated by forbidding the export of money from France, thus cutting off a large part of papal revenues. Philip went on to encourage the pope's Italian enemies, the powerful Colonna family, to rebel. At the same time, the English king Edward I, in much the same boat, declared all tax-delinquent English clergymen outlaws. Confronted with this crippling resistance, Boniface was compelled in 1297 to concede that in time of necessity–a necessity determined by the king–a ruler could tax the clergy of his realm without approval from Rome.

The final break was precipitated by the arrest by Philip of the bishop of Pamièrs on a rather flimsy charge of treason. Boniface protested and summoned the bishops of France to a council in Rome to consider the state of religion in France. He also sent a letter to Philip, urging him to provide justice to his subjects. Philip's counselors, lawyers of middle class origin who believed that the king's will was law, arranged a clever coup. They burned the original letter and circulated a forgery in which Boniface was made to claim total authority, temporal as well as spiritual, as France's overlord. This forgery had the desired effect: feelings in France ran high against Boniface.

In 1302, Boniface replied to this maneuver with one of his own, by issuing another decree, *Unam sanctam*. In it he reasserted his authority as a Christian leader to correct moral evil–even in the conduct of a ruler. This was not a new position. But the last sentence of Boniface's document, probably intended merely to support this traditional position, took a form that caused consternation in many quarters and seemed to justify Philip's forgery. Boniface wrote: "We declare, state, define, and pronounce that it is absolutely necessary for salvation that every human being be subject to the Roman Pontiff." This, on the face of it, was a revolutionary statement.

Philip responded by declaring the pope guilty of heresy, blasphemy, simony, gross and unnatural immorality, magic, and murder. The king also sent his agents throughout the kingdom to purge the Church in France of those who opposed him. And it was then that, to silence Boniface's protests, Philip sent his right-hand man, Guillaume de Nogaret, to Italy to join with Sciarra Colonna in an attempt to take the pope prisoner.

2. *The Babylonian Captivity at Avignon*

After Boniface died in humiliation, his successor, a saintly Dominican, Benedict XI, absolved Philip, who declared himself penitent for his misdeeds. But Benedict was unable to regain the ground the papacy had lost, for he died in 1304, after a reign of only eight months.

Among the cardinals assembled to elect Benedict's successor, the majority favored a pope who would resist the French. But they failed by a single vote to elect their man, and so, in 1305, a compromise candidate was chosen. He was the archbishop of the French city of Bordeaux, who took the name Clement V. Clement was an accomplished canon lawyer, a competent administrator, and a skillful negotiator. But he was a weak and vacillating man whose advisors were often in the pay of the French king. A sign of things to come was Clement's decision to be made pope in France in the presence of Philip the Fair. Philip browbeat Clement into remaining in France and appointing French cardinals.

The extent of the king's power over the pope is shown by the suppression of the Knights Templar, a crusading order whose wealth attracted the cupidity of Philip and Guillaume de Nogaret. On October, 13, 1307, all French members of the Order were arrested and charged with a long list of heinous crimes. Dumfounded by the accusations, which were being systematically spread throughout the kingdom by Philip's agents, the Templars were told that the pope had abandoned them and that they could either confess their guilt and be pardoned or else face the prospect of hideous torture and death. Placed in this dilemma, many of them, including the Grand Master of the Order, chose to plead guilty. Clement V protested that the Templars, being members of the clergy, should be tried in ecclesiastical courts. Since those courts did not employ torture, many of the accused now retracted their confessions. Nogaret threatened the pope, who then gave his consent to the civil proceedings the French government had initiated. Fifty-four Templars were quickly condemned as "relapsed heretics," for having retracted their original confessions. The next day they were slowly roasted alive, and most of the remaining Templars hastened to admit their guilt. Philip brought new pressure to bear on the pope to dissolve the Order, and when the Council of Vienne (1312) did this, the French king seized the Templars' property in France. The former Grand Master, Jacques de Molay, was condemned to life imprisonment. When he protested that his only crime was to have betrayed the Order to save his own life, he was burned at the stake instead.

The aftermath of the affair was extremely damaging to the papacy. Philip had been able to coerce Clement by threatening to dig up the body of Boniface VIII and conduct a posthumous trial. To prevent this, the pope not only retracted *Clericos laicos* and *Unam sanctam* but publicly praised Philip for the zeal for the Church he had shown in attacking Boniface. The manner in which all these things were done left an indelible impression that the pope had become a puppet in the hands of the French king. The prestige of the papacy suffered a grave setback, and its ability to serve as an effective symbol of Christian unity was much diminished.

The later years of Clement's reign witnessed another development–the establishment of the papal residence at Avignon. There a huge palace was built and an elaborate court installed by Clement and his immediate successors. Most of these popes remained under substantial French influence, although the city was not actually part of France at that time. This period of absence from Rome is known as the "Babylonian Captivity" of the popes–a reference to the exile of the Jews in Babylon in the sixth century B.C. It witnessed a further loss of authority for the papacy because nations other than France lost confidence in the impartiality of the papal court. Another development that reflected discredit on the Avignon popes was their nepotism, the practice of granting high and remunerative offices in the Church to their relatives.

Much resentment was also caused by the financial policies of the Avignon papacy, which resorted to many new and ingenious devices to raise the ever larger revenues needed to support the ever more elaborate bureaucracy which now developed. Though the Avignon popes were not wicked men, they seemed far more concerned with the institutional structures of the Church than with the spiritual welfare of the Christian flock. Among the clergy there was much grumbling at the imposition of new and ever increasing papal levies. For example, a fee was now imposed whenever a clergyman assumed the office of bishop or a post of comparable dignity, and the payment amounted to half the first year's income of the office. Every newly created archbishop had to pay for his *pallium*, the strip of wool worn over his vestments to indicate his rank. An additional fee was to be paid if the new prelate received his consecration at the papal court. Bishops were required to attend the court at Avignon at regular intervals, and on these occasions still another fee was assessed.

Special taxes were imposed on most other church offices, and an army of papal agents was recruited to collect them. These agents, as well as their bureaucratic supervisors at Avignon, were highly unpopular with the clergy, especially since it was known that a massive multiplication of official positions had bred graft and corruption at the papal court. Nor was it good for priests' morale to learn that rich men could now purchase high church offices so as to enjoy the incomes attached to them. These high churchmen passed the burden of papal exactions on to the lower clergy who, in turn, were sometimes forced to curtail their charitable and educational work or to charge fees for baptisms, weddings, funerals, and other services in order to maintain themselves.

Yet, despite all this taxation, the Avignon papacy was in a state of chronic financial crisis. Its revenues were never sufficient to support the horde of officials, dignitaries, pensioners, and relatives who swarmed through the great palace. Great sums were also spent in waging fruitless wars to regain control of the pope's territories in Italy, then in a state of chaos. To raise these sums the popes not only taxed the higher clergy but also assumed, whenever possible, the power of appointing bishops. This was an infringement on the right of election of bishops that had been won by the church reformers of the High Middle Ages. In addition, the new practice often resulted in the choice of bishops who were not native to the country of their new dioceses and who consequently had little knowledge of the language of their flock or of local problems and customs. All too often these appointments went to those who had won favor by their service at the papal court, and these men were frequently despised for their foreign ways when they arrived as bishops, abbots, or canons in Spain, England, or Germany.

3. The Great Schism

Everyone but the French wished the pope to return to Rome. In 1377, in response to these desires, Gregory XI did go back to Italy. Once there, however, he was dismayed by the anarchy which prevailed and was about to return to Avignon when he suddenly died. The Roman populace then set up a clamor for the election of a native of their city as bishop of Rome. The cardinals chose a compromise candidate who was an Italian though not a cardinal. The new pope took the name Urban VI. Much to everyone's surprise Urban, who had been considered a pliant tool of the curial cardinals, turned out to be a strong pope bent on sweeping reform. He began energetically setting things right by correcting abuses at the very summit of the hierarchy: the cardinals, the papal court, and the bishops. This was too much for the French cardinals, who left Rome. Soon afterwards, they elected another pope, who took the name Clement VII and established himself and his court back at Avignon. There were exchanges of anathemas and mutual excommunications, and for some forty years there were at least two lines of claimants to the see of Peter.

It is difficult for us even to imagine the confusion wrought by this great division, or schism. So tangled were the conflicting claims that no one could be completely certain who was the legitimate pope. All over Christendom bishop rose up against bishop, abbot against abbot, and priest against priest. France acknowledged the pope in Avignon, while England, which was at war with France, chose Rome. Scotland, often at odds with England, chose Avignon, as did Spain and southern Italy, while central and northern Italy opted for Rome. The Empire was divided, a reflection of the political fragmentation of Germany. The rest of Europe gave its allegiance to Rome. Nearly everywhere the fundamental consideration was local political interest and not the welfare of European Christendom as a whole.

The effects of the schism were little less than catastrophic for the Church. The feuding popes were far too busy maintaining themselves to undertake a thorough reform of the Church. Nor did they have the power to impose reforms because of the divided state of that Church. The real winners in the struggle were the temporal rulers who seized the opportunity to exact concessions from the popes in return for their support. This gave kings and princes an ever-increasing power over the Church.

4. The Conciliar Epoch

Responding to a growing sense of desperation over the plight of the Church, the theological faculty of the University of Paris drafted a memorandum in 1393. The document they issued suggested three possible ways to end the schism: simultaneous resignation by both claimants to the papacy, arbitration between them by a jointly chosen group, or the convocation of a general or ecumenical council of the Church. Since the first two alternatives proved impracticable, the third method came to be regarded as the only one feasible. So support grew for the convening of a council that would, if need be, depose both popes and replace them with a single pontiff.

In March of 1409, twenty-four cardinals (fourteen "Romans" and ten "Avignonese"), accompanied by some three hundred leading clergymen, held a meeting at Pisa. They voted to depose both popes and elected Alexander V in their stead. "Oh, happy choice! Peace had been restored! Oh, pacific union!" So rejoiced the University of Paris. But the unforeseen now happened: both the Roman and the Avignon popes refused to abdicate, and instead of two contending popes of doubtful legitimacy, there were now three.

These events gave great impetus to the view, called the Conciliar Theory, that a general or ecumenical council, subject not to the pope but to the will of the whole Church, was responsible for the reform and healing of that Church. Impressed by the growing popularity of this doctrine, the emperor Sigismund now issued a call for a general council to meet in his territories. His appeal was widely heeded, and, during the course of the year 1414, representatives from all parts of western Christendom and all three rival papal camps streamed toward the little south German town of Constance. Eventually crowded together there were no fewer than thirty-three cardinals, nearly 500 bishops, some 2,000 representatives of the universities, and about 5,000 priests, not to mention ambassadors from every court, forty dukes, thirty-two princes, and over 500 knights–each nobleman and prelate escorted by a retinue of servants and horses.

This great assembly had a triple purpose: to end the Schism, to reform the Church, and to oppose the heresies that had recently been gaining ground. Only the first of these aims was seriously pursued and successfully achieved. Reform was found to be too complex and too challenging for so large a body. The Council's sole "success" in dealing with heresy was to imprison the Bohemian priest John Hus, who had rashly denounced the vices of the clergy in his homeland. This was the sort of criticism that, in the twelfth century, had won Bernard of Clairvaux the leadership of Church and society, but times had surely changed. Hus also opposed the crusade indulgence being preached by the Pisan pope John XXIII, and objected to the pope's use of the money raised to finance a military attack on King Ladislas of Naples. Hus had come to Constance protected–he thought–by a safe-conduct issued him by Emperor Sigismund. This availed him not at all. The Council Fathers found him guilty of teaching heresy and had him burned at the stake. And they did virtually nothing to bring about the reform which would have cut out the ground beneath dissent.

5. *The Papal Restoration*

Although no great reform of the Church had resulted, the schism had been ended and the popes had resumed their residence in Rome. The Council of Constance elected Martin V in 1417, and the new pope received widespread support. He and his successor, Eugenius IV, devoted their pontificates not to eliminating corruption but to fighting the conciliar theory. Their efforts were successful since conciliar government by committee was by that time largely discredited because of its ineffectiveness. By about 1455 the pope was free from any important check on his authority by other clergymen. By this time, however, the papacy was almost completely powerless outside its own central Italian territory, for in all countries of Europe temporal rulers had profited by the century-long weakness of the popes to limit the competence of church courts, get their hands on the revenues of the clergy, and tax the wealth of the Church. When bishoprics fell vacant, the kings collected the episcopal revenues until a successor was consecrated. The appointment of church officials became more and more subject to royal control. Churchmen were now regularly brought to trial in secular courts and forbidden to appeal to the pope for assistance. For most practical purposes, temporal rulers had assumed powers that made them the administrative heads of their respective national churches, reviving–on a national scale–the caesaropapism of late antiquity and of early medieval times.

The condition of the Church in the Late Middle Ages was always confused and often chaotic. The popes of the fourteenth and fifteenth centuries had turned their backs on the reforming ideal that had brought them leadership in the High Middle Ages. The popes' overriding concerns seemed to everyone to be the pursuit of ever increasing power and wealth. There continued to be many who sought reform, like Catherine of Siena (1347–1380), who labored mightily to bring the popes back to Rome and ensure peace among bickering Italian city states. And one of the modern world's most influential books of spiritual guidance, *The Imitation of Christ*, was written during this time, counseling humble withdrawal from self-promotion and loving service to others.

Would-be reformers and reform movements appeared everywhere in late medieval Europe, but they lacked the cohesion and direction that spiritual leaders like Bernard or popes like Innocent III had once provided. A very few reformers, like the Englishman John Wyclif (c. 1330-1384), sought to realize their ideals outside of, and in opposition to, the institutional Church. A far greater number of people, however, increasingly directed their energy toward secular goals. Religion was still very important to late medieval people, but it had ceased to be the focus of all life's activities, as it had been for so many in the High Middle Ages. Christianity was in the process of becoming compartmentalized as an activity suitable mostly for Sundays.

B. The Failure of the State

Given the failure of the institutional Church to bring order to the life of the Late Middle Ages, we can surely understand why many looked to the state for answers to their pressing problems. But the various political institutions of the period failed to respond to that hope.

1. The Dissolution of the Empire

During the thirteenth century, the Roman Empire had ceased to be an effective political entity. Frederick II, the nominal ruler of the Empire from 1215 to 1250, spent less than two years of his reign in what had been the heart of the Empire, in Germany, and concentrated his considerable talents on building a state in the warmer and more cosmopolitan lands of southern Italy and Sicily. In his absence, the great lords of Germany–both ecclesiastical and lay–had a free hand to govern their territories in what were now nearly sovereign states. Then, when Frederick's Hohenstaufen dynasty died out in 1254, nineteen years passed without a universally recognized emperor. By the end of the thirteenth century, there was no longer one Germany but only "the Germanies." From this time on, the "Holy Roman Empire of the German Nation," despite its new and grandiose title, was little more than a loose coalition of independent states. By 1803, there were some 112 of them, and Napoleon Bonaparte administered the *coup de grâce* to this anachronism in 1806.

2. The Strengths and Weaknesses of the French Monarchy

France in the Late Middle Ages moved in almost the reverse direction from Germany. From a loose collection of virtually independent feudal principalities, France had become, by the time of Louis IX (reigned 1226-1270), a powerful state under the increasingly centralized control of an efficient and respected monarchy. Only fifteen years after the death of the monarch who would be canonized as Saint Louis, his grandson Philip IV (also called Philip the Fair) ascended the throne and occupied it for nearly thirty years (1285-1314). We have already met this same Philip as the formidable antagonist of Pope Boniface VIII.

Under Philip the French monarchy reached a new height. During his reign the royal courts were so reliable that the justice they dispensed came to be preferred to that obtainable in feudal or ecclesiastical courts. The high court, or Parlement of Paris, had so much business before it that it sat in permanent session from 1308 onward. The income of the crown increased as a result, for litigants paid judicial fees, and the power and prestige of the king were correspondingly enhanced. To support his army and administration Philip sought to raise additional money by a variety of other means, levying feudal dues, harbor and customs duties, income taxes on the clergy (despite the pope's objection, as we have seen), new income and property taxes on the laity, confiscating the property of Jews and of the Templars, and, finally, taking loans from Italian bankers, which he later repudiated. Philip habitually got his way by lies, trickery, and brute force. He left the French monarchy with a reputation for unscrupulousness and injustice.

After Philip's death, all three of his sons reigned in brief succession and died without male heirs. In 1328, their cousin Philip of Valois succeeded to the throne as Philip VI, founding a new dynasty that lasted until 1589.

With the accession of Philip of Valois, an exhausting dynastic conflict known as the Hundred Years' War broke out between France and England. As a result of royal intermarriages, the kings of England were descended from the same ancestors as the Valois kings of France. This provided the English kings with a basis for contesting the Valois claim to the French crown. This dynastic dispute, together with clashing commercial interests in Flanders, gave rise to more than a century of episodic struggles. From 1340 to 1360, from 1369 to 1375, and from 1414 to 1453, the English devastated various parts of France and won battle after battle, but they were unable to govern effectively the lands they conquered.

Both monarchies exhausted themselves in these struggles, taxing their subjects to the very edge of revolt and sometimes even beyond, overstraining their credit, and slipping into repeated bankruptcies that proved ruinous to many of the leading banking houses of Europe. The English kings were sometimes able administrators and military leaders, while the French kings proved themselves feeble, inept, cowardly, and sometimes even insane. By 1400, the French monarchy was much weaker than it had been in 1300. It had lost control of much of the territory ruled by Philip the Fair and had seen the remainder devastated by armies, bandits, and swarms of ex-soldiers who had either deserted or been dismissed when funds to pay their wages ran out. Worse yet, by mid-century had come the onset of the Black Death which devastated a French population already suffering from near starvation.

3. *English Successes and Failures*

The political history of England roughly paralleled that of France in the Late Middle Ages. But the English Parliament in this period acquired a role in government hardly matched by the French institution that was its closest equivalent, the Estates-General. By the reign of Edward I (1272-1307), Parliament had come to provide political representation for a considerable part of English society: not only the great lords and prelates, but also representatives of knights and townsfolk were customarily in attendance. Cooperation between these groups frequently made it possible for Parliament to attain its objectives–such as the removal of an obnoxious royal minister or the redress of some administrative grievance.

So firmly established was the position of Parliament as an integral part of English government that its approval was deemed essential for any important change in law or policy, and its strength was so great that the institution could survive even the absolutism of the Tudor kings after 1485. The barons of the late medieval England, however, were too disunited to provide effective government through Parliament, and the kings of the period were often politically inept. Factions and corruption in high places became the rule rather than the exception.

The century following the death of Edward III in 1377 was a sorry time for England's people, despite evidences of institutional growth. A widespread revolt of peasants and city laborers led by Wat Tyler was momentarily successful in 1381, but king and nobles put it down so mercilessly that the lower classes found their lot even worse than before. There were also bloody wars with the Welsh, the Scots, and the French, the last ending in the loss of the last of England's holdings on the continent. Then the country was subjected to a series of civil wars (1453-1485) known as the Wars of the Roses because each faction took either a red or white rose as its emblem. The adherents of Richard of York and the followers of Henry of Lancaster fought a war of mutual extermination for no higher aim than power and spoils. A significant part of England's nobility was physically liquidated; whole families were wiped out, leaving no male heirs to succeed to their titles. Only in 1485 was the remote claim of Henry Tudor to the crown accepted, mainly because he won the last great battle at Bosworth Field and because the country was too weary to protest.

The peace and order, the security and justice, that in the High Middle Ages had been provided by the cooperative efforts of Church and state were, in the Late Middle Ages, only a memory. In England, France, Germany–and indeed in all the lands of Europe–the institution which held out the greatest promise of providing peace and justice, the state, had failed to live up to the hopeful expectations of the people. The effects of this painful loss were evident in the economic, social, and cultural life of the period.

C. Economic and Social Upheaval

In dramatic contrast to the vigorous expansion of the preceding centuries, the frontiers of Europe had ceased to move outward by about 1250, and after 1300 they began to contract. Alexander Nevsky, the Christian ruler of Russian Novogorod, halted, in 1242, the eastward advance of knights and missionaries to the Slavs and Balts not yet converted. The recently recovered city of Jerusalem was lost two years later, and, in 1291, Acre, the last Christian foothold in the Holy Land, was overwhelmed. By 1300, all the conquests of the crusaders, excepting only a few toeholds in Greece, had been lost.

Underlying much of the financial stringency of the Late Middle Ages was a general economic recession. Manufacturing and trade stagnated or shrank, and one result was that ambitious, warring governments could not collect sufficient revenues to support their administrative bodies and war machines. There was nothing else for these governments to do than repudiate their debts. This caused not only the ruin of many bankers but a general tightening of credit and a further slowing down of general business activity.

Then, in the mid-fourteenth century, came widespread disaster–the Black Death. Although the nature of the disease is now in dispute, we do know that it spread most rapidly in crowded towns and the more prosperous, more heavily populated rural areas. Its ravages were terrible. Beginning in Mediterranean lands in 1347, the pandemic spread northward, in 1348, to France, Spain, the British Isles, and Scandinavia, and eastward to Germany, Poland, and Russia. The disease raged for three years before its effects began to moderate, possibly owing to the development of immunity, possibly as a result of the simple fact that the inhabitants had been thinned out to the point that the disease was no longer easily communicated. It lingered on for years, however, and produced no less than five secondary outbreaks of great severity between 1350 and 1400. Sporadic recurrences, especially in cities, persisted until the early eighteenth century. The death-rate for Europe in the mid-fourteenth century was appalling: between one-third and one-half of the people died in many districts. Throughout Europe as a whole, it is probable that one out of every four or five people lost their lives between 1347 and 1350, and whole towns were wiped out or abandoned. The total population of Europe, which had been about seventy million in 1300, was reduced to some forty-five million by the year 1400.

The effect of the Black Death on the Church was near catastrophic. Many priests and bishops deserted their flocks and fled the ravages of disease. The flocks thus abandoned–at least those that survived–felt betrayed. The prestige of the clergy suffered still another blow. The clergy who stayed faithfully at their posts or rushed in to fill the gaps left by those who had fled contracted the disease themselves. Bishops who lost priests through death or desertion and religious orders whose ranks were similarly depleted were desperately intent on recruiting replacements, but the recruits who responded were often ill-educated and badly motivated for their new pastoral positions.

At every level of late medieval society, Europe suffered severe dislocation–and not only from the Black Death. The upper class of warriors, which had once provided protection and justice, was now divided between ruling princes and increasingly impoverished knights. Members of the lesser nobility found that their fighting prowess qualified them only for occasional employment as mercenaries, and the great princes turned from them to middle-class lawyers to serve as their administrators. The chivalric code of the high medieval knight and the ethos of courtly love were maintained only as entertaining games for the increasingly indolent noble men and women of the great courts.

Some members of the middle class found employment in the service of the princes' courts, but as a rule manufacturers and merchants did not thrive in the Late Middle Ages. The bankers who supplied capital to these business people suffered repeated failures themselves. Many of the greatest banking houses of Europe went bankrupt between about 1300 and 1350, including the Buonsignori of Siena, the Ricciardi of Lucca, the four leading banks of Florence, and the two chief financial houses of Pistoia. A number of these firms had advanced huge sums of money to monarchs like Edward III of England and Philip IV of France, and, when these kings defaulted on their debts, the bankers were forced to the wall.

The manufacture and distribution of goods in late medieval Europe were transformed by a shift from the guild system of owner-producers to the development of an urban proletariat. The masters in the guilds serving the most prosperous industries–like fine cloth manufacture in Florence–prevented journeymen from becoming masters by charging impossible fees for promotion. Only the favored relatives of the masters were admitted the highest level of the industry. Frustrated journeymen sometimes joined members of less powerful guilds in seizing control of town and city councils. Civil wars sometimes resulted, those in Italy often settled by the proletariat's installation of an imported dictator.

Because of a worsening climate, the effects of endemic warfare, and the loss to disease of large numbers of farmers, agricultural production plummeted in the Late Middle Ages. Whole families became extinct, much land reverted from cultivation to the wild, and overworked mines were abandoned. Europe was shrinking geographically. Large territories in the Balkans were lost to the Turks, and the once flourishing Norse colony on Greenland died out from starvation.

The Jewish population of late medieval Europe also saw a drastic decline. Persecution came easily to the Christian people of a diminishing Europe who sought a scapegoat for the suffering they were enduring. Jews were accused of poisoning wells and thus spreading the Black Death, despite papal pronouncements that the disease killed Jews and gentiles indiscriminately. Rulers of increasingly centralized and powerful monarchies one by one ejected Jews from their realms, taking care to ease their journey by seizing all their wealth. Then, in the sixteenth century, the Spanish Inquisition, an agency of the crown, began to burn Jews as heretics. All this was a symptom of a new direction in European culture, one which in the sixteenth century would see Catholics burning Protestants, Lutherans slaughtering Anabaptists, Calvinists executing Servetus the unitarian, and English kings and queens burning, beheading, and disemboweling all of these by turns.

X. THE MIND OF THE LATE MIDDLE AGES

Some Useful Data

1263-1321	Dante Alighieri, Florentine poet
1243-1328	Augustinus Triumphus, Parisian scholar
1316-1334	reign of John XXII, pope
c. 1275-1342	Marsiglio of Padua, Parisian scholar
1304-1347	Francesco Petrarcha, man of letters
c. 1285-1349	William of Ockham, Franciscan scholar
1342-1352	reign of Clement VI, pope
1350-1429	Jean Gerson, Parisian scholar
1417-1431	reign of Martin V, pope
1431-1447	reign of Eugenius IV, pope
1401-1464	Nicholas of Cusa; reformer, cardinal, and bishop of Brixen
1471-1484	reign of Sixtus IV, pope
1445-1510	Sandro Botticelli, Florentine painter
1503-1513	reign of Julius II, pope
1452-1519	Leonardo da Vinci, artist and scientist
1475-1564	Michelangelo Buonarroti; sculptor, architect, and painter

The late medieval Church and state failed to provide conditions conducive to political, economic, or religious security. This failure led to widespread personal disorientation and pessimism during the fourteenth and fifteenth centuries. That pessimism, that demoralization, was reflected in popular psychology, in the arts, and in religion. A morbid preoccupation with death appeared in much of the art and literature of the period. A scene that frequently decorated the walls of parish churches was the frenzied "Dance of Death," a depiction of a skeleton leading away a line of frightened dancers. The victims were often nude, wearing only head-gear–papal tiaras, bishops' miters, princes' crowns, and scholars' caps–to indicate the role in society from which they had been snatched.

The late fourteenth and early fifteenth centuries also saw the rise of black magic, witch cults, devil worship–and, inevitably, an equally hysterical reaction in the form of witch hunts. These phenomena were to reach their peak in the sixteenth and seventeenth centuries and were to plague backward areas of Europe down to the nineteenth century. Perhaps the superstitions of late medieval people are understandable, for they gave some meaning to a world that seemed to offer little other hope.

A. Political Thought and Papal Power

The search for security took other forms as well. Given the failure of the Church and state to provide that security, and given the sometimes ferocious conflict between those institutions, the scholars of the time faced substantial issues of definition. What was the nature of the Church and of the state? How was each to be governed? What were the proper relations between them? The role of the papacy in the Church, the authority of the state, and the source of the state's authority were all burning issues. The range of thought on these question was wide, and the disagreements were deep.

At one extreme of the political and ecclesiological spectrum of the time stood a treatise on ecclesiastical power written about 1320 by the Parisian professor Augustinus Triumphus of Ancona. Augustinus held that the pope is both the head and body of the Christian commonwealth–in effect, that the pope is the Church. The pope, wrote Augustinus, possesses the keys that unlock the doors to salvation, and only through the pope are the people given supernatural life. One practical consequence of this position was that the pope could by his own authority choose the emperor or depose him. Augustinus' views were understandably popular with popes. And his views were translated into the ceremonies of the contemporary papal court. The pope's headdress, the tiara, was topped with a golden crown. The pope, clad in imperial purple, was preceded in processions by imperial banners. The pope's coronation as temporal and spiritual ruler now eclipsed his consecration as bishop of Rome.

At the opposite end of the spectrum of political thought stood Marsiglio of Padua (c. 1275-1342). Marsiglio had been rector–we would say president–of the university at Paris in 1312-1313, but was forced to yield to papal pressure and flee Paris in 1326. Pope John XXII's ire had been aroused by Marsiglio's treatise *The Defender of the Peace* (1324). Peace, for Marsiglio, is the precondition of order in the state and the prerequisite for human happiness—both in the good life of this world and in the salvation of the next. Marsiglio was convinced that the fundamental challenge to that peace, and therefore to the good order of Church and state, is the papal pretension to absolute power and the corruption that results from the attempted application of this unjustified claim. To combat this usurpation, the people, who are the source of law, bestow power on a temporal ruler, who must maintain peace and order. Marsiglio's Church is the totality of the faithful, not the clergy alone. This was surely a traditional view in the High Middle Ages, though it was upsetting to fourteenth-century proponents of papalism. Though Marsiglio saw the priesthood as of divine origin, he considered the hierarchy of popes and bishops a human creation. The people of God who are the Church should appoint the clergy and convoke a general or ecumenical council to reform both erroneous Church teachings and corrupt practices. These positions of Marsiglio's elicited the furious condemnation of a whole series of contemporary popes.

Another fourteenth-century thinker who drew the ire of the Avignon popes was William of Ockham (c. 1285-1349). William was not only the greatest logician of his time but also a Franciscan who supported the "Spiritual" party within his order. The Spirituals advocated a total commitment to the absolute poverty that had been the lifestyle and teaching of Saint Francis. That teaching, we have seen, ignored the need for housing, for medical care, and for education in an order comprising many thousands of men. To support their position, the Spirituals declared that Jesus and his apostles had possessed neither individual nor collective property. And this "apostolic poverty," they claimed, should be mandatory not only for Franciscans, but for all clergymen of whatever station. Pope John XXII (1316-1334) declared the doctrine of apostolic poverty to be heresy. Since an earlier pope, Nicholas III, had in endorsed apostolic poverty in 1279, the Spirituals introduced the doctrine of papal infallibility in an attempt to nullify Pope John's condemnation. Theologians and canonists of the High Middle Ages had insisted that the pope could fall into doctrinal error and be deposed for his fall. Pope John XXII followed this tradition in dismissing papal infallibility as a "pestiferous doctrine." He then repeated his rejection of apostolic poverty.

William of Ockham's response was to declare that John XXII and his papal successors were heretics. William taught that the pope did not possess the supreme authority in temporal matters that papal supporters claimed. William also denied that the pope possessed "fullness of power" over the Church as well, noting, for example, that no pope could command Christians to observe virginity or absolve spouses committed to each other of their marriage bond. Unlike Marsiglio of Padua, however, William did believe the papacy was of divine institution, created to serve the people of God. That community of believers was, for William, the sole arbiter of correct doctrine.

Between the extremes represented by the papalism of Augustinus

Triumphus and the anti-papal position of Marsiglio of Padua were a host of thinkers torn by their loyalty to the traditional doctrines and structures of the Church and their revulsion at the corruption found everywhere in the Church–and especially at the papal court. Among them was Dante Alighieri (1263-1321), the Florentine poet who has left us the splendid spiritual masterpiece *The Divine Comedy*. Dante subscribed to the mutual interdependence of the spiritual and temporal orders. He believed this harmony had been destroyed by the papal usurpation of temporal power. His solution to the chaotic conditions which resulted from papal pretensions was a restoration of the monarchy embodied historically in the Roman Empire.

Still more moderate was the position of Jean Gerson (1350-1429), professor and sometimes chancellor at the university at Paris. Gerson hoped to bring about moral reform in the Church through a refocusing of priestly education. He saw his fellow teachers less interested in truth than in the quest for novelty. He wished to replace the sterilities of late scholastic theological discourse, which he saw as mostly irrelevant and divisive, with immersion in the study of Scripture. Because moral reform was Gerson's chief concern, he supported any system of Church government that seemed likely to bring that about. He was adamant in his belief that the true head of the Church was Christ, even in the presence of his papal vicar. The Church could choose that vicar through a general council, even without the assistance of cardinals.

Perhaps the greatest late medieval mind to address the question of Church and state was that of Nicholas of Cusa (1401-1464). Nicholas had been a delegate to the Council of Basel called by Pope Martin V in 1427. That council had fought Martin's successor, Eugenius IV (1431-1447), declared him deposed, and asserted its authority over the whole Church. Endless debate and increasing disorder led Nicholas to the papal camp. Nicholas served as papal legate (or ambassador) to Constantinople, where he worked for reunion with the Greek Church. He assumed an active reforming role as papal legate in Germany, Bohemia, and the Low Countries, where he presided over local and provincial councils. His service won him a cardinal's hat, and he was also installed as bishop in the Alpine diocese of Brixen. He had proven himself a reformer throughout his life, and his fidelity to the pope was never in doubt. But he maintained to his dying day that the pope is a servant of the Church, not her master.

In his *De concordantia catholicae* (a treatise on universal harmony), Nicholas described the Church as the "community of the faithful," as the extension of Christ in time and eternity. Nicholas believed in the fundamental freedom of each individual person–a freedom expressed through participation in the Church. Nicholas saw the pope as the steersman of the ship of Saint Peter, and, as he is the one charged with setting its course, his participation is necessary to legitimate church legislation. But the pope does not have the power to legislate independently of the whole Church, and the power of bishops derives not from the pope but from God. For Nicholas all forms of government, both ecclesiastical and temporal, arise from the consent of the people.

The political theorists of the Late Middle Ages employed reason, both theologically–by applying it to the content of Revelation–and philosophically–by using it to analyze the data provided by the senses, the data learned through experience of the physical world. But those same thinkers surely cast doubt on the efficacy of rational inquiry by their radical disagreements on the political and ecclesiastical questions of fundamental and critical importance to the time.

B. Late Medieval Religious Life

Philosophy and political theory, theology and science, are pursuits engaged in by intellectuals who can retreat to their ivory towers in times of disorder and strife. But what of the ordinary people whose Christian faith remained firm in the face of the failure of Church and state, whose faith withstood the economic and social upheavals of the Late Middle Ages? As we have seen, for many late medieval people life had become compartmentalized, and for them their religion had to compete with other often unrelated concerns. But most fourteenth- and fifteenth-century Europeans thought of themselves as sincere Christians, and there is plenty of evidence that they practiced their religion with fervor.

But the forms that religion took were vastly different from the ways Christianity had been practiced in the High Middle Ages. Late medieval popular religion was intensely concerned with the insecurity of sinfulness. It was less concerned with the cultivation of an interior life of love than with devotionalism, with a dedication to external actions intended prevent damnation to Hell or shorten the sinner's time in Purgatory.

The Mass, the liturgical service surrounding the sacrament of the Eucharist (or Communion), ceased to be the central event in sincere Christians' lives. There were good reasons for this, I think. The Mass had become increasingly inaccessible to most people, whose role in the liturgy was reduced to distant observation of the priest's back as he mumbled in a language unintelligible to most. Some form of Latin had been the mother tongue of many people in the western part of Europe during the Early Middle Ages. That tongue had been replaced in the High Middle Ages by the various vernacular languages, but most members of the upper and middle classes of that time could understand enough Latin to follow along in the liturgy. Even the uneducated could sing along with major parts of the Mass, notably the Lord's Prayer, as the music of the early and medieval Church was designed to be sung by everyday people. The simple melodies of plain song, of Gregorian chant as it is also called, had been sung in unison by all worshippers.

But in the Late Middle Ages, Church music became more and more a matter of professional performance. The Mass music of the time was polyphonic, with many different melodic lines being sung at once. The second tenor line in one fourteenth-century Mass had the melody and words of a contemporary barroom ballad, and was sung in French. The people could not sing this polyphonic music, and despite the appreciation they may have had for the beauty of the compositions sung, they could not understand the words obscured by the complex sound.

The priests and other clergy in cathedrals and other large churches were now often separated from the laity by a rood screen, a wall built across the width of the church. It was called a rood screen because the wall was topped with a crucifix (the Old English word for which was *rood*). At the very time the clergy were losing their credibility with lay people because of clerical corruption, those clergymen sought to enhance their status through separation from their charges, the laity.

Lay people filled many of their religious needs by joining pious confraternities devoted to the veneration and cultivation of one of a host of saints assigned to special spheres of competence. Artists prayed to Saint Luke; the athletically inclined attended masses at altars dedicated to Saint Sebastian. Bakers had Saint Elizabeth of Hungary as their patroness; bankers relied on the intercession of Saint Matthew. Every occupation had its favorite saint: musicians looked to Saint Cecilia, dancers to Saint Vitus.

The bones and scraps of clothing thought to belong to these saints were credited with miraculous power and venerated with fervor. This led to a traffic in relics which resulted in many aberrations. There were perhaps as many as seven right arms of John the Baptist in circulation in late medieval Europe. The crown of thorns, pieces of the True Cross, the tablecloth used at the Last Supper, pieces of the tablets which Moses broke, were all available for veneration. The cathedral at Aachen boasted–as did many other churches–of its possession of the swaddling clothes in which Mary wrapped her son Jesus. The cathedral of Cologne served as a pilgrimage site for those who wished to be blessed by viewing the gifts of the Three Magi. Cologne also possessed a vial of the Virgin's milk, as did several other churches. Perhaps the most powerful of all these relics was that of the Holy Foreskin, which, it was said, had survived Jesus' circumcision and been saved.

The people of the Late Middle Ages followed their high medieval forbears in taking the humanity of Jesus seriously. But the aspect of that humanity which meant most to hungry and plague-ridden people was the physical suffering of Christ. The instruments of Jesus' torture–hammers and nails, crowns of thorns and scourges–became the focus of depictions of Christ in sculpture and painting.

The belief that Jesus was really present in the eucharistic bread distributed at Mass had led high medieval churchmen to encourage frequent reception of communion. In the Late Middle Ages, however, that very presence of Christ led to widespread avoidance of communion. A people burdened by pessimism about human nature and fearful for the consequence of their sin sought to avoid Saint Paul's threatened condemnation of those who communicated unworthily. But they seized the opportunity of viewing the communion wafer whenever possible. The practice grew rapidly of installing a eucharistic wafer in a monstrance, a splendidly decorated altar vessel with a transparent center. It was widely thought that viewing the "Sacrament"–even by those in a state of sin–somehow conferred saving power. Nicholas of Cusa, the fifteenth-century cardinal, complained to the reform councils over which he presided that the Eucharist "was instituted as food, not as an item of display." No one listened.

The fear and awe aroused by Jesus' presence in the Eucharist was enhanced by a radically increasing emphasis on Jesus' role in the Last Judgment. He is the one who will reward the virtuous and condemn sinners to Hell. In an age that viewed humans as seriously, almost fatally, flawed by original sin, the best all but a few people could hope for was the reprieve of Purgatory. In the High Middle Ages, Jesus had been seen as the merciful Mediator between God the Father and human beings. Late medieval people sensed a pressing need for an advocate with Jesus the awesome judge.

Who better to turn to than Jesus' mother Mary? Those who came before the seat of judgment occupied by Jesus could plead with his mother for the protection of a mediatrix. In the twelfth century Mary had been viewed primarily as a model of humility and loving obedience; in the thirteenth Mary was increasingly seen as an intercessor. By the Late Middle Ages, Mary had become the Queen of Heaven. A frequent depiction of her coronation as queen was a large statue of Mary shown as the central figure on a cross. God the Father occupied the left cross bar of this cross, while God the Son, Jesus, from his position on the right cross bar, joined his Father in placing a crown on the Queen's head. Above fluttered a dove, representing the Holy Spirit. Critics of this depiction referred to its subject as the Holy Quaternity.

C. The Scandal of Indulgences

Nervous sinners also sought other ways of mitigating the effects of their actions, among them recourse to indulgences. Indulgences had begun as an innocent practice in the twelfth century. They were then merely a statement by any ecclesiastical authority that a certain pious activity–from helping install a new roof on a church to enrolling in a crusading pilgrimage–was a meritorious act. That activity–if done in a spirit of genuine repentance, and preceded by confession of guilt–would make up for the evil brought into the world by one's sin.

Indulgences were to become a central part of the religious life of the Late Middle Ages. The fourth of the Avignon popes, Clement VI (reigned 1342-1352), contributed the classic description and justification of indulgences in a decree of 1343. Ironically, the central image around which Clement structured his decree was a treasure chest–ironic because Clement was one of the most politically active and financially rapacious popes of his century. According to Clement, through the "precious blood" of Jesus, which he "shed as an innocent victim on the altar of the cross," God the Father "acquired a great treasure for the Church." Although it was "an infinite treasure,...the merits of the blessed Mother of God and of all the elect...are known to have supplied their increment." The agent who portioned out this infinite treasure was the pope–and he alone, for he, as the sole successor of Peter, was "the bearer of heaven's keys." The recipients of this largess were those "truly penitent," those who had confessed, those who had performed some meritorious act of reparation. The meritorious act that soon eclipsed all others was the contribution of money to a fiscally strapped papacy.

Contemporary theologians were puzzled. If the acts of reparation done by Christians were truly meritorious, why did they need the treasury? If it were the treasury that made their acts meritorious, did this not deny the freedom of the will–a freedom always considered necessary to good works? And if the will's choice were crucial in determining the goodness or merit of an act, why did Christian folk need the pope's authority to gain access to God's mercy?

In 1476, Pope Sixtus IV compounded these misgivings. He decreed that indulgences were henceforth applicable to the souls suffering in Purgatory. By this act, the jurisdiction claimed by the popes over the Church Militant–the Church struggling in this world to attain the next–was extended to papal control over life after death in the Church Suffering. Still more disturbing to many theologians was Sixtus' assertion that indulgence buyers need not be repentant for their sins or confess them. This seemed to make money, not merit, the means to the release of souls from Purgatory and their entrance into Heaven.

But what seemed to be magic to theologians was embraced with enthusiasm by most late medieval lay people. They were told that, when their coins clinked into the money box of the papal indulgence peddlers, their dear relatives' souls would fly away to Heaven. They eagerly contributed.

D. Renaissance and Humanism

A startling contrast to the pessimism and despair which characterized the Late Middle Ages is the intellectual stance contemporaries called "humanism" and the movement we call "Renaissance." Since the late eighteenth century, the "Renaissance" has been popularly held to be a historical period marking the transition between the medieval and modern worlds. The dates of this "period" no one has clearly delineated. It began, some have suggested, about the year 1300. Others hold that dates as late as 1475 mark its start. The ending of this age is still more nebulous, ranging from 1517 to 1600–and sometimes later. It is difficult to delineate a historical period when the dates advanced for it are so indeterminate and vague.

"Renaissance" is, of course, the French word for rebirth. And the classical work on the subject, Jacob Burckhardt's *Civilization of the Renaissance in Italy* (1860), saw the Renaissance as a rebirth of the long-ignored classical culture of ancient Greece and Rome. We can easily recognize the difficulty with Burckhardt's thesis in that classical culture was an essential and enduring component of medieval Christian culture. The typical response to this objection is to say that it was not until the Renaissance that classical culture was understood in its "true" context–a secular context in which "man is the measure of all things." Proponents of this position label as "humanism" the secularism that characterized the transitional period between the Middle Ages and the modern world.

In the pages which follow, we shall explore what humanism meant to some significant authors and artists of the fourteenth through sixteenth centuries. And those authors and artists we shall query will be men identified by their contemporaries as the outstanding representatives of those disciplines, literature and art, central to the spirit of humanism.

1. *Humanism in Literature: Petrarch*

Francesco Petrarcha (or Petrarch) lived from 1304 to 1347, and was praised by his contemporaries as "the father of humanism." Although an Italian, Petrarch spent a great part of his adult life as a bureaucratic functionary in the papal court at Avignon. Petrarch was a bitter critic of the corruption of that court. "Here," in Avignon, he wrote, "reign the successors of the poor fishermen of Galilee who have strangely forgotten their origin." The popes and their cardinals, he continued, are "loaded with gold and clad in purple." They live in "luxurious palaces and on heights crowned with castles, instead of under a boat turned upside down for shelter." These "fishermen" employ "worthless parchments, turned by a seal into nets used to catch hordes of unwary Christians."

Petrarch found refuge from this "slavish luxury" in fictional conversations, conducted by letter, with the long-dead authors of classical antiquity. Yet the letter for which he is most famous is one he addressed to the bishop of Borgo San Sepulcro–though intended for all to read. This work is usually entitled *The Ascent of Mount Ventoux*, for it tells the tale of his expedition into the French Alps.

Petrarch tells us first of his search for a companion. After rejecting several candidates, Petrarch selected his brother, a Carthusian monk, a member of an order that had successfully maintained its rigorous ideals throughout the Late Middle Ages. With his brother, Petrarch set out. His brother chose a difficult climb, a straight and narrow path, leading directly to the top. But Petrarch three times chose an easier path, a roundabout route which took him ever lower. He then realized that "no human ingenuity can alter the nature of things or cause anything to reach a height by going down."

The ascent of the mountain became, for Petrarch, a symbol of the human "journey toward the blessed life." In his reflection on that journey Petrarch asks himself and his reader: "What then holds you back?" He answers: "Nothing except a choice of a path which seems easier, leading through low and worldly pleasures." In the end, Petrarch concludes, the sinner must "climb the steeper path, under the burden of deeds foolishly deferred, to its blessed culmination." To choose to "lie down in the valley of your sins" will lead to "an eternal night amid constant torments."

Strengthened by this reflection, Petrarch attacked the climb with resolve and reached the summit. There he rested and read from the book which was his constant comparison, Saint Augustine's spiritual autobiography, *The Confessions*. In Petrarch's letter describing his experience, he also quotes Vergil and Ovid and "the pagan philosophers" as well as saints Paul and Augustine. For Petrarch, as for the ancient Christian writers Justin Martyr and Clement of Alexandria, no fundamental contradiction exists between classical and Christian thought. For Petrarch, as for Bernard and the other twelfth-century humanists, the beauty and the precision of ancient thought are means to better understanding of a loving God. Petrarch's purpose in writing his letter, he tells us at its end, is to convince his readers that they must "direct themselves at last toward the single, true, certain, and everlasting good."

2. *Humanism in Art: Michelangelo*

I suspect that, if we asked our friends to name a Renaissance artist, the answer most often given would be Michelangelo. And that answer would serve well our purposes here, for Michelangelo Buonarroti (1475-1564) was prized by his contemporaries as an outstanding–perhaps the most outstanding–painter, sculptor, and architect of his time.

Michelangelo was, of course, the architect of Saint Peter's basilica. Though his design was but imperfectly realized, it reflects Michelangelo's intent to create on a massive scale the appearance of an ancient Roman temple. The content of Michelangelo's creation–the purpose he had in mind for the structure–is equally obvious: it is a church that serves as a gigantic worship space. The style is classical, the content (or purpose) Christian.

Michelangelo's sculptures are surely among the world's finest. The statues which seem to stand out above the rest are the magnificent *David* and the moving *Pietà*. The City Fathers of Florence, Michelangelo's native city, commissioned his *David* in 1501, and he worked on the eighteen-foot statue for three years. The artist's inspiration was clearly classical, though it is the David of the Old Testament who is portrayed. Once again we recognize a fusion of classical form and religious content. This fusion is still more apparent in the *Pietà* (probably 1498-1500) which now stands in a side chapel of Saint Peter's basilica. This portrayal of Mary embracing the body of Christ recently removed from the cross is clearly Christian. The nearly nude body of Jesus is rendered with the structure and musculature of an ancient Greek god.

Michelangelo seems to have had little taste for painting and accepted only reluctantly Pope Julius II's commission to decorate the ceiling of the Sistine Chapel. The chapel was part of the papal palace next to Saint Peter's. The ceiling was eighty-five feet above the floor and encompassed an area of some seven hundred square yards. To cover this enormous space, Michelangelo labored for four years. He tells us of his great discomfort in accomplishing this work in one of his many poems:

> My beard turns up to heaven.
> My neck arches in, fixed upon my spine....
> A rich embroidery bedews my face from
>   brush drops thick and thin.

Hating his task and intent on finishing it as soon as possible, Michelangelo paused from his labors only when exhausted. For a period of weeks, he neglected to remove his boots, and they pulled the skin off his feet when he was finally persuaded to change his clothes. A story, perhaps apocryphal, is told that Pope Julius II (1503-1513)–better known for his skill in battering down city walls with artillery than for his social graces–was so dissatisfied with what he regarded as Michelangelo's slow pace that he threatened to throw him off the scaffolding. Michelangelo ignored him, and so the pope climbed up to the artist's high perch and beat him with his cane.

Michelangelo's finished ceiling grandly displays the creation of the universe, and the creation of man and of woman. It depicts the sin of Adam and Eve and their expulsion from paradise. Noah and David, Esther and Judith are among the artist's splendidly portrayed Old Testament figures. The prophets of the Jewish and Christian tradition are shown side by side with sibyls, the prophets of classical mythology.

Why did Michelangelo endure the pain of his unwanted labors and the contempt of his papal patron? We can gain some insight into Michelangelo's motive for painting by pondering his sonnets. One of them goes like this:

> From thy fair face I learn, O my loved Lord,
>> That which no mortal tongue may rightly say.
>> The soul imprisoned in her house of clay,
>> Helped by thee, to God hath often soared....
> Lo, all the lovely things we find on earth
>> Resemble for the soul that rightly sees
>> That Source of bliss divine which gave us birth.

Michelangelo saw the universe and his own artistic creations as reflections of God's glory. Therefore he wrote that "loving loyally, I rise to God and make death sweet by thee." Michelangelo's mastery of classical form, his extensive knowledge of classical philosophy and mythology, all served his deep longing for the happiness of salvation.

3. Humanism and Science: Sandro Botticelli and Leonardo da Vinci

Sometime around 1485, Sandro Botticelli painted *The Birth of Venus*. This work depicts the Roman goddess of love arising from the sea, clothed only in a few breezes. Our first reaction to this painting is surely that the subject seems to glorify sensuality rather than encouraging us to love God. But Botticelli did indeed aim at winning us to the Christian life of love. For Botticelli, the central figure, Venus, was an allegorical representation of God's love–perhaps better, of God *as* Love. Botticelli hoped to attract us to Love by the beauty of his painting. And in this we come close to the meaning of humanism for Petrarch and Michelangelo, as well as for Botticelli. Through beauty, the beauty of classically inspired literature and art, they hoped to communicate what they saw as the fundamental truths of human existence, the truths taught by Jesus of Nazareth.

But neither beauty nor, certainly, Christianity were the central concerns of Leonardo da Vinci (1452-1519). Leonardo's paintings are stunningly beautiful, and many depict religious topics–his *Virgin of the Rocks*, for example. But we need not look very far to discover that Leonardo's motivation in creating these artistic works was fiscal, not religious. In his widely appealing *Last Supper*, Leonardo saw merely an exercise in perspective. The discovery and application of scientific knowledge was Leonardo's passionate pursuit. His notebooks are filled with sketches of jacks, clocks, and automatic turnspits. Helicopters, tanks, and bat-like flying machines abound on the pages of the notebooks. Detailed studies of human anatomy, from muscles to eyeballs, are the result, we are told, of the dissection of corpses collected by his aides in the back streets and alleys of Milan. Outrageous as it may seem, we cannot count Leonardo as a Renaissance artist–not if what we mean by "renaissance" is a devotion to humanism.

The Late Middle Ages was a time in which the cultural synthesis of the High Middle Ages was breaking down. Politics and religion competed for loyalty; credulous superstition existed side by side with profound spirituality. Three differing views of human nature and its potentiality existed in ever increasing hostility: the pessimism and despair which characterized much of the theology of the time, the joyful embrace of infinite human possibilities that informed Christian humanism, and the calculating analyses which forged the coming of a scientific world-view.

XI. THE PROTESTANT REFORMATION AND EUROPEAN CULTURE

Some Useful Data

1513-1521	reign of Leo X, pope
1464-1531	Huldrych Zwingli, Swiss reformer
1523-1534	reign of Clement VII, pope
1469?-1536	Desiderius Erasmus, humanist and reformer
1490-1545	Albrecht von Hohenzollern, elector/archbishop of Mainz
1483-1546	Martin Luther, theologian and reformer
1509-1547	reign of Henry VIII, king of England
1547-1553	reign of Edward VI, king of England
1519-1556	reign of Charles V, emperor
1553-1558	reign of Mary, queen of England
1509-1564	John Calvin, theologian and reformer
1558-1603	reign of Elizabeth, queen of England

A. Martin Luther

On October 31, 1517, Martin Luther, a professor of theology at the university at Wittenberg, posted ninety-five theses on the door of the local castle church. This door was covered with such notices, for it served as the university bulletin board, and discussions of theses on all sorts of topics were a standard means of instruction at a medieval university. Luther's ninety-five theses, however, centered on the topic of indulgences–a hot issue in 1517.

The reason for this heat was that some five years before, in 1513, Albrecht von Hohenzollern, though not a priest, had become archbishop of Magdeburg and administrator of the see of Halberstadt. Albrecht was but twenty-three at the time and too young to hold either office legally. To circumvent this violation of canon law, a costly papal dispensation had been purchased. Albrecht's ambitions were inflamed still more the following year, in 1514, when the death of the archbishop of Mainz left that important see vacant. To become primate (or first bishop) of Germany was desirable in itself. In addition, the archbishop of Mainz was an elector–one of the seven great princes who, since the thirteenth century, had chosen the Roman emperor. Albrecht's older brother was elector of Brandenburg, and thus two out of the seven votes would be in the hands of the Hohenzollern family. Of course Albrecht had no intention of giving up Magdeburg and Halberstadt. Pluralism was against canon law. So, to obtain an exemption from Pope Leo X (1513-1521), Albrecht promised an enormous bribe of 10,000 gold ducats, to which was added papal taxes of 14,000 gold ducats–in modern terms, many millions of dollars.

Leo had no scruples about accepting the bribe. His clerical career had been advanced through the liberal use of money and influence by his father Lorenzo "the Magnificent" de' Medici, the *de facto* ruler of Florence. Leo had been made a clergyman at the age of seven; among his many clerical positions–and sources of income–had been the abbacy of Saint Benedict's monastery at Montecassino. When he was only thirteen, Pope Innocent VIII had named him a cardinal. In 1513, Leo was elected pope, and in that office he distinguished himself by his lavish lifestyle. His favorite activities were hunting and the theater; so, to support his life of pleasure, Leo was wont to traffic in indulgences. He also saw in the indulgence trade a way out of the enormous expense entailed by the building of a new and grander Saint Peter's basilica.

Leo and Albrecht struck a deal. They would launch a massive effort to sell indulgences, informing the public only of the pious cause, constructing the new Saint Peter's. The proceeds from this campaign, however, would be split down the middle: half going to Albrecht to relieve him of the burden of his debts, half going to Rome to support Leo's building of the most massive church in Christendom. A corps of indulgence preachers spread out over Germany under the leadership of a Dominican friar, Johannes Tetzel. Copies of Leo's indulgence decree were carried into cities and towns in elaborate processions. All church services were forbidden so the local people could attend rallies at which Tetzel would proclaim:

> How many mortal sins do you commit each day, how many in a week, how many in a year, how many in the course of your entire lifetime? These sins are well-nigh numberless, and those who commit them must suffer endless punishment in the burning pains of Purgatory.

Having heightened people's panic, Tetzel offered the remedy: purchase from the preacher of a document with which "you will be able at any time in life to obtain full indulgence for all penalties imposed upon you, and at the hour of death to receive a full indulgence for all your penalties and sins." Those in the audience concerned for their relatives could purchase an indulgence for them as well–in this case without the need for repentance or confession. A reliable witness has recorded Tetzel's sales-pitch: "As soon as the coins ring in the chest, the soul for whom the money is paid will fly straight up to Heaven."

One of the few cities in the Empire into which the indulgence preachers were *not* allowed was Wittenberg, in which Luther lived and taught. The reason is not edifying. The ruler of this land, Elector Frederick the Wise, had a splendid collection of relics, housed, ironically, in the very church whose door was to serve as the posting place for Luther's theses. In Frederick's rich collection of 18,970 relics there were thirty-five pieces of the True Cross, a vial of Virgin's milk, a piece of the burning bush seen by Moses on Mount Sinai, and 204 parts of the bodies of the Holy Innocents slaughtered by King Herod. All these could be viewed by anyone with the entrance fee, a payment rendered still more attractive by the already existing indulgence, associated with only one visit, of 1,902,202 years and 270 days. Grace, thus quantified, was already on sale in Wittenberg. Frederick was too wise to allow Tetzel's competition.

Even so, many of Wittenberg's nervous citizens stole across the nearby border to hear and pay Tetzel. Some of them were Luther's parishioners, for he was a priest as well as a professor, and Luther took his pastoral responsibilities seriously. But the underlying reason for Luther's theses was his theologian's need to address the rationale behind indulgences.

Luther's theses were posted, as he put it, "with the aim of elucidating the truth" about indulgences through a disputation among his fellow theologians at Wittenberg. Luther's theses, of course, were posted in Latin, clearly not intended for popular consumption. Luther's purpose was threefold: to clarify the Church's teaching on indulgences, to expose and reform the shoddy practices employed by indulgence preachers, and–perhaps surprising to us–to affirm the authority of the institutional Church and encourage a revival of respect for it.

Theses 13 and 18 provide a good example of Luther's contribution to the theology of indulgences. In them Luther asserted that the souls in Purgatory are "already dead to canon law," because the pope's acknowledged authority over the Church on earth does not extend to the afterlife. But, said Luther in Thesis 25, "the pope acts most rightly in granting remission to souls [in Purgatory], but not by the power of the keys [granted to Peter by Christ] but through his intercession for them." On the other hand, Luther maintained that indulgences granted to those who are still living are "by no means to be despised," since they are "a declaration of divine remission."

When he turned to the practices of the indulgence preachers, Luther's measured theological analysis became more vehement. Thesis 75 thundered out: "To think that papal indulgences have such power that they could absolve a man even if he had violated the Mother of God is madness!" Theses 45 through 50 all began with "Christians should be taught that." The first of these continued: "whoever sees anyone in need and, passing the needy one by, gives money for indulgences, is purchasing instead the anger of God." The last of these, Thesis 50, contained a barb directed against Leo X: "Christians should be taught that, if the pope knew about the exactions of the indulgence preachers, he would prefer that Saint Peter's basilica be burned to the ground rather than built up with the skin, flesh, and bones of his sheep."

The indulgence trade, Luther alleged, injures the prestige of the Church and the pope in the eyes of all. Thesis 81: "The laxity in controlling pardon preaching makes it no easy thing, even for the learned, to protect the reverence due to the pope." Thesis 82 illustrates the kind of question lay people had been asking: "Why doesn't the pope empty Purgatory out of the highest sort of love and because of the great need of the souls there? That would be the most just of all reasons. Why does he instead redeem an infinite number of souls for the sake of that most deadly thing, money, to be spent on building a basilica–that being a very slight reason indeed?" In Thesis 90, Luther concluded this line of reasoning: "To repress those scruples and arguments of lay people, and not resolve them with reasons, is to expose the Church and the pope to the ridicule of their enemies."

With his ninety-five theses, Luther showed himself no enemy of Church or pope. The theses were not the first salvo in a Protestant assault on Catholicism. Nor does the initial response to Luther's theses–quickly circulated in translation–support the view that they indicated apostasy. Of course Tetzel and his troop of indulgence peddlers were furious, but Leo X's response was bored indifference to what he termed "a monks' quarrel." The bishop of Brandenburg, Luther's own bishop, approved of the theses. Bishop Adolf of the nearby diocese of Merseburg went further. He urged that Luther's theses "be posted in many places" to warn the poor "against Tetzel's humbuggery and hoaxes."

The following years saw increasing controversy centered on the person and thought of Martin Luther. In 1518, Luther attempted to calm the waters by writing to the pope, addressing him as "Holy Father." The letter rehearsed the "scandal to ecclesiastical authority" created by the perverse preaching of indulgences. Luther insisted that his theses were, from the first, questions to be discussed, not doctrines he taught. He ended his letter with words of reverential submission: "I acknowledge your voice as the voice of Christ, who reigns and speaks through you."

In the following year, in Leipzig, Luther engaged in a public debate with Johann Eck, a professor of theology at the university at Ingolstadt. Before the debate, Luther presented a new set of theses. The twelfth reveals the direction his thought was moving and was to bring him condemnation from many quarters: "The very feeble decrees of the Roman pontiffs that have appeared in the last four hundred years attempt to prove the Roman Church is superior to all others. Against them is a history of eleven hundred years, the text of divine Scripture, and the decree of the Council of Nicaea." Eck's response was to label Luther a heretic, as did the theological faculties of several universities.

The next crucial year was 1520, a year in which Luther published three of his most well-known works. The first was written in German, an *Open Letter to the Christian Nobility of the German Nation*. It began:

> The Romanists have built, with great ingenuity, three walls about them. With these they have always defended themselves so that no one has been able to reform them, and this has been the cause of terrible corruption throughout all Christendom.

The first of these walls repels attempts by temporal powers to encourage reform. The Romanists, the canon lawyers of the papal court, "have said that the temporal power has no jurisdiction over them and that the spiritual power is above the temporal." The second wall restricts the Bible: "When the attempt is made to admonish them on the basis of Holy Writ, they object that no one but the pope can properly interpret Scripture." And the third wall obstructs episcopal attempts at reform: "If threatened with a general council, they answer with the fable that no one can call a council but the pope."

In the process of assaulting these walls, Luther cited Saint Peter, asserting that "through baptism we are all consecrated to the priesthood." On this position early Christian and medieval theologians had agreed, but it clearly offended the clerical mindset of the Late Middle Ages. Against the second wall, the assertion that popes alone can interpret Scripture, Luther hurled the long held position of theologians and canon lawyers that the pope can err, asking: "Has not the pope erred many times?" Astute theologians at Paris could remember that their fourteenth-century predecessors had condemned Pope John XXII for heresy. Against the third wall, the assertion that only the pope can call an ecumenical or general council, Luther pointed out that the very first such council, the Council of Nicaea, "was neither called nor confirmed by the bishop of Rome." All this was a clarion call to the lay lords of Germany to resist papal attempts to subvert reform.

Luther's other two fundamental works of 1520 were *The Babylonian Captivity of the Church* and *On Christian Liberty*. In the first, written for theologians, Luther accepted the high medieval definition of a sacrament as an external sign of spiritual grace, a sign instituted by Christ. According to Luther, on the scriptural evidence there were three sacraments, not seven. These were baptism, penance, and communion. Transubstantiation Luther considered "an invention of human reason." He vigorously affirmed the Real Presence of Christ in the eucharistic bread and wine, but could accept no merely human explanation of how this was so. Concerning Baptism he quoted the scriptural promise: "Those who believe and are baptized shall be saved." About Penance he wrote: "Private confession is wholly commendable, useful, and, indeed, necessary."

Pope Leo's response came in the form of a papal decree "Arise, O Lord," condemning Luther as a heretic. To Catholic theologians all over Europe the decree was a source of profound embarrassment, for Leo's list of Luther's "heresies" included condemnation of historically accurate statements, of universally accepted Catholic beliefs, and of positions which Luther had never held. In the course of his condemnation, for example, Leo asserted that the existence of Purgatory could be proved from the Bible.

The reaction of lay and ecclesiastical lords to Leo's decree was mixed. In some places copies of the papal document were torn to pieces. The Catholic dukes of Bavaria asked that Leo's verdict against Luther be suspended, and numerous bishops opposed its circulation. On the other hand, in several cities Luther's works were burned.

B. Luther and Erasmus

What brought about the final break between Luther and Rome was not, he later wrote, those "irrelevant points about popery, purgatory, indulgences, and other similar baubles." Addressing the biblical scholar Desiderius Erasmus in 1525, Luther continued: "You, and you alone, have seen what was the great hinge upon which the whole matter turned. And therefore you attacked the vital concern at once. For this I thank you with all my heart." Those words come from the beginning of Luther's fundamental and monumental work whose very title indicates this "hinge": *On the Bondage of the Will*.

"The human will," wrote Luther, "is, so to speak, a beast. If God sits on the beast, it wills and goes where God wills. But if Satan sits on the beast, it wills and goes where Satan wills. It is not within the beast's power to choose either rider." With this Luther was denying the possibility of free choice. The human will is not free, he asserted; it is in bondage.

From this profoundly negative anthropology, Luther turned to the fundamental nature of reality. "God," he wrote, "is that Being for whose will no cause or reason can be ascertained." God is totally free; he need not act according to reason or logic. It follows from this that "what God wills is not right because he is or ever was bound [by reason] so to will." The governing principle of the universe, Luther concluded, is not the *Logos* or Reason which early Christian authors thought it was. Instead, "what takes place is right because God wills it so." The ethical implications of this position are earth-shattering. If God willed us to murder, for example, then murder would become virtuous. The only way we can know this or anything else is through faith. Reason helps us not at all.

"As for myself," Luther wrote, "I openly confess that I would not wish to be given free will–even if that were possible. I would not wish to have control over anything which pertains to my own salvation." If he had this control, he knew he would not be able to ward off Satan's assaults. Neither Luther nor anyone else could resist these attacks, and thus no one relying on free will would be saved. Freedom is a serious threat to our psychological security. "Even if there were no dangers, conflicts, or devils" to threaten him, Luther wrote, if he possessed freedom "I should be compelled to labor under a continual uncertainty, for whatever I would do there would remain doubts about whether my deed pleased God or whether he demanded still more." Luther had learned through many years' experience the extreme psychological stress of a scrupulous conscience.

Luther welcomed the fact that humans have no freedom of choice in matters of salvation:

> God has taken my salvation out of the way of my will, and has made it his own concern. It is not my deeds or way of life that will save me, but only his grace and mercy....Hence it is certain that in this way–even if not all will be saved–some, perhaps many, will be saved. By the power of "free will" no one at all could be saved, and all would perish forever.

Our good works bring us no merit that pleases God; rather God, in his mercy, pardons our weakness and evil deeds. He then grants us salvation by his free gift of grace. Luther believed all people can rest secure in their lack of freedom to effect their own salvation. The devastating effects of the Fall–our lack of freedom, our inability to discover ultimate reality through reason, our insecurity–are all overcome by grace.

This is the true meaning, Luther believed, of Saint Paul's statement that "humans are justified by faith." So emphatically did he believe this that Luther added the word "alone" to this phrase from the letter to the Romans. "Justified" signifies "being made just" which means "saved." The "faith" in Paul's phrase does not mean the acceptance of a statement on the authority of its source. "Acceptance" is a choice of the will, and, lacking a free will, we have no such power. So Paul's "faith," Luther concluded, must mean God's grace, for faith is indeed a gift. Thus, the "great hinge" of Luther's teaching is that we are saved only by God's grace–and not by our own freely chosen good deeds. Luther never wavered from this, the cornerstone of his whole theology.

The man to whom Luther's treatise on the will was addressed was Desiderius Erasmus (1469?-1536). Erasmus was a scholar whose early interests focused on the classical literature of antiquity. He directed his considerable learning to a new, critical edition of the Greek New Testament. Erasmus believed all Christians should have access to the Bible in their own language and could use the insights gained through reading Scripture to give meaning and direction to their lives.

Erasmus was also a bitter critic of the corruption in the Church of his time. He denounced far more vehemently than Luther the corruption of the pope and the papal court, the simony practiced by bishops and his fellow priests, and the preaching of those who trafficked in indulgences. When Johann Eck and his followers attacked Luther as a heretic, Erasmus remarked that Luther's views could hardly be heretical since they were the same as those of Augustine of Hippo, Bernard of Clairvaux, and Nicholas of Cusa. But Luther's denial of a role for free will in one's salvation Erasmus could not tolerate as a humanist whose anthropology reflected the positive view of human nature he shared with the humanists of the twelfth century.

As a biblical scholar, Erasmus began his treatise *On the Freedom of the Will* with a consideration of what Scripture seems to say about this now-disrupted faculty. The gospel's account of the prodigal son (Luke 15:11-32) Erasmus found especially instructive: "How could the prodigal son have wasted his inheritance had it not been his to do with as he pleased?" This affirmation of free choice is balanced by an affirmation that free will is God's gift: "What the prodigal son possessed, he received from his father." And Erasmus added the admonition: "We too must remember that all our natural powers are gifts of God."

The prodigal's demand for his share of the inheritance and his departure from the family farm were seen by Erasmus as the sin of pride. That is, he said, "quite simply to give oneself credit for one's natural powers, and then use them, not to obey God's commandments, but to satisfy one's carnal lusts"–both choices freely made. The hunger experienced by the prodigal son Erasmus explained in spiritual terms: as the sinner's God-inspired self-knowledge, his self-hatred resulting from that knowledge, and his regret for having left his father. The son's inner doubts about facing up to his sin Erasmus understood as "the human will adapting itself to the motivating grace also called prevenient." The father who runs out to meet his returning son is "the grace of God which allows our will to do good when we have decided to do it."

I find it helpful in understanding Erasmus' theology of grace to imagine it as a three-act play with two cast members. Before the play begins, God prepares the stage by creating the human being and endowing her or him with many powerful attributes–among them a will that possesses freedom of choice. Center stage in the first act belongs to God, who motivates the human being to choose the good through prevenient grace, the gift that precedes human choice. The protagonist of the second act is the human being, who is free to choose the good or to reject it. The action in the third act is God's gift of another grace: the power to accomplish the good when chosen.

"But why," Erasmus was asked, "should you leave a place for free will?" He answered: "So we can justly accuse the wicked who, through their own decisions, place themselves outside divine grace." So too, affirming free will "acquits God of false charges of cruelty or injustice." Erasmus thought that, if Heaven is our destination, it is by God's grace that we get there. If our fate is Hell, it is our own fault for choosing evil.

We have met Erasmus' view of grace and free will before when discussing the anthropology of Bernard of Clairvaux. Erasmus knew Bernard's treatise *On Grace and Free Choice*. He also knew Bernard's source, Augustine of Hippo's work bearing the same title. Erasmus thought that, through his approach, "free will can be preserved, at the same time that we avoid flagrant confidence in our own merits and the other dangers seen by Luther." Erasmus joined Luther in rejecting the theology of grace that dominated the thought of the time. This was the view–called semi-pelagian in the sixteenth century–that human beings are completely free to make choices and that their good choices require God to grant the grace to effect those choices. Luther saw the Church of his time teaching this heresy–and so he felt forced to disassociate himself from the institutional Church responsible for that heresy, as well as for the pernicious reliance on external practices that followed from the heresy. But Erasmus thought Luther had overreacted by rejecting free will altogether. This then is the fundamental theological dispute that was to separate Catholic from Protestant.

C. John Calvin

The followers of Martin Luther are by no means the largest group of Protestants. That preeminence belongs to the Calvinists, followers of Jean Cauvin or John Calvin (1509-1564). The Reformed Churches of Germany and the Netherlands, the Huguenots of France, the Presbyterians of Scotland, are all Calvinist. Calvinism has also exercised a strong influence on the theology of the Church of England. We most often think of Calvin and Calvinists holding to the doctrine of predestination. Actually they believe in double predestination, the idea that God has determined from all eternity who goes to Heaven, who to Hell. This position is, however, a corollary of their insistence on the sovereignty of God and their acceptance of justification by faith alone–a doctrine we tend to associate with Luther. Both Lutherans and Calvinists taught both doctrines, which are opposite sides of the same coin. Both Lutherans and Calvinists–and all but a handful of other Protestants–believed that the Fall, the Original Sin of Adam and Eve, had catastrophic effects on the human condition. Human beings were incapable of knowing fundamental reality and the nature of the good–except by faith alone. The human will was in bondage to sin and thus could not choose the good. Thus, the Protestantism of the sixteenth century–and, as we shall shortly see, the Catholicism as well–was the fruition of the anthropological pessimism of the Late Middle Ages.

A serious question was raised by the Calvinist adherence to the doctrine of predestination. If your fate in the afterlife has been predetermined by God, why should you strive to be good? Yet, if you lived in Calvin's Geneva, you would be fined and perhaps imprisoned for failing to live up to the city's stringent regulations against vice. You could not swear or offer a drink to your friend. Nor could you drink yourself during the long hours of Calvin's sermons. Dancing or singing "immoral, dissolute, or outrageous songs" would result in imprisonment.

Calvin's solution to this apparent inconsistency was significant for his culture and has played a role in ours. He made a distinction between justification and sanctification. Justification, and hence salvation, is out of our hands and in

God's. But sanctification, advancement in holiness, is the joint task of God and human beings. By living according to God's commandments and the regulations of Church and state, you can become more and more holy–though that holiness will have no effect whatsoever on your salvation. But God had surely denied Heaven to the wicked; surely he has selected the blessed from the ranks of those he foreknew would become holy. This conviction should inspire Christians, Calvin thought, to strive to be good.

But the itch to know what fate awaits even the holy–for not even all these are predestined to Heaven–would lead later Calvinists to look for signs of their salvation. In nineteenth-century Europe and America, for example, rich Calvinists saw their wealth as a sign of salvation, and this agreed nicely with the *laissez-faire* liberalism which they most often adopted. A much more sinister example of "covenant theology," as this search for signs of salvation is called, is the rationale for the *apartheid* imposed on the black inhabitants of South Africa by white Afrikaaners. It was clear to these good Dutch Calvinists that God has placed the "mark of Cain" on black people, a mark made visible by the color of their skin. Whiteness thus becomes a sign of salvation, an idea John Calvin would have denounced vehemently.

D. Cultural Influences and Consequences

Few sixteenth-century people were aware of the theological niceties at the heart of the Protestant-Catholic debate. For most of those who opted for the "reformed" as opposed to the "old" Church, clerical corruption was a major factor in their decision. For example, many of the good citizens of the north German port city of Lübeck were offended by the beer and brothel business run by the canons of their cathedral. It did not help that those canons–and, indeed, all the clergymen of Lübeck–were exempt from paying taxes.

In the grander political arena of kings and princes, religious reasons often seemed secondary in the choice of church affiliation. Some rulers, notably the princes of northern Germany, profited from becoming Lutheran through their acquisition of lands independently ruled by neighboring bishops. At the very least, those princes and the kings in Scandinavia–as well as many city governments–could and did gain control of the churches within their domains. Catholic princes, like the dukes of Bavaria, did the same, both exercising control over a much weakened Catholic Church within their domains and acquiring neighboring ecclesiastical principalities. Some rulers, like the king of France, so completely controlled the Catholic Church in their land that they saw no point in converting to Protestantism.

Economics played a role in defining the denominational map of Europe. The many German principalities of an Empire reduced to a shadowy existence had had no powerful ruler to protect them from papal exactions, including the trade in indulgences. The monied burghers of Germany–especially the wealthy citizens of politically independent towns–resented the outflow of cash to Rome. So they cut off that flow by introducing Protestantism into their territories and by controlling their Churches closely. In all Protestant lands the government replaced the Church in providing services such as education and health care, paying for those services by confiscating church properties.

The legacies of the Protestant Reformation are many, and we shall examine but a few of the most important of them. On the other hand, some ideas often viewed as the legacy of the reformers were not their beliefs at all. For instance, it is widely held that the reformers insisted on the supremacy of Scripture as the source of Christian doctrine. They did indeed hold that no doctrine was valid unless based on Scripture, but they knew that the reading of Scripture could lead to "many unfounded interpretations." These are words from Luther's preface to his splendid 1522 translation of the New Testament. In this preface, Luther offered guidelines for reading the Scriptures. "Which," he asked, "are the true and noblest books of the New Testament?" Luther answered: "Saint John's gospel and his first epistle, Saint Paul's epistles, especially Romans, Galatians, and Ephesians, and Saint Peter's first epistle are the books that show you Christ and teach you all that is necessary and salvatory for you to know." But there are some books that Luther would rather we did not read. Foremost among these is "Saint James' epistle [that] is really an epistle of straw, compared to these others, for it has nothing of the nature of the gospel about it." The reason for Luther's resistance to this epistle is that James insists that "faith without works is dead." Since Scripture is difficult to interpret and sometimes misleading, there must be a higher authority than Scripture in discerning the truths of the Christian faith. That authority, all sixteenth-century scholars would agree, is the author of Scripture, the Holy Spirit. Not one of those scholars would agree with what has come to be known as the "Protestant principle," that each person has the right to interpret the Bible as he or she sees fit. An assertion of that position would have led to burning at the stake everywhere in Europe and by all denominations. For who can interpret Scripture save God alone? Surely not humans, whom the Fall has made intellectually inept.

But assigning the Holy Spirit the role of ultimate arbitrator has its problems. As we have seen, charismatic knowledge, the gift of the Holy Spirit, has been accepted by Christians throughout the ages, and has caused as many problems as it has solved. This was apparent in the eucharistic controversy between Luther and Zwingli.

Huldrych Zwingli was born in 1464, just a few weeks after Luther, and died in 1531 at the battle of Kappel while leading the army of Protestant Zürich against its Catholic enemies. Zwingli was as successful in leading the reform of the Church of extreme southwestern Germany (now Switzerland) as Luther was in the reformation in the northeastern part of that land. It seemed sensible to unite their efforts. At the Marburg Colloquy of 1529, agreement was reached on a wide range of doctrinal issues. The sticking point, however, was the Eucharist. Luther held that the Real Presence of Christ was somehow contained in the communion bread and wine, whereas Zwingli insisted that the Lord's Supper was simply a commemorative event. Both appealed to Scripture. Luther pointed to Jesus' declaration at the Last

Supper: "This is my body." Zwingli cited Jesus' command: "Do this in commemoration of me." Luther declared that "This is my body" could not be taken any way but literally, though he one time expressed the wish that this "popish" position were not so. Zwingli dismissed Luther's literal interpretation in favor of a symbolic meaning. Luther rejected Zwingli's literal interpretation of the commemoration quotation. Both appealed to the Holy Spirit as the source of their interpretation, but apparently the Spirit had not spoken to at least one of them.

The problem of biblical interpretation has plagued Protestantism to this day, and disagreements over doctrine have repeatedly led to schism. A whole welter of Protestant denominations has resulted—each denomination appealing to Scripture and the Spirit as the sources of their teaching.

E. A New Approach to Politics

In 1525, violence broke out among the peasantry of southern and central Germany. Resentment had been smoldering for a good hundred years. What we now call the Peasants' Revolt involved resistance by farmers to their landlords' attempts to reimpose manorial rights. These had fallen into disuse during the labor shortage that followed the worst days of the Back Death. Monasteries and manor houses were looted and burned, while their inhabitants were extremely lucky to escape with their lives. The rampaging farmers saw their revolt coinciding with Luther's resistance to the Catholic Church, and they appealed to him for support. What they got was a savage condemnation, a treatise *Against the Robbing and Murderous Peasant Gangs*. It began: "With three horrid sins against God and their fellow humans have these peasants burdened themselves, for which they have deserved all sorts of death for body and soul."

The peasants' first sin was disobedience. Having "sworn to their true and gracious rulers to be submissive and obedient...they have deliberately and sacrilegiously abandoned their obedience and have thereby forfeited body and soul, as perfidious, perjured, lying disobedient wretches are wont to do." To oppose authority is "sacrilegious," because secular authority is sacred. Thus, the peasants deserve death, not only of body in this present life, but of soul in the next.

The peasants' second sin was rebellion: "They cause uproar and sacrilegiously rob and pillage monasteries and castles that do not belong to them." Luther condemned these actions as evil and asserted: "It is right and lawful to slay at the first opportunity a rebellious person." "Therefore," he concluded, "whosoever can should smite, strangle, and stab them, and remember that there is nothing more poisonous, pernicious, and devilish than a rebellious person."

The third sin of these rebels was blasphemy, for "they cloak their frightful and revolting sins with appeals to the gospel, calling themselves Christian folk, swearing allegiance to their gang, and compelling people to join them in such abominations." These pernicious people are "blasphemers and violators of God's holy name, and serve and honor the devil."

Inspired by these condemnations, the princes and townspeople of central and southern Germany drowned the revolt in a sea of blood. Many historians have reacted with horror, not only to the bloody retribution but also to Luther's supposed inconsistency. They find that Luther's call to religious freedom at variance with his opposition to political and economic freedom. But religious freedom was not Luther's goal. He did not believe in freedom of the will, and he taught that the Holy Spirit must direct helpless humans into orthodoxy.

There is another reason why Luther's position makes sense and belies the belief of nineteenth-century Romantics and Liberals that Luther supported religious freedom. Luther felt compelled to reject the divine authority of the Catholic Church because it taught heresy and was thus the agent of Satan. Medieval political theory had affirmed divine sanction for the state, and this Luther retained. In a treatise entitled *On Secular Authority*, Luther wrote: "A true Christian...submits most willingly to the rule of the sword. He pays his taxes, honors those in authority, and serves, helps, and does all he can to further the government." To replace the Church as the counterweight to a sinful and unjust state, Luther affirmed the direct and exclusive action of God.

The medieval theory of a social contract between ruler and ruled Luther rejected. He likewise discarded the medieval position that the people have the right to resist an unjust ruler and, if necessary, to depose him. For Luther, the person and authority of the ruler are sacred, and the ruler is responsible only to God. This was a long leap toward the early modern belief in the divine right of kings–a belief that would be more completely developed in the seventeenth century.

F. The English Reformation and the Growth of Secularism

Perhaps the most far-reaching and inexorable change in European culture apparent after the sixteenth century was a growing secularism, an increasing attention to the things of this world. The Reformation was not the cause of this. The reformers were all intent on reviving and intensifying a religious view of the world. But the course of the sixteenth century saw a significant shift in values. That shift is well illustrated by the course of the English Reformations.

From the beginning of his reign, Henry VIII was a pious and theologically sophisticated ruler who governed the Church and state in his sixteenth-century realm with the same sort of intense activity and meticulous control as Charles the Great had exhibited in the eighth and ninth centuries. But Henry had a problem. He was only the second king of the Tudor dynasty to rule England, and he needed a son to cement his family's hold on the throne. Henry's queen, Catherine of Aragon, had borne Henry a number of children, but only a girl named Mary lived beyond infancy. Henry determined to rid himself of Catherine by having his marriage to her annulled. This would free him to marry a lady of the court, Anne Boleyn.

Henry argued that Catherine and he were not really married, since Catherine had been engaged to Henry's older brother Arthur, who had died before coming to the throne. Henry's marriage to Catherine had been, to be sure, contrary to canon law, but a papal dispensation from that law had been granted by Pope Julius II in 1503. This dispensation was contrary to a mandate recorded in the Old Testament book of Leviticus, Henry contended, and his violation of that divine ordinance had brought down God's displeasure in the form of Catherine's failure to produce a male heir.

Henry petitioned Pope Clement VII to retract the dispensation. However, the authorities cited against Henry's petition were numerous, many of them referring to a passage in Deuteronomy mandating marriage to a brother's widow. Perhaps more important was the fact that Henry was, in effect, asking the pope to declare that his predecessor had exceeded his authority by issuing the original dispensation. A practical reason Clement could not respond favorably was that he was a virtual prisoner of the emperor Charles V, who was Catherine's nephew.

Frustrated, Henry shifted the focus of his campaign. He pressured his prelates–the bishops and abbots of England–to declare him "protector, single and supreme lord, and as far as Christ's law allows, supreme head" of the English Church. Only one prelate, John Fisher, the bishop of Rochester, resisted–and he ended up a head shorter. In November of 1534, the English Parliament declared "that the king our sovereign lord, his heirs and successors,...shall be taken, accepted, and reputed the only supreme head on earth of the Church of England." The "Supreme Head" then put aside Catherine and married Anne.

Doctrinally nothing had changed. Already in 1521, Henry had written a book against Luther affirming that there are truly seven sacraments. On receiving this book, the pope had named Henry "Defender of the Faith," a title still held by British monarchs. In 1539, Henry issued *Six Articles* of faith. The pope himself could hardly have issued a more Catholic document. Henry endorsed transubstantiation as the only proper explanation for Jesus' presence in the eucharistic bread and wine. Henry argued, contrary to the claims of the continental reformers, that the wine need not be given to the laity. He required celibacy of priests and demanded that vows of chastity be observed. "Private masses," with no congregation present, were declared "agreeable also to God's law." And the practice of confession to a priest was affirmed as "expedient and necessary."

When Henry died in 1547, his nine-year-old son was crowned king. The regents who ruled Edward VI's England were men who had rejected Catholicism for Calvinism, and the kingdom became a refuge for persecuted continental Protestants. Church properties were secularized, and an English-language *Book of Common Prayer* became the only accepted guide in worship. Justification by faith alone was affirmed, as was Scripture as the sole source of doctrine. The government saw to it that the doctrine of Purgatory was rejected, as was prayer to the saints and transubstantiation. England had become a Protestant nation.

When Edward died in 1553, his elder sister, Catherine's daughter Mary, was proclaimed queen. Mary attempted a restoration of the Catholic faith, seeing to it that Catholic bishops replaced Edward's Protestant prelates. Mary has often been referred to as "Bloody Mary," and she deserves that sobriquet, for some three hundred people were burned as heretics during her reign. By that standard, however, all the rulers of Europe, Protestant and Catholic–and surely Mary's sister and successor Elizabeth–should be called "bloody." The sixteenth century was an age of ferocious intolerance on all sides.

In 1558, Elizabeth, daughter of Anne Boleyn, succeeded her half sister. Elizabeth's long reign, lasting until 1603, was a period of enforced political stability, of rapidly expanding manufacture, of bold overseas colonization, and of the growing ascendancy of the English navy. Elizabeth was a strong willed and highly intelligent ruler. She was also completely unscrupulous. It is no accident that Machiavelli's *Prince*, a handbook on gaining and keeping power by any means, was translated into English at Elizabeth's court.

Whatever Elizabeth's closely guarded opinions in religion, she brought about a religious settlement that was nothing short of a work of art. Adherents of virtually every denomination–Calvinists, Lutherans, and Catholics–could find something to please them in Elizabeth's *Thirty-nine Articles*, issued in 1563. There are references to justification by faith alone side-by-side with an affirmation of prevenient grace. Predestination is affirmed without denying freedom of the will. In consuming the eucharistic bread and wine we partake of the Body and Blood of Christ, although–we discover a few paragraphs later–that partaking is "only after a heavenly and spiritual manner." Clergy are named as bishops, priests, and deacons in Article XXXII, though they were referred to as "ministers" in Article XXVI. In short, Elizabeth created a religious document that was the basis of a new sort of all-inclusive denomination, a denomination that we now call Anglican. Elizabeth's only interest was in stability and order, and, if a document could be created that would keep virtually everyone content or, at least, quiet, she would create it. Even "Puritans," dissidents within this English Church, were tolerated, if they were but loyal. Displays of disobedience–whether political or religious–to the monarch, now styled "Supreme Governor" of the Church, were met with brutal force.

Reflection on the religious preferences of the Tudor dynasty reveals a rapidly changing culture. From 1509 to 1534, Henry VIII was a Catholic in communion with Rome; from 1534 to 1547, Henry enforced a Catholicism headed by himself–now an English Catholic. Edward VI's brief reign, from 1547 to 1553, was characterized by Calvinism. Mary was very Roman Catholic during her short time as queen from 1553 to 1558. And Elizabeth made the Church of England Anglican. From the last years of Henry's connection with Rome, 1534, to the first year of Elizabeth's Anglicanism in 1558, there is a span of but twenty-four years. During this brief period, England experienced five different official versions of Christianity.

Many English clergymen managed to keep their posts throughout all these changes. On the river Thames, not far upstream from Windsor Castle, sits the village of Bray. The vicar of the church in Bray was, in the sixteenth century, a man named Simon Aleyn. Simon survived the changing religious policies of the Tudors by shifting his allegiance with each new monarch. This feat has inspired a verse attributed to Simon: "And this is the law I'll maintain 'til my dying day, sir, that whatsoever king shall reign, still I'll be Vicar of Bray, sir."

Simon's desire to remain in his sequestered and lovely retreat is understandable. But it also illustrates a growing phenomenon of the time: an increasing indifference to denominational differences. This shifting view stemmed from a growing secularism. From Simon's time to the present, each century has seen an ever-increasing growth of commitment to the idea that happiness is found in the things of this world. That revolutionary idea would remove Christianity from the cultural center of western civilization and banish it to a peripheral position. New relationships between Christianity and culture would need to be hammered out.

XII. CATHOLIC REFORMATION AND COUNTER-REFORMATION

Some Useful Data

1417-1431	reign of Martin V, pope
1503-1513	reign of Julius II, pope
1513-1521	reign of Leo X, pope
1521-1523	reign of Adrian VI, pope
1523-1534	reign of Clement VII, pope
1483-1542	Gasparo Contarini, cardinal from 1535
1534-1549	reign of Paul III, pope
1491?-1556	Ignatius of Loyola, founder of the Society of Jesus
1500-1558	Reginald Pole, cardinal from 1534
1476-1559	Gian Pietro Carafa, pope as Paul IV from 1555
1524-1597	Peter Canisius, Jesuit missionary to Germany
1552-1610	Matteo Ricci, Jesuit missionary to China
1552-1623	Paolo Sarpi, Venetian reformer
1564-1642	Galileo Galilei, physicist and astronomer

Historians have long debated whether to characterize the radical changes in the sixteenth-century Catholic Church as the Catholic Reformation or the Counter-reformation. The latter view has much evidence on its side: considerable energy was devoted by contemporary Catholics to the rejection and refutation of Protestantism–sometimes by harsh measures. On the other hand, there were many Catholics, clerics and laity alike, who saw the Protestant schism as just punishment for the Church's wide-spread corruption. Many Catholic theologians decried the careless and sometimes misguided doctrinal stances of their Church–especially in the matter of grace and free will. These Catholic reformers were open–often eager–to converse with their "separated brethren" on both doctrine and practice. The reaction to Protestantism by the popes of the time ranged from initial indifference to vigorous attack.

A. The Range of Papal Reaction

The ecclesiastical politics of the fifteenth century had prevented the popes of that day from embracing reform–even though some of them were sincere reformers. The Council of Constance had ended the Great Schism in 1417, by electing a single pope, Martin V (1417-1431), who received universal acceptance. But Martin and his successors fought the edicts of Constance and succeeding councils with every weapon at their disposal. Constitutional restraint on a papacy conceived as an absolute monarchy was anathema to these popes. Their claim to supreme jurisdiction over all the Church was incompatible with the aspirations of conciliar constitutionalism and reform efforts. The papacy had become the target of reform rather than its leader.

Ironically, the tactic these fifteenth-century popes employed was to turn to the leading secular rulers of the time. In return for recognition by those rulers of a theoretical papal supremacy over all the churches, the popes of the period granted those rulers ecclesiastical powers in their realms that made them in practice the heads of national and territorial churches. The popes' abdication of real power was less important to them than acknowledgment of their theoretically supreme power over the universal Church.

In the process, the "Supreme Pontiff" became little more than an Italian prince, the ruler of the Papal States in central Italy. This task consumed enormous energy–allowing little time or concern for Church reform. Julius II, who reigned from 1503 to 1513, made the pretense of calling a reform council, but spent most of his energy attacking the Italian states that surrounded his Roman possessions. Julius was reckoned by many as a very successful pope because he was one of the best military men of his time. Celebrating his capture of the city of Bologna, Julius rode into that defeated town without either bishop's miter or papal tiara. His true commitment was displayed by the full suit of heavy armor which he proudly wore. Julius' mode of exercising papal power earned him the slashing condemnation of Desiderius Erasmus. In a short, satirical piece, *Julius Excluded from Heaven*,

Erasmus portrayed the swaggering warrior-pope prevented from passing through the heavenly gates by his predecessor, Saint Peter.

Julius' successor, Leo X (1513-1521), was far too engaged in enjoying the perquisites of papal power to concern himself with reform of the Church. As we have seen, this pope's condemnation of Luther was based not on an understanding of that reformer's theological positions but on Leo's clear perception of Luther's potential challenge to papal power.

Leo's successor, Adrian VI, was sincere in his desire for reform, but his mere twenty months on the papal throne allowed no time for the effective pursuit of reforming action. And Adrian's successor, Clement VII (1523-1534) was far too involved in peninsular politics to even consider the need for reform, much less sense its urgency.

In 1536, Pope Paul III issued a reforming edict. But its aim was not to reform the Church Universal or even the church in Italy. His goal was simply to weed out church corruption in the city of Rome. The content of Paul's edict shows how badly that cleansing was needed. Paul began by forbidding his clergy to wear clothing "adorned with gold or silk," though canons, priests, and other "ecclesiastical dignitaries are permitted to wear velvet, silk, or damask." No one is to be ordained a priest "who does not possess...the requisite qualities" although the edict omits any enumeration of those qualities. Those clerics attached to the principal churches of Rome were commanded to "assist at the divine services" conducted in their churches and to "preserve due reverence in choir." Pastors should minister to the needs of their flocks—or else hire someone to do it for them. Those priests, Paul commanded, "should celebrate Mass at least once a month." The goals of Paul's directive surely seem modest to us—and perhaps painfully obvious.

Heresy was not ignored in the counter-reformation components of Paul's edict. Priests were directed to "preach against heretics, especially against Lutherans." To make sure that that heresy—or any other—should not take hold in Rome, Paul commanded the establishment in Rome of an institution long dormant, the Inquisition: "Those who think evil of the faith and, as a result, are under suspicion of heresy, shall be examined by the appropriate ecclesiastical judges and punished accordingly."

There was another pertinent product of Paul's pontificate—one much more important because it embraced reform of the whole Church. In February of 1537, a Select Committee of nine cardinals and other prelates appointed by Pope Paul made its detailed report to him. The Committee pulled no punches, pointing out that exaggerated claims of papal power and the avarice of popes were the source of most of the abuses plaguing the Church. The corruption of the popes, they forcefully stated, was the result of the secularization of that spiritual office, turning papal pastors into political princes.

The Committee attacked the ignorance and immorality of many of the clergy, "as a result of which," they said, "reverence for divine worship has not only lessened but has become almost extinct." To combat this, the Committee urged bishops to exercise "care and diligence" before ordaining clerical candidates.

"Moreover," they asserted, "each bishop should provide for his church a professor to instruct those candidates in both letters and morals, as the laws demand." The laws to which the Committee referred had been on the books since the days of Charles the Great, but they had been ignored by the majority of bishops for the previous two hundred years.

"There is another prevalent abuse," the Committee declared. "Not only one but several bishoprics are conferred on or entrusted to the most reverend cardinals." Clearly the flocks in those bishoprics were ill served by this pluralism, but, more fundamentally, "the offices of cardinal and of bishop are incompatible. For it is the duty of a cardinal to assist the pope,...but it is the duty of a bishop to feed his sheep." The Committee, four of whom were cardinals, clearly recognized that the historical role of the cardinal was that of a Roman clergyman, without the status "prince of the Church" that cardinals had in the previous two centuries attained.

The Committee also urged that bishops and priests be required to reside in and serve the churches for which they had been chosen. The radical solution for absenteeism–radical in terms of the practice of the time–was that the offender would be denied the income attached to the office.

Religious orders received an even harsher condemnation: "The fact is that many are so corrupt that they are a great scandal and do great harm." The solution proposed is abolishment, "not by decree but by forbidding them to admit any new members."

The Committee concluded their long and detailed list of reforms to be accomplished with a plea to the pope: "Under your leadership may we see the Church of God purged, beautiful as a dove,...to the everlasting glory of your name." This appeal was apparently heard, for, in 1537, Pope Paul appointed another commission that actually undertook to reform some of the worst abuses of the papal bureaucracy–an effort, however, largely unsuccessful.

B. Three Reforming Cardinals

Two members of this reform commission, Cardinal Contarini and Cardinal Carafa, had also served on the Select Committee that had detailed the necessary reforms. On that Committee they had been joined by an Englishman, Cardinal Reginald Pole. The attitudes and activities of these three men illustrate well the wide range of Catholic reform.

Gasparo Contarini has been called "the soul of the Catholic Reform in Rome." He was born in 1483 of a patrician family of Venice, and was educated in the classics as a Christian humanist. While still a young man he participated in the political affairs of his powerful city-state, and served his country as ambassador to the Imperial court in Germany from 1521 to 1525. Early in his life he exhibited an intense and deeply felt commitment to the goal of reform. In 1516, for example, he wrote a moving description of the ideal pastor for a friend who had been newly appointed as bishop of Bergamo.

Though Contarini was still a layman, Pope Paul III named him a cardinal in 1535, and he spent the rest of his life as the leader of the reform party in the papal curia. He served as chairman of Paul III's Select Committee on Reform, and it was he who induced that pope to appoint the reform commission that attempted to carry out the program of the Select Committee.

Throughout his reform ministry, Contarini displayed a remarkable understanding of the doctrinal position of Protestants, and he consistently worked for both reunion and reform. He worried that the Christians of his day were more concerned with "defending their own views and refuting those of their opponents" than with growth in the humility and love which would make their faith fruitful. During the years 1540 and 1541, Contarini served as papal legate to a series of conferences between Protestant and Catholic theologians held in Germany. The two sides reconciled many of their differences, but both Luther and the pope rejected their agreements.

Shortly before his death in 1542, Contarini presented to the pope a document describing the way of life of men aspiring to found a new religious order, the Society of Jesus. Contarini thus lived to see papal commissioning of a powerful agent of reform, the order commonly called the Jesuits. At his death, however, Gasparo Contarini was under suspicion of heresy generated by his fellow cardinal Gian Pietro Carafa.

Cardinal Carafa, the future Pope Paul IV, was born in Naples in 1476, a member of one of the great noble houses of the kingdom. Through the patronage of his uncle, Cardinal Oliviere Carafa, Gian Pietro was made archbishop of Chieti, a town in central Italy. There he exerted himself in a largely successful effort at reform. In 1524, having renounced all his sources of clerical income, Carafa joined a newly formed society of clerics, the Theatines, a group which renounced all income and property and sustained itself only by begging. After being named a cardinal by Pope Paul II, Carafa served with Contarini on Paul's Select Committee on Reform and then on Paul's reform commission. Carafa was also entrusted with diplomatic missions to England and Spain.

In 1555, at the age of seventy-nine, Carafa was elected pope, as Paul IV. "A man of irreproachable life, but dreaded for his severity," he issued strict reform regulations for the papal curia and for the church in the Papal States. He enforced equally strict measures against simony, demanding that the papal court dispense spiritual benefits without payment. Paul also reduced radically the expenses of his papal household. But his notion of reform was totally at odds with the movement toward reform encouraged by humanists like Contarini. As a cardinal, Carafa had equipped his residence with detention cells and torture devices. His zeal for the activities of the Roman Inquisition was matched only by his enthusiasm for a new instrument for the repression of thought, the Index of Forbidden Books. Paul insisted that all the works of Erasmus be included. Paul forced Jews in the Papal States to live in ghettos and wear yellow hats as signs of their perfidy and even kept one of his cardinals in prison because he thought that prelate's attitude toward dissent was too conciliatory.

Paul was an adherent of an extreme theory of papal power. He saw himself as the ruler of all Christendom. His pursuit of political power for the papacy led him to efforts to destroy the Spanish presence in southern Italy, and he set up his nephews as princely rulers in the Italian peninsula. His alliance with France against Spain led to the "Carafa War," which only served to display the papacy's military and political impotence.

Because Queen Mary of England had entered the war on the side of Spain, the pope declared war on newly re-catholicized England. Paul then deprived Reginald Pole, his former colleague on the Select Committee on Reform and now archbishop of Canterbury, of his position as papal legate to England. Paul demanded that Pole present himself in Rome, insinuating that he was under suspicion of heresy. Only the queen's refusal to allow Pole to leave England saved him from an unknown but presumably harsh fate.

Reginald Pole was, by all accounts, a man of deep piety. He was born in 1500, a relative of King Henry VIII. He was named a cardinal in 1534, and, in 1538, he published in Rome a work entitled *On the Defence of the Unity of the Church*, which earned him the hatred of King Henry. Pole's family too suffered from their opposition to Henry's estrangement from Rome; Pole's mother Margaret was imprisoned in 1541, then executed.

In 1544, Paul III named Pole one of three cardinals who were to preside over the sessions of the reform Council of Trent. Pole's address to that body, made in January of 1546, is a truly remarkable document. Pole first apprised the bishops assembled of "the efforts that are expected of this holy council,...the uprooting of heresies, the reformation of ecclesiastical discipline and of morals, and, lastly, the fostering of the external peace of the whole Church." However, Pole warned: "if we think these things can be accomplished by us or by any other than by Christ himself,...we shall err in the foundation of all our actions, and we shall provoke still further the divine wrath." With this insistence on the necessity of grace, Pole placed himself, with both Erasmus and Luther, on the side of Saint Paul and Saint Augustine. "We who have the office of fathers," he told his assembled audience of bishops, "must act in everything by faith and hope and place our trust in the power of Christ,...whose ministers in all things we acknowledge ourselves to be."

"What shall we do," Pole asked, "so that we can now become adequate ministers of Christ in renewing the Church?" Imitate Christ in taking on themselves the sins of all, he informed the assembled bishops. But, whereas Christ took on the sins of humankind out of his overwhelming generosity and love, "we must take upon ourselves the sins of all, not in generosity but in justice." For all the evils plaguing the Church, Pole insisted, "we churchmen are in great part the cause."

Heresies have sprung up because "we have not tilled our field as we ought," and so "we are no less the cause of these growing weeds than if we ourselves had sown them." The corruption in the Church requires no extensive inquiry into its cause, for we bishops "cannot even name any other cause but ourselves." The strife, domestic and external, plaguing the people of Europe are "scourges to punish our sinning." "Of these conflicts," Pole declared, "we cannot deny that we are the chief cause." The first step in Church reform, therefore, must be that we churchmen "confess our own sins and those of the princes and the people,...for the sins of priests, princes, and people are intertwined into such a rope that we can hardly search out the sin of one class without laying bare the sins of another."

When he returned to England after Mary's 1553 accession to the throne, Pole continued his reform activities. As papal legate to England, he formally absolved Parliament for its schismatic legislation. He exercised his newly acquired status as archbishop of Canterbury in restoring and reforming the Catholic Church in England. The English Church council over which he presided obliged bishops to reside in their dioceses and to preach. It organized teams of preachers to serve the people in much the same way that the now dispersed Franciscans and Dominicans had done. He and his council called for the establishment of seminaries to educate young men aspiring to the priesthood.

Pole did not, however, escape the sixteenth-century penchant for persecution. He aided his sovereign in the persecution of Protestants, resulting in the death of 273 of them. Despite this, Pole was seen in Rome as too moderate. As we have seen, Pope Paul IV deprived Pole of his legatine authority and, hinting at heresy, summoned him to Rome. Queen Mary protected her reforming archbishop from the pope until queen and archbishop went to their graves–both on November 17, 1558, within twelve hours of each other.

C. The Council of Trent

It took twenty-eight years from the late October day when Luther first raised his call to reform until a council was convened to respond to that call and to the hopes of an entire generation of Christians. The chief obstacles to action were papal memories of fifteenth-century conciliar opposition to absolute monarchy in the Church. The man who faced up to these fears and, in 1542, called for a reform council was Pope Paul III, the same pope who had made the first steps toward reform of his Roman diocese and who had commissioned the Select Committee on Reform to which we have so often referred. The site for the council was the south German city of Trent. It was situated on the southern side of the Alps where the pope thought the council would be relatively free from outside interference but close enough to Rome to allow his domination of its deliberations and decisions. It was also a location which appeased the emperor, since it was within his domain.

The number of bishops who actually appeared at Trent for its first session in 1545 was painfully small. Deliberations were postponed until twenty-five bishops appeared. By 1547, when the first phase of the council ended, there were still only seventy bishops present, and three quarters of these were Italians. Three bishops came from France, and from Germany only the proxies of the archbishops of Mainz and Trier. The second period of the council (1551-1552) saw a somewhat better balance among the bishops represented, for now there were thirteen German bishops present. But far more were absent than in attendance. The numbers grew to 109 cardinals and bishops during the third period of council deliberations (1562-1563), still a mere fraction of the prelates who could have come. Although the council meetings were strung out over a period of eighteen years, the council fathers actually sat for little more than a total of three years.

Persuading bishops to travel to Trent was only the first difficulty. In the absence of any agenda, the topics to be discussed were hotly debated. Paolo Sarpi (1552-1623), a Venetian church reformer, tells us in his *History of the Council of Trent* that the emperor and his German colleagues were sure that "points of doctrine could not be touched on with any hope of success, because it was first necessary to get rid of corruption...by a solid reformation." They judged that no one would accept the doctrinal declarations of a corrupt clergy. The papal party and those of a counter-reformation persuasion "thought it fit to begin with doctrine and then pass to reformation." "Rooting out heresies" was their highest priority. Eventually both doctrine and reform were considered in all the meetings of the council, though the tension between reformers and counter-reformers continued.

The doctrinal decisions of Trent were directed against Protestant theological questioning and dissent. Those decisions solidified many Catholic teachings that, during the Middle Ages, had been open to various interpretations. Doctrinal uniformity was now considered the only way to achieve unity. Any dissent or dissenter was rigorously condemned: "If any one says that, after the reception of the grace of justification, guilt is so remitted...that no debt of temporal punishment remains to be discharged either in this world or in purgatory,...let him be consigned to damnation."

The council's decisions on the life of the Church were similarly reactionary and protective of late medieval practice. The liturgical reforms stemming from this defensive mentality brought to the Mass a strict uniformity that emphasized its character as a sacrifice rather than a eucharistic meal. The priest was to face away from the people and recite the words of the Mass in Latin. The role of the laity was only to observe unintelligible mysteries; any sense of participation in a communal celebration was denied them.

And so the laity were left to practice their faith primarily through the extraliturgical devotions that had been their primary religious outlet during the Late Middle Ages. Devotions to the Queen of Heaven, and to a whole corps of saints specializing in the specific needs of individual worshipers, were continued, indeed forcefully mandated, in opposition to any "protestantizing" attempts at reform. Although the office of indulgence preacher was abolished, the Council of Trent declared, virtually without discussion:

> Since the power of conferring indulgences has been granted to the Church by Christ, and since the Church from earliest times has made use of that divinely bestowed power, this holy council teaches and commands that the use of indulgences...is to be retained in the Church. This council consigns to damnation those who assert that indulgences

are useless.

Clearly the council fathers were more intent on theological orthodoxy than historical accuracy.

The range of conciliar concerns covered virtually every imaginable theological topic. Nevertheless, there was one pressing concern that the council failed to address: the nature of the Christian Church and the role of papal power within it. The procedure of the council did answer the papal part of this question–at least implicitly. The popes of the period insisted that reform of the papal court and administration was not within the competence of the council–an implicit declaration that the functions and actions of the popes were immune from alteration by any agency of the Church save themselves. The fact that the council submitted its decisions to the pope for confirmation gave him the power to veto its actions. Indeed, the papal decree of 1564 which did confirm the canons and decisions of the Council of Trent declared that the pope alone had the right to interpret those canons. This illustrates the counter-reformation papacy's aggressive centralization of power. The popes of the period had the clear intention of subordinating the bishops to their direct control and asserting their supremacy in temporal affairs as well. How little this program succeeded–at least until the nineteenth century–we shall see.

D. The Society of Jesus

On August 15, 1534, seven young men met in the Chapel of Saint Denis at Montmartre in Paris. With their leader, Ignatius of Loyola (1491?-1556), the small group pledged themselves to personal spiritual development and the spiritual welfare of humankind. To those ends, they made vows of poverty and chastity and also made a commitment to missionary work in the Holy Land. Since the last proved impossible, they placed themselves and their ministry at the disposal of the pope. Though opposing Protestantism was not their original intent, they were eventually to become leaders in both Catholic reform and counter-reformation efforts.

The order grew rapidly. In 1541, there were but ten members of the Society of Jesus who elected Ignatius their superior and pledged him their obedience. At Ignatius' death in 1556, there were just under one thousand Jesuits, and, by 1624, there were more than sixteen thousand. Perhaps more impressive than the numbers is the quality of the young men who were attracted by the order's sense of total commitment to God. That commitment was reflected in its motto: "To the Greater Glory of God." The Society provided a place for men of intelligence, individuality, and flexibility. Each Jesuit was imbued with a spirit of commitment to his mission, expressed through obedience to his local superiors, to the father general in Rome, and through him to the pope. Jesuits, however, were also trusted to employ their own insights and methods in carrying out their assignments. That trust was earned through a splendid intellectual and deeply spiritual education.

Ignatius of Loyola had been a soldier as a young man in Spain, and military images came readily to his mind. In 1547, he wrote in this vein to the young Jesuits attending the order's college at Coimbra in Portugal. "More than anything else," he declared, "I wish you to be animated by a pure love of Jesus Christ...and the longing for the salvation of the people he has redeemed." This love and longing led to the enlistment of young men in the service of their Lord, for, he wrote, "you are his soldiers, soldiers with extraordinary pay." That pay, Ignatius continued, includes "all that you are and possess by nature, all the components and perfections of your soul and body." That pay is further enhanced by "the spiritual gift of the Lord's grace which he has bestowed on you with liberality and benevolence." The soldier who gives his life for his Lord will receive the ultimate pay: "the ineffable gift of his glory that he keeps ready and prepared for you."

All this talk, though couched in military terms, betrays a positive anthropology, a view of humankind more attuned to the humanism of the High Middle Ages than to the pessimism and despair that characterized much of the contemporary thought of both Protestants and Catholics. In his Coimbra letter, for example, Ignatius cited Saint Paul and Saint Bernard in urging his audience to temper their spiritual zeal with discretion. Overly zealous persons load themselves with burdens that make their ministry difficult or impossible. Ignatius concluded that "he who desires to be good to others should be good to himself,...following a middle path between the extremes of tepidity and indiscreet fervor."

The young men selected to study at Coimbra–and all those aspiring to serve God in the order–had to meet high intellectual, moral, and physical standards. They were also chosen for their sociability and adaptability. The young men spent two years as novices engaged in a spiritual process of discernment and formation that culminated in taking temporary vows of poverty, chastity, and obedience. Then came seven years of intellectual preparation called the Scholasticate. This involved mastering a liberal arts curriculum which emphasized philosophy, followed by a stint as a teacher or tutor, and culminating in several more years of theological education. The young men were then ordained priests and sent off for a year of intense spiritual growth called the Tertianship. After two more years of ministry, the young Jesuits could be invited to make solemn profession in the order. This long and demanding route to full membership in the order was a reflection of the Jesuit conviction that intellectual maturity, combined with a life of prayer and meditation, is necessary to the service of God and effective ministry to the people of God.

The ministries of the Jesuits were many. Among these education soon took a major place. Jesuits not only served as professors at all the universities of the Catholic world, they established many colleges of their own, primarily in German-speaking lands. Rome saw the foundation of the Gregorian University, which attracted candidates for the priesthood from all over Europe. To provide room and board for these students, the order established Roman residences that housed various national groups: German-Hungarian, Greek, and English, for example. Jesuits also built and ran excellent preparatory schools. Princes often employed

Jesuits as tutors to their sons. In all of Jesuit education, a major aim was to encourage, through humanist literary studies, a sophisticated command of language and expression.

Jesuits served both princes and ordinary folk with their popular preaching. They aimed at sermons that were simple and direct and that stressed morality and practical Christianity. One Jesuit, Peter Canisius (1524-1597), witnessed the success with which Luther had reached children and parents alike through doctrinal compendia called catechisms. In response, Peter created immensely popular Catholic catechisms, published in various forms for people of all ages and levels of education.

Jesuits were also popular as confessors. They aimed at restoring sinners to virtue and stimulating in them a desire for a deeper spiritual life. The same goals motivated a widespread network of Jesuit retreat houses, places where laity, clergy, and members of other religious orders could renew and intensify their spiritual life and confidence.

The text around which Jesuit retreats were built was a book by Ignatius himself, the *Spiritual Exercises*. Originally devised for use by Jesuits, it was soon adapted for all sorts of people leading all sorts of lives. Through meditation, the retreatant was led to an awareness of the horrors of sin, the meaning of Christ's life and death for his or her salvation, and the significance of Christ's Resurrection and Ascension. This highly structured meditation, characterized by an intense use of the imagination, was intended to lead the retreatant to an understanding of God's plan for him or her and to the embrace or "election" of that plan. The *Exercises* show Ignatius' certainty that grace is necessary for human happiness, but they also reflect an optimistic view of the role of free choice in the human acceptance of that grace.

E. Matteo Ricci and the Mission to China

In 1581, a young Jesuit named Matteo Ricci, with a handful of his confrères, settled in China near the city of Canton. Believing, with the sixth-century pope Gregory the Great, that Christianity could be expressed through any culture, these Jesuits dressed in the saffron roles of Buddhist monks. Five years later, in 1586, they had won only forty Chinese to Christianity.

They then saw that, although Buddhism was the religion of many Chinese, their culture was based on the ethical principles of the ancient scholar Confucius (550?-478 B.C.). Ricci and his companions eagerly learned the Chinese language and studied the works of Confucius and other Chinese sages. Ricci wrote of the results of this study: "In ethical matters Confucians agree with us Christians almost completely." The Jesuits then doffed their saffron monastic dress and donned the robes of Confucian scholars.

Ricci's little company earned great prestige among educated Chinese by their scientific knowledge. Ricci wrote: "If we teach them our sciences, not only will they succeed as very eminent men, but through those sciences we can easily lead them to our holy faith." During extensive and intensive conversations with Confucian scholars, Ricci did not hide his Christian faith, but he gained such a knowledge and appreciation of Chinese thought that he was able to write a treatise on Confucianism that became a classic of Chinese literature.

Ricci was convinced that the Chinese "were inclined toward piety...and followed the natural law much more faithfully than did Europeans." In the books written by Chinese intellectuals, Ricci declared, "we find very few points contrary to human reason and, indeed, many things conformable to it." Ricci concluded that, just as Thomas Aquinas had reconciled Aristotle with Christianity in the thirteenth century, so too could a reconciliation between Confucianism and Christianity be successfully accomplished in his day.

"Since the Chinese highly prize science and positions based on reason," Ricci wrote, and since "many important persons have great esteem for the integrity of our lives, our converts now number in the thousands." Ricci recognized that Chinese society was directed from the top, and so he rejoiced when, in 1601, the emperor gave the Jesuits a house in the capital city of Beijing and allowed them to build a nearby church for worship by the some two hundred Christians in that city. At the time of Ricci's death in 1610, there were some 2,500 Christians in China, many of them of noble rank.

Soon after the death of Matteo Ricci, a controversy arose in Europe over his acceptance of traditional cultural practices in Chinese Christian life. For example, Ricci saw no problem with the practice of honoring ancestors and sages like Confucius. These practices, Ricci thought, were civil and filial, not religious. Ricci's successor saw the practice as idolatry and banned it. Despite Pope Alexander VII's approval of Ricci's position in 1656, a later pope, Clement XI, condemned "Chinese rites" in 1704. This effectively shut off the flow of Chinese converts to Catholic Christianity, for accepting the faith of the Westerners now meant repudiation of the rich cultural heritage of China. Ricci's optimism about the power of reason to bring all people to much of the truth, and his confidence that all cultures were good and hence compatible with Christianity, were rejected. So, even on the other side of the planet, the pessimism of the Late Middle Ages, of the fourteenth through sixteenth centuries, had triumphed over the optimism of the High Middle Ages.

F. The Condemnation of Galileo

Another indication that the world of Bernard of Clairvaux and Thomas Aquinas had come to an end is the case of a professor of mathematics, Galileo Galilei of Pisa (1564-1642). After long observation and study, Galileo boldly asserted that the sun stood still and that the earth moved around it. For this he was denounced and summoned before the Roman Inquisition. In 1616, that august body declared that Galileo's position was "philosophically foolish, indeed preposterous, and, because contrary to Scripture, theologically heretical."

The passage of Scripture that proved Galileo's heresy to the inquisitors was the tenth chapter of Joshua. There is related the story of Joshua and the Israelites' victory over the Amorites. The battle was so exhausting that the day threatened to end before the Israelites could slaughter all their opponents. "Then," the Scripture declares, "Joshua spoke to the Lord,...and he said in the sight of Israel: 'Sun, stand still at Gibeon and, you moon, in the valley of Aijalon. And the sun stood still...until the nation took vengeance on their enemies." Now, reasoned the inquisitors, if it takes a miracle to make the sun stand still, it follows that the normal state of the sun is motion–obviously motion about the earth. Though condemned to life imprisonment, Galileo recanted his "heresies" and was then sentenced to spend his days under house arrest. His works were placed on the Index of Forbidden Books and not removed until 1822.

Galileo's recantation, though hardly heroic, is surely understandable. His true position we know from a letter he wrote, in 1615, to Cristina di Lorena, the grand duchess of Tuscany. In it Galileo declared his conviction that the words of Scripture are true. "But," he added, "who could insist with complete certainty that the Bible always limits itself to the strict and literal meaning of words when it mentions only incidentally the earth, water, the sun, and other created entities?" Restraint is all the more necessary when Scripture speaks about those entities "in a way that has no bearing on the primary purpose of Holy Writ, which is service to God and the salvation of souls." The natural world about us should be investigated "through sensory experience and logical demonstration," not by citing passages from Scripture. "Both Nature and Holy Scripture proceed from the Word of God," he said, Scripture "being the dictate of the Holy Spirit," and Nature "being the completely obedient executrix of divine Law."

Galileo thus affirmed that human knowledge is attained through the parallel though distinct methods of reason and faith. This had been the position of Bernard of Clairvaux and Thomas Aquinas. In his optimism concerning human ability to ascertain truth Galileo was no revolutionary. It was his opponents, the Roman inquisitors, who were the innovators–they and theologians both Protestant and Catholic who doubted the ability of the human intellect to know very much at all about the universe.

XIII. MOVEMENTS TOWARD MODERNITY

Some Useful Data

1574-1589	reign of Henry III, king of France
1589-1610	reign of Henry IV, king of France
1567-1622	Francis de Sales, bishop
1575-1629	Pierre de Bérulle, cardinal
1611-1632	Gustavus II Adolphus, king of Sweden
1547-1638	Cornelius Jansen, bishop
1585-1642	Armand Jean de Richelieu, cardinal and chief minister of France
1608-1657	Jean-Jacques Olier, theologian
1627-1704	Jacques Bénigne Bousset, bishop
1635-1705	Philipp Jakob Spener, theologian
1643-1715	reign of Louis XIV, king of France
1663-1727	Hermann Franke, educator
1713-1740	reign of Frederick William I, king of Prussia
1769-1774	reign of Clement XIV, pope
1740-1780	reign of Maria Theresa, empress
1703-1791	John Wesley, founder of Methodism

The seventeenth and eighteenth centuries saw the growth of secularism and the decline of the Christian religion as a force in Western culture. After these centuries we may no longer speak of the interaction of Christianity and culture. In the modern world, Christianity and the churches that are its institutional expressions would be, for the most part, reduced to reacting against secular culture and to have little or no influence on it.

A. Antecedents of the New World

The development of a largely secular culture did not happen overnight, of course. Indeed, it had already begun when the late medieval Church forfeited much of the confidence of Christians by its corruption and misdirection. Even during the revival of Christian zeal that accompanied the Protestant and Catholic reformations, the hold of religion on the European conscience was slipping, and the state was rapidly replacing the Church as the institution which expressed western values. Some examples are in order.

March of 1562 saw the beginning of the protracted "wars of religion" in France, the last phase of which is called "The War of the Three Henrys." At war were Catholics and Calvinists (in France often called Huguenots). But the fact that the "three Henrys" led the three warring factions indicates that more than religion was involved. The Catholic Henry III (ruled 1574-1589) was the third of Catherine de' Medici's sons to reign and be ruled by her. Unlike his elder brothers, Henry threw off his mother's strong influence, but his cause and crown were ultimately lost through inaction or misdirected activity. One of his rivals was also Catholic, Henry of Guise, the leader of the violently anti-Protestant "Catholic League." This Henry had led a Paris mob in the slaughter of Huguenots during the Saint Bartholomew's Day massacre of August 24, 1572. Opposing both was Henry of Navarre, the Huguenot leader. In the end, it was this Henry who survived the others, but the acceptance of a Protestant as king by the overwhelmingly Catholic French was problematic at best. So Henry took what he called the "perilous leap" and converted to Catholicism. Questioned by dismayed Huguenots, Henry–now King Henry IV–is supposed to have said: "Paris is worth a Mass."

That was in 1589. Only twenty-nine years later, in 1618, occurred the "Defenestration of Prague." Those "defenestrated"–pitched out the window of the Hradčany palace in the Bohemian (now Czech) capital of Prague–were the agents of the new king of Bohemia, the emperor Ferdinand II. The "defenestrators" were the leaders of the Calvinist resistance to local Catholic authorities. The rebels elected a fellow Protestant, the elector Frederick, as king of Bohemia. In the Bohemian phase (1618-1623) of the Thirty Years' War which followed, powerful Lutheran states refused to help Frederick, contending that Calvinists were less than Christian. Frederick's reign lasted but a year–hence his sobriquet "the Winter King." He had been defeated resoundingly at the battle of White Mountain, not far from his erstwhile capital of Prague.

The next phase of the Thirty Years' War exhibited the same confusing sort of inter- and intra-denominational rivalries. This phase, which lasted from 1624 to 1629, began when King Christian IV of Denmark took up the Protestant cause. However, the most powerful Lutheran state in Germany, Brandenburg-Prussia, fought on the side of the Catholic emperor against the Danes. It seems the Lutheran faith of the Danes was not sufficiently orthodox, as it did not adhere fully to Luther's teaching on the eucharist. It is just barely possible that Danish ambitions for territories in northern Germany clashed with the expansionist policies of Brandenburg.

On the Catholic side, there were two armies in the field. One, under the command of Count Tilly, defeated the Danes in 1626. Tilly served not the emperor but the Catholic League, which had been formed by a party of German Catholic princes to oppose the political ambitions of the Catholic emperor. The other, the emperor's army, served Ferdinand under the leadership of a colorful mercenary, Count Albert von Wallenstein. At the point of seeming victory over the Protestant army, Ferdinand dismissed Wallenstein, who had urged a peace settlement that ignored denominational differences. Once more religion and politics were enmeshed in confusing and often contradictory ways.

On July 6, 1630, King Gustavus II Adolphus of Sweden marched into Germany to rescue the Protestant cause. The Protestant princes of Germany refused to accept his leadership, however, until Gustavus Adolphus forced them to do so. Thus reinforced, the Swedes beat Tilly in 1631. They overcame Wallenstein as well, in 1632, but Gustavus Adolphus lost his life in the battle, and two years later the imperial army defeated the Swedes.

The chief diplomatic and financial supporter of Sweden had been His Eminence Cardinal Armand Jean de Plessis de Richelieu, the chief minister and real power in King Louis XIII's France. With the Swedish defeat Richelieu decided that France must enter the war–on the Protestant side. The French phase of the Thirty Years' War (1635-1648) saw the Swedes defeating the imperial forces and the French victorious over their Catholic co-religionists, the Spanish allies of the emperor. Religion, in the end, was ignored, and political power proved the only interest of the Roman cardinal, Richelieu.

The Peace of Westphalia that followed showed the true colors of France and all the other states. The Holy Roman Empire of the German Nation was virtually destroyed–the French goal. The mighty medieval Empire was reduced to three hundred independent states–by 1800, over 1,200–most of them postage-stamp-sized principalities ready to be licked by France. France and Sweden took large chunks of German territory, and still more Church lands were taken over by secular states. The pope's protests were ignored. Indeed, he was not even invited to take part in the deliberations. To none of the international treaty conferences that concluded the wars of the seventeenth and eighteenth centuries was a pope invited. He was everywhere treated only as a foreign potentate–by Catholic states as well as Protestant. The primary goal of the rulers of those states was terrestrial power, not celestial bliss, and they treated the churches in their realms–Catholic, Lutheran, Calvinist, or Anglican–as state departments of religion. The pope, who had once served as the moral arbiter of Europe, was reduced to the status of the ruler of a fourth-rate power. This reduced status exactly mirrored the pope's almost exclusive concern with his central Italian principality.

B. Gallicanism, Febronianism, and the Jesuits

As rulers of Europe ignored the pope as a political power, so too the Churches in their realms–Protestant, of course, but also Catholic–refused to acknowledge the pretensions of the pope to universal supremacy in the Church. In May of 1682, the French Assembly of Clergy formulated Four Articles. The first denied that the pope possessed authority over temporal affairs. The second affirmed the superiority to the pope of general or ecumenical councils–a statement reviving the position of the Council of Constance in 1414. The Assembly rejected the authority of any papal decrees that had not been accepted by the French Church. The fourth article rejected the infallibility of the pope when he acted without the agreement of the whole Church. King Louis XIV (ruled 1643-1715) declared the Four Articles the official doctrine of the French Church and ordered that they be taught in all universities and seminaries. Together these doctrinal statements and decisions of the French Church (in Latin, *ecclesia gallicana*) constitute what has come to be called Gallicanism.

Gallicanism was not confined to Gaul. In Germany the same view of the Church came to be called Febronianism. The father of Febronianism was a scholar and bishop, Nicolaus von Hontheim (died 1790), who wrote an influential book on the Church (first published in 1763) under the pseudonym Febronius. The book declared that the pope's claim to supreme authority over the Churches was false; not he alone but all bishops were successors of the apostles. The ultimate source of doctrine, Febronius asserted, was the Holy Spirit speaking through the Church in a general or ecumenical council. The pope, he granted, was the foremost symbol of unity in the Church, but papal rights claimed beyond that were spurious. Febronius conscientiously sought precedents in the early and medieval Church for his positions, and he hoped that one result of the reforms he advocated would be an opportunity for dialogue with the Protestant churches of Germany.

Rome reacted to the book with condemnation, of course. But significantly, twenty-six German bishops refused to publish the papal decree. In 1786, the archbishops of Cologne, Trier, Mainz, and Salzburg met at Bad Ems, a Rhenish resort, and offered a twenty-two point reform program for the Church. Reflecting Febronius' influence, the archbishops saw the cornerstone of this reform in the independence of episcopal authority from Roman control. This teaching on the nature and structure of the Church was an integral part of the theological education at German universities until the middle of the nineteenth century.

The only significant group even slightly interested in supporting the remaining pretensions of the papacy to supremacy in the Church was the Society of Jesus. Their reward for this position was expulsion, in 1764, from France, Spain, and Portugal. In 1769, a man pledged to the suppression of the Jesuits was elected pope–in large part because of that pledge. After his election, Clement XIV spent the next three years wavering in indecision, fearing, he claimed, that the Jesuits would poison him if he took the final step. The papal decree suppressing the Jesuits was written by the Spanish ambassador to Rome and issued by Clement in 1773. The Father General of the Society was thrown into jail, where he died a miserable death. Some twenty thousand priests and brothers were removed from their ministries. Hundreds of Jesuit houses and schools were closed, not to be reopened until 1814. The weakness of Clement XIV and the weakness of the papacy as an institution were painfully exposed.

C. The King as Christ

In 1627, a boy was born to a well-to-do family in the French town of Dijon. His name was Jacques Bénigne Bossuet, and a brilliant future awaited him. As a lad of thirteen years, his father obtained for him a post as canon of the cathedral of Metz. At the ripe old age of twenty-five, he was made archdeacon of the Metz diocese. As archdeacon he was the bishop's principal judicial officer, presiding most often over marriage cases. This duty was not burdensome since most of the people of Metz were Huguenots who were understandably reluctant to submit their marital troubles to a Catholic court.

As a result, young Bossuet had plenty of time to devote himself to his passion: preaching. Bossuet thus trained himself for the pulpit, a center of influence in a land with no popular assemblies through which information could be shared and decisions disseminated. In 1659, Bossuet tried out his newly-developed skills in Paris. So successful was he that King Louis XIV appointed him chaplain to the Chapel Royal, in which post he preached with great effect to the royal court on state occasions. As a reward the king appointed him bishop of a diocese in far southwestern France, in Gascony.

Being so remote from the seat of power in France was not at all to Bossuet's liking, and he eagerly accepted Louis XIV's next appointment as tutor to the dauphin, the French crown prince. Among the many books that Bossuet produced in this period was one written for his charge entitled *Politics Drawn from Holy Scripture*. In this book, addressed to "Monseigneur le Dauphin," Bousset affirmed that "there are four essential characteristics or qualities of royal authority." The first of these is that "royal authority is sacred." Since "all power comes from God," it is clear that "God established kings as his ministers and reigns through them over the people." Thus "the royal throne is not the throne of a man, but the throne of God himself."

The second characteristic flows from the first: "The person of kings is sacred" and, therefore, "any attack on them is a sacrilege." Indeed, since "God causes kings to be anointed by his prophets [the priests], the title of Christ [the anointed one] is given to kings." The consequences are that "one must guard kings as sacred objects," and that "he who neglects to guard them is worthy of death." That is why "royal authority must be absolute," and, therefore, "the prince owes an explanation to no one for what he commands." Thus, "when the ruler has judged, there can be no other judgment." As for his subjects, "it is necessary to obey princes as justice itself,...for they are gods."

This new political theory, the "divine right of kings," carried on the thought of Luther and was based on a virtually identical anthropology. Bossuet, as a Catholic, could not say with Luther that humans are depraved–primarily because it was Luther who had said it. But Post-Reformation Catholicism took such a dismal view of the Fall's effects that human beings were seen as riddled with sin, just as Luther and Calvin had believed them to be. Diseased human beings require an absolute power to heal them. Bossuet agreed with all the political thinkers of the ancient and medieval worlds that the purpose of the state is to provide justice. Bossuet, however, defined justice as subjection to the ordering power of a state ruled by God's minister, the king. If justice is defined as absolute order, then personal freedom is clearly an absurd goal.

Bossuet was well aware of the most pressing objection to his politics: what if the king is not just? For Bossuet the very question contains a contradiction. Since God is infallibly just and the king is God's agent on earth, whatever God decrees through the king is by definition just. Resistance to the king's decisions is not simply illegal; it is sacrilegious. This position was popular with the king, who made Bossuet bishop of the prosperous diocese of Meaux, where he served as the "spokesman of his age."

D. A Revived Caesaropapism

Although Bossuet's political theory was conceived within a theological context, it gave supernatural sanction to the already growling power of an increasingly secular state. That divine authority was exercised ruthlessly over the Churches in most of the lands of Europe, Protestant as well as Catholic.

Throughout the seventeenth and eighteenth centuries, the rulers of Catholic countries gained an ever increasing hold on the Churches in their realms. Princes claimed and asserted the power to nominate bishops, and this meant in practice that they appointed them. Rulers administered–and sometimes appropriated–the revenues of a diocese whose bishop had died. Many kings prohibited the publication of papal decrees within their realms. In Austria, in 1744, the empress Maria Theresa went so far as to redraw unilaterally the boundaries of dioceses and parishes. Prelates and priests often served as a significant part of the civil bureaucracy. They provided the authorities with information about people and problems in their area, and they communicated from the pulpit the decrees and propaganda of the state, while preaching submission to that state. Catholic Europe became a welter of national churches with little communication between them and related to the pope in little more than name.

In the Protestant parts of what was still nominally the Holy Roman Empire of the German Nation, most of the principalities were miniscule and only a few attained moderate size. In all of them the Churches were largely dependent on the ruler. The rulers appointed ecclesiastical councils that effectively controlled the Lutheran bishops–in some states called superintendents. There was little separation between the spiritual and secular in those realms, and the ruler exercised authority over both. Sometimes, as in Brandenburg-Prussia in 1730, a ministry for church affairs was established as an integral part of the state's structure. Lutheran liturgy, its order of worship, was subject to King Frederick William I's interference, and the king attempted to determine the contents of the sermons preached by the Calvinist pastors in his realm.

The Church of England was likewise subject to the state in this period. Whether the dominant influence within that Church was sympathetic to traditional modes of worship or with Puritan zeal wished to rid the Church of all relics of "Romanism," including bishops, the Church was an established Church. As such it was subject to the state, whether to king or parliament. The religious and political rights of "Non-conformists," whether Protestant or Catholic, were strictly curtailed, and a fine was levied on those who failed to attend the local parish. The kings and, later, leaders of Parliament appointed bishops, almost invariably for political reasons, since bishops sat in the House of Lords, the upper house of the British Parliament.

Everywhere in Europe the Church functioned as the state's department of religious affairs. However, there were advantages, most churchmen thought, to state control of religion. The established church–be it Catholic, Lutheran, Calvinist, or Anglican–enjoyed a monopoly of public worship. Only members of that church were allowed to hold office or otherwise participate in public affairs. The state treated heresy or apostasy as criminal offences. Blasphemy and adultery–and, in Catholic states, missing Mass, and in Protestant cities like Geneva, missing worship services–were punished by fines or imprisonment. The state provided financial support for the churches, either by paying its clergy or, more usually, by enforcing payment of tithes. These matters, of course, concern congregational discipline and institutional functions. But, we are bound to ask, what of the spiritual life of Christians in this age? How was Christianity lived in this emerging modern culture?

E. Pietism and Protestant Spiritual Life

In all Christian denominations, the state Churches emphasized external adherence to the local orthodoxy and rigid moral conformity. The vivid memory of the religious conflicts of the Reformation era was constantly reinforced in sermons and tracts. Deviations from "proper" belief were readily taken as assaults on orthodoxy. Conformity had largely replaced religious fervor, and enthusiasm was regarded with deep suspicion.

This was surely true of the German Lutheran Churches. Church doctrine was narrowly defined and rigidly defended. Christian morality was publicly enforced, and deviation resulted in unforgiving and sometimes brutal punishment. Luther's lively liturgy had become dull and uninspiring.

In 1675, Philipp Jakob Spener (1635-1705) published a book called *Pia desideria*. The book's subtitle indicates its intent and purpose: *Heartfelt Desires for a God-pleasing Improvement of the true Protestant Church*. For Spener and the "Pietists" who followed him, Christianity was not the intricate system of abstract doctrines which he saw being taught by mainstream "Lutheran Orthodoxy." Christianity was rather the practice of a way of life that would transform the individual Christian. Genuine conversion would lead to rebirth. The means to this reinvigoration of Christian life, Spener taught, was a simplicity and fervor which would make preaching relevant, thus enlivening worship services that had become formal and lifeless. Daily Bible reading by all, supported by frequent group discussions, would lead each believer to meditation on his or her own life and open them up to illumination by the Holy Spirit.

The Pietist concern for a deepening of the religious life of the individual did not preclude intense attention to the betterment of society. Pietists founded all sorts of charitable institutions: orphanages, schools for the poor, and centers for fellowship, among others. They also established a printing press that produced inexpensive editions of the Bible, song books, prayer books, and devotional guides. They also invested much time, money, and energy in overseas missions, notably in south India. A group of Pietists was also sent to America, where they organized the nascent Lutheran Church.

In 1694, a leading Pietist, Hermann Franke (1663-1727), founded a university at the town of Halle, not far from the Saxon capital of Leipzig. This center of learning fostered a theology that concerned itself less with doctrinal controversy than with individual spiritual growth within a Christian community–a community deeply conversant with the Bible. At the height of its success in the early eighteenth century, some 1,200 students attended the university's theological school each year. The influence of Pietism on contemporary culture was powerful. The university at Halle was the first to be concerned with teacher training, and there new educational theories were put forth and new pedagogical methods explored. The language of instruction in all departments was German, not Latin, which may have contributed to the growth of the hitherto meager literary production in the modern German language. Perhaps influenced by the numerous edicts which everywhere prohibited their meetings, Pietists early on denounced princely absolutism.

Critics of Pietism claimed that the introspection characteristic of Pietist spirituality led to a morbid preoccupation with the state of one's soul. Critics also feared–with some reason–that emotion played so strong a role in Pietist spiritual life that the role of the intellect in that life was disparaged.

F. Methodists and English Evangelicals

Emotion was also suspect in the Church of England of the time, and most Anglicans recoiled in horror from what they called "enthusiasm." The liturgy of the established Church was rigidly formal. It provided a comfortable way of worship for the landed gentry and monied middle class, but failed to excite the fervor of many members of the working classes.

Candidates for ordination to clerical statues in the Church of England were required to present themselves to their bishop. At that time, bishops most often lived in London, and so a trip to that capital was frequently a necessary prerequisite to ordination. There were no widely accepted standards for that ordination–either of character or education–and after ordination parish clergy rarely received any supervision. Many clergymen held more than one ecclesiastical office, and this pluralism led to absenteeism, so that many churches were served by poorly paid and poorly educated clerical substitutes. Reform was urgently needed, but the close association of the Church with the state meant that the very bishops and other members of government with the power to effect reform were occupied with political problems of much greater interest to them.

There were two great movements toward reform in eighteenth-century England. In one, Methodism, the leaders started their spiritual journey within the Anglican fold but by force of circumstances forsook this ecclesiastical home. The other was Evangelicalism, which remained within the Church though attempting to alter it radically in both doctrine and practice.

John Wesley (1703-1791) was one of nineteen children, the offspring of an Anglican clergyman and his wife. John and his brother Charles attended Oxford University, where they founded a student society, known as the Holy Seekers, devoted to Bible study, prayer, and fellowship. When attending a meeting of Pietists in 1738, John heard a talk about God working in the human heart through faith. He felt his heart "strangely warmed" and became convinced, he tells us, that Christ "had taken away my sins, even mine, and saved me from the law of sin and death."

Wesley's ecstatic message of forgiveness was viewed as "enthusiasm" by Anglican clergymen who closed the doors of their parish churches to him. But he continued his ministry by preaching in fields or wherever and whenever people were willing to listen. He preached some forty thousand sermons, often in camp meetings. These services were accompanied by the splendidly straightforward hymns composed by brother Charles. Although the brothers' goal was to encourage a deeper Christian life within the established Church, that Church could not abide Wesley's disregard for parish boundaries, his claim to gifts from the Holy Spirit, and his assumption of the power to ordain fellow ministers.

Wesley was a charismatic preacher, who addressed his sermons to crowds largely composed of lower middle class shopkeepers and artisans and of impoverished and often unemployed laborers. His dramatic oratory aroused the emotions of his listeners, who responded with confessions of sin, shouts of joy, songs of thanksgiving–and sometimes convulsions.

Few charismatic speakers have possessed Wesley's genius at organization. He exhorted his hearers "to form themselves into a sort of little society, to meet once or twice in a week, in order to reprove, instruct, and exhort one another." The groups, called "classes," usually of twelve members, exercised oversight over the small community and were responsible for collecting "class money," a penny a week donation from each member. Wesley formulated a set of rules for these members. They were to read the Bible regularly and pray privately. They were to participate in the public prayer and many other activities of the society, while seeking to convert others to the "methodical" way of life which gave rise to the name "Methodist." Wesley not only provided his flock with that discipline of life but also a sense of worth and belonging that many of them had never before experienced.

Methodists quickly followed Wesley's lead in works of loving service to their neighbors. He–and they–built dispensaries, homes for widows, and schools for poor children. Wesley and the Methodists concerned themselves with the evil effects of alcoholism and indolence, and by their well-regulated life offered a pattern of hope to those on the margins of society.

John Wesley's theology of grace was neither Lutheran nor Calvinist. It rather resembled the Catholic position in its emphasis on the power and responsibilities of free choice. On the other hand, Evangelicalism, though founded at the same time as Methodism–the eighteenth century–and serving similar religious needs, was theologically very different. Evangelicals were ardent Calvinists who affirmed the total depravity of humankind. Justification, and hence salvation, was by God's grace alone, not through the initiative of human choice.

There was a strong puritanical streak in the Evangelical moral stance. Idle amusements of many kinds were condemned–cards, the theater, and dancing, for example. All these activities distracted genuine Christians from the serious business of life and from frequent reflection on death. Their source of inspiration was, of course, the Bible, which they read with uncritical literalism. Evangelicals also found intellectual pursuits distracting and even dangerous.

Evangelicalism provided a meaningful way of life for many. Its adherents' piety, earnestness, and fervor, their concern for the poor, the fallen and downtrodden, were otherwise rare within the contemporary Church of England. As a result, Evangelicals constituted the most vital and active component of the established Church.

G. Early Modern Catholicism

Catholic spirituality in the seventeenth and eighteenth centuries exhibited a bewildering array of forms and options. Many of these "schools" of spirituality were identified with and taught by the most influential religious orders of the time. For example, the Jesuits practiced Ignatian spirituality, Carmelites the path to perfection described by Teresa of Ávila and John of the Cross. We shall here discuss two of these schools: one the French School, was heir to the pessimism of the Late Middle Ages and Luther; the other was a direct descendent of the humanist spirituality of Bernard of Clairvaux and Desiderius Erasmus. We shall begin with the latter.

Francis de Sales was born, in 1567, in Savoy, a mountainous land lying between France and Italy. After studying the liberal arts with the Jesuits at Paris, Francis did doctorates at Padua, in civil and canon law–to please his father–and in theology–to please himself. Receiving his ordination to the priesthood in 1593, he was then named head of the cathedral chapter of Geneva. He did not take up residence in that city, however, for Geneva was the world capital of Calvinism. Francis did visit and preach to the Calvinists in Chablis, the area northwest of Geneva. His success in this mission led to his appointment as assistant bishop, and then, in 1602, as bishop of Geneva.

Francis spent his life in preaching and writing, and he was a much sought after spiritual advisor. His ministry was often exercised through letters, and it was said that, when Francis wrote, he wrote not only about something but to someone. Francis' books, *An Introduction to the Devout Life* (1609) and *Treatise on the Love of God* (1616) were so popular that edition after edition was printed. All his works show Francis' deep insights into the problems and possibilities attending the search for holiness. Those works, especially his letters, show the sensitivity and kindness–indeed tenderness–with which he treated everyone. Francis lived in a world in which his affability, his admiration for and gentle understanding of others, led to deep friendships.

The God in whom Francis passionately believed was a gentle God, a God with profoundly maternal care and concern for his children. Francis saw God as so loving human beings that he bestowed his saving grace on each and every person–a position not popular with contemporary theologians, Catholic or Protestant.

As a consequence of his belief in divine benevolence, Francis sought mightily to make the means to perfection accessible to all Christians everywhere. He wrote in the preface to his *Introduction to the Devout Life:*

> I want to teach people who live within their families in crowded cities, women who live at home amid domestic cares, men who live under the pressure of public affairs in their professional life....It is a mistake, it is a heresy indeed, to wish to exclude a life of devotion from the soldier's camp, from the artisan's workshop, from the courts of princes, from the homes of married people.

This call to universal holiness presupposed an anthropology as optimistic as that of Bernard of Clairvaux or Desiderius Erasmus. Francis was following the path of a devout Christian humanism that saw love as central to human happiness.

"Love," wrote Francis, "is spiritual fire, and when it breaks into flame, it is called devotion." A devout life, he thought, involved no special spiritual exercise;

it is simply loving and serving God and neighbor with all one's heart. The devout life could be lived by persons with all sorts of vocations and occupations. Like Saint Bernard, Francis taught that the true Christian should lovingly observe the duties dictated by the calling of her or his life. Thus Christian perfection does not consist, for Frances, in the extreme forms of asceticism widely practiced in his day in monasteries for women. Francis and his good friend Jane Frances de Chantal founded, in 1610, a community in which young women and widows would live without being walled up. Francis and Jane made it clear that this community was open to those unable or unwilling to accept the rigorous austerities of other orders.

Francis taught that, with the exception of sin, the greatest evils encountered in the spiritual life are anxiety and sadness. To overcome these evils, Francis recommended a life of prayer under the direction of a person of love, learning, and prudence. Mediation, prayer, frequent communion, and spiritual reading were practices accessible to people in all walks of life. This sort of response to God's love would help make better lovers of everyone.

Francis' spirit and spirituality would have found a happy home in twelfth-century Europe. But he was a lone voice crying in the wilderness of the seventeenth century. No disciple or successor carried his vision onward. Indeed, everything he stood for, all that he proposed as a pathway to happiness, was rejected by most of his contemporaries–certainly by the proponents of so-called French school of spirituality.

The spiritual founder of that school was Pierre de Bérulle, born in 1575 of an aristocratic family in the château of Sérilly, not far to the southeast of Paris. He was educated by Jesuits and at the university at Paris, and was ordained priest in 1599. Appointed honorary chaplain to the king, he was a trusted advisor to several members of the royal family. Because Bérulle was the leader of the pro-papal party at the French court, King Louis XIII chose him, in 1625, to conduct negotiations with the pope in Rome. There Bérulle was successful in obtaining a dispensation that allowed Princess Henrietta Maria to marry an Anglican, King Charles I of England. In 1627, Bérulle was made a cardinal for his services. Two years later he died at the altar while saying Mass.

Bérulle was always deeply concerned with the renewal of priestly life in France. He saw essential to this goal the introduction of seminaries for priestly formation that had been mandated by the Council of Trent but not implemented in France. To realize this goal, one of Bérulle's followers, Jean-Jacques Olier (1608-1657), founded the Society and seminary of Saint-Sulpice. This Parisian seminary was to influence priestly formation on both sides of the Atlantic.

Even before Bérulle's ordination he had written a book that exposed the basis of his spirituality and that of his followers: *A Brief Discourse on Interior Abnegation*. The view of human beings revealed there is completely negative. Because of the Fall, human reason is darkened to the point that it is incapable of attaining authentic knowledge save by grace. Bérulle's pessimism about human possibilities was so severe that it is difficult to discover what place there is in his thought for the will's cooperation with grace. In short, we humans are but sin and abomination.

Bérulle's world is thoroughly evil. The disordered things of this world are but vanity and illusion. All that the world values, like wealth and honor, friendship and affection, should be the objects of our revulsion and rejection. This world is informed and governed by the severe justice of an avenging God.

That God is completely transcendent, and to him is due the constant adoration of humankind. As the Second Person of the Trinity, Jesus is likewise transcendent and impersonal. This is the first "state" of Christ. The second "state" is that of the Incarnate Word. In the Incarnation Christ emptied himself, and we must initiate that self-emptying through self-abnegation. In the Incarnation, the Sacred Humanity of Jesus was annihilated, and we must experience annihilation of our own self-interest and self-love so we can be clothed with Christ. Through this process of self-annihilation, we take on the divine states of Christ by hating our flesh and loving pain, suffering, and persecution. Béruille's disciple Olier added that even our eating and drinking must be kept to an absolute minimum. Through a life of rigorous asceticism and self-punishment we realize our uselessness, our dependence, our poverty.

Even more important in our daily practice must be adoration of Christ in his third or eucharistic "state." This devotion centers on Christ as Priest and Sacrifice and explains why Bérulle insisted that only ordained priests can hope for high levels of holiness. This seventeenth-century rigorism led, in the eighteenth, to a movement that took the French school's principles to their logical end and earned the repeated condemnation of churchmen–even those much influenced by the French school.

Cornelius Jansen (1547-1638) was a university professor who became bishop of Ypres in 1636. He died of the plague only two years later, leaving the manuscript of his major work unpublished. This work, titled *Augustinus*, aimed at reconciling the vexing problems of grace and predestination in the light of Saint Augustine's thought. This work was the foundation stone of a movement that stirred passionate controversy until the middle of the eighteenth century.

Jansenists taught that human nature is fundamentally corrupt due to Original Sin. And thus we are totally incapable of choosing between good and evil. Proper choices and actions are the result of grace alone. This grace is given only to those predestined to Heaven, and thus only they can benefit from the Redemption and be saved.

Jansenist moral theology displayed a thorough-going rigorism. Jansenists taught that perfect contrition–sorrow for sin stemming from absolutely selfless love–is necessary for absolution within the sacrament of penance. Pure love for God is necessary for a worthy communion. The primary practice of the Christian life is the performance of penitential acts.

Although Jansenism ceased to be a force in the French Church by 1750, its name lives on in Catholic spirituality to this day. The name is now assigned to the sort of spirituality characterized by an extremely negative anthropology and by an extremely rigorous moral theology which sees sin everywhere and in everyone. It also teaches that pain is the path to virtue and that humiliation of their subordinates is the proper task of pastors and religious superiors. This "Jansenism" became the dominant spirituality of the Catholic world until the middle of the twentieth century. And it is not dead yet.

XIV. ENLIGHTENMENT AND REVOLUTION

Some Useful Data

1578-1657	William Harvey, English biologist
1627-1691	Robert Boyle, English physicist
1642-1727	Isaac Newton, English physicist
1694-1778	Voltaire, French *philosophe*
1712-1778	Jean-Jacques Rousseau, French political and educational theorist
1729-1781	Gotthold Ephraim Lessing, German dramatist
1713-1784	Denis Diderot, French *philosophe*
1729-1786	Moses Mendelssohn, German Jewish philosopher
1740-1786	reign of Frederick II, king of Prussia
1768-1790	reign of Joseph II, emperor
1774-1793	reign of Louis XVI, king of France
1737-1794	Edward Gibbon, English historian
1743-1794	Jean de Condorcet, *philosophe* and political leader
1758-1794	Maximilien Robespierre, French political leader
1769-1821	Napoleon Bonaparte, French emperor
1800-1823	reign of Pius VII, pope
1743-1826	Thomas Jefferson, American politician and president
1797-1840	reign of Frederick William III, king of Prussia
1818-1897	Jacob Burckhardt, Swiss art historian

The Enlightenment was not a period of time, any more than was the Renaissance. The Enlightenment was not a philosophical system, despite the fact that its proponents are called *philosophes*. The Enlightenment was an intellectual movement that saw its first flowering in the late eighteenth century, and, in a very real sense, its French form–on which I shall concentrate–has dominated western thought ever since. Even those who have rejected the Enlightenment have been mightily influenced by it. It is Enlightenment thought, not Christianity, which has defined modernity–for better or for worse.

The fundamental word and concept in Enlightenment thought is "progress." The man who, more than any other, made "progress" the watchword of the *philosophes* was Jean Antoine Nicholas de Condorcet (1743-1794). Like many of the *philosophes*, Condorcet was educated by Jesuits; he then distinguished himself as a mathematician. He held high office in several revolutionary governments after 1789. In October of 1793, he was tried *in absentia* and condemned to death by the radical government which had succeeded to the seat of power in France. He then spent some nine months hiding from arrest and execution. It was during this time–a time, one would think, of fearful suspense–that Condorcet wrote an incredibly optimistic assessment of the human condition, *The Progress of the Human Mind*.

A. The Notion of Progress

The people of antiquity held a view of history that was cyclical, featuring ever recurring situations and events. The ancient Hebrews saw things in a radically different way: their view of history was linear. Time had begun with God's creation of the cosmos, and the central event in the history that had followed was the Exodus, God's deliverance of the Hebrews from Egypt. All subsequent history was related to that event. When God revealed the Law to his people on Mount Sinai, he reminded Moses: "I am the Lord, your God, who brought you out of the land of Egypt, out of the house of bondage. You shall have no other gods besides me." History was directed toward an end: there would come a time when God would send the Messiah to lead his people.

The Christian view of history was an adaptation of the Hebrew version. There was a beginning to time in the creation. There was a central event in time as well, an event that gave meaning to all others. This central happening was the Incarnation of the Second Person of the Trinity as Jesus–who was the Messiah, the Christ. The end of time will bring the apocalyptic Second Coming of Christ, when all humans will be raised from death to new life.

Like so many of its components, the Enlightenment held an understanding of history that was a secularized version of the Christian. For Condorcet and the *philosophes*, history is both linear and progressive: the world has been getting better and better over the ages, that is, more and more enlightened. It will continue this progress, until–in a day not far off–a state of perfection will be realized, not in the next world, but in our own.

Since the past was darker and the future will be more enlightened than the present, the study of history was almost completely useless to the *philosophes*. Yet two of them wrote enormously influential works of history. Edward Gibbon (1737-1794) wrote his six-volume *Decline and Fall of the Roman Empire* over the years 1776 to 1778. For Gibbon the glories of antiquity were destroyed by the pernicious otherworldliness of the Christian religion. All the creative energies of ancient Greece and Rome had been directed toward happiness in this world and had been misdirected by Christianity toward an imaginary afterlife. Thus the barbarous "Dark Ages" overtook Europe. The line marking upward progress was, then, not a straight line. Progress stagnated when religion ruled. Fortunately, the *philosophes* thought, the "Dark Ages" had been succeeded by the Renaissance, an early age of enlightenment characterized by a rebirth of the glories of ancient Greek and Roman secularism. We have already met the proponent of this point of view in Jacob Burkhardt and spoken of his book *The Civilization of the Renaissance in Italy* (1860).

The basis for the overwhelming optimism displayed by Condorcet and his fellow *philosophes* was their understanding of the so-called Scientific Revolution. There is no doubt that the seventeenth century had seen scientific breakthroughs of a spectacular sort. Isaac Newton (1642-1727) had formulated and described mathematically the fundamental laws of motion: inertia, acceleration, and action-reaction. These laws, and Newton's reflections on gravitation, had appeared in 1687 in his *The Mathematical Principles of Natural Knowledge*. Just a bit earlier, William Harvey (1578-1657) had discovered the basic principles of the circulatory system, and he published his ground-breaking work *On the Motion of the Heart* in 1628. In 1661 appeared Robert Boyle's *Skeptical Chemist*. In this work and others Boyle explored the nature of gases and supported the emerging atomic theory by pointing to the possibility of creating a vacuum.

It seemed to Condorcet that all of reality would soon be known by applying the methods expounded by Newton and utilized by the other scientists of his era. The details of Newton's scientific methodology–his application of logic to mathematically analyzed and expressed sense data, and his insistence on the principles of simplicity and uniformity–were unknown to the *philosophes*. Nor did they know the antecedent of Newton's method in the thought of the thirteenth-century philosopher Robert Grosseteste. Details such as these were irrelevant for the *philosophes*, for they held to the simplistic notion that by reason, and reason alone, humans can know all things. By the simple application of reason, all of society's ills could and would be solved as readily as the secrets of the physical world had been disclosed.

B. Enlightened Cosmology and Anthropology

The universe in which the *philosophes* lived was, of course, rational and hence accessible to the human mind through its exercise of reason. Most *philo-*

sophes, those we call Deists, thought the existence of the universe required the existence of an entity variously called the Prime Mover, the First Cause, or the Necessary Being. This is the language of Thomas Aquinas, a vocabulary the *philosophes* may have learned from their Jesuit teachers. But the sophisticated proofs which Thomas offered were ignored as unnecessary by the *philosophes*. As we have said, few *philosophes* were philosophers, though they were enthusiastic social reformers. The Prime Mover of the *philosophes*, unlike that of Thomas, did not concern itself with its creation, for it had set in motion a perfect, rational world that needed no further attention. The Prime Mover was sometimes likened to a Celestial Clockmaker who had made the Perfect Clock–and then walked away from it. To pray to such an entity would be absurd, the Deists thought. The Prime Mover ignores us, and it is only rational for us to ignore the Prime Mover.

The Enlightenment defined human beings as rational animals, a definition derived from Aristotle and Aquinas. But the *philosophes* stressed the "rational" component of the definition more than had their philosophic predecessors. As we know, they confidently–perhaps naively–asserted that all of reality could be eventually known by reason. Since they did not believe in a moral "Fall," they rejected the idea that Original Sin had darkened the human intellect.

C. The Origin of Evil

Unaffected by any superstitious primeval sin, the human will is completely free to choose human destiny. Of course, what human should–and shall–choose is the good clearly seen through reason. Human happiness requires no supernatural intervention–indeed, there is no such thing as the supernatural, save in the clouded minds of ignorant people. Ignorance, for the *philosophes*, is the only evil; enlightenment leads inevitably to happiness.

How is it, then, that we suffer evil, that we are in ignorance? All the pain, suffering, and injustice that humans endure has been inflicted on humans by two evil institutions, the Church and the state. The *philosophes* thought that unenlightened governments must be overthrown and replaced with an institution enlightened by reason. The Church does not need replacement; it needs annihilation. *Écrasez l'infâme* ("wipe out the infamous thing") was the battle cry provided by Voltaire (1694-1778), the most famous advocate of the Enlightenment. One of his disciples, Denis Diderot (1713-1784), added: "The world will not be happy until the last king is strangled in the entrails of the last priest."

What Voltaire and his fellow *philosophes* did not consider were questions they did not bother to ask. If humans have been free from all evil since the beginning of the species, how is it that evil institutions arose, since institutions are human creations? How have the tyranny and oppression inflicted on humans by the state arisen? The superstition and ignorance inculcated by the clergy seem difficult to explain if all humans–including, presumably, clergymen–have always been good by nature.

D. Religious Intolerance and Enlightened Toleration

Philosophical inconsistencies aside, there was still much about the contemporary Churches which could arouse the ire of thinking people. Both Protestant and Catholic Churches upheld the idea of the depravity or near-depravity of human beings. There was a strong component of anti-intellectualism in all the denominations–some going so far as to teach that faith was the only source of true knowledge. Jews and Christians alike read the Bible so literally that their leaders taught absurdities at odds with even the most elementary science. But the most powerful argument against the claims of religion was the inhumanity with which the adherents of all the religions treated each other. Christians, in particular, were not known for their love for one another.

In Voltaire's brilliant essay *Religion*, he told a story of being awakened one night by an archangel who led him on a journey through history: "He transplanted me," wrote Voltaire, "to a desert all covered with piled-up bones." Before the first pile, the archangel said: "These are the twenty-three thousand Jews who danced before a calf, along with twenty-four thousand killed while fornicating with Midianite women." The inhumanity of the Jewish God was matched by the brutality of Christians. Voltaire is shown "the bones of Christians slaughtered by each other because of doctrinal disagreements." Likewise, the archangel informed him: "Muslims have been sullied with the same inhumanity."

Much further on, the archangel led Voltaire to "a man of gentle, simple countenance, who seemed to me to be about thirty-five years old,...his feet swollen and bleeding, his hands too, his side pierced, and his ribs flayed with whip cuts." The man informed Voltaire that it had been by "wicked priests and wicked judges" that he had been killed. His death had not been due to his desire to teach a new religion, for "all I said to them was 'Love God with all your heart and your fellow-creature as yourself.'" Voltaire asked: "If one loves God, one can then eat meat on Friday?" The figure answered: "I always ate what was given me."

Voltaire allowed his story to end only after the practices of Catholicism were derided and dismissed with brilliantly witty satire. Since Voltaire was French, his most stinging barbs were directed against the traditional faith of his countrymen. But Voltaire and his fellows were convinced that all religions were frauds. The toleration the *philosophes* preached stemmed from the rejection of all religions, not out of respect for the various virtues of each.

E. Enlightened Politics

With what or whom should the last unenlightened king be replaced? All the *philosophes* agreed that it was essential that enlightened men should govern.

Through their rational rule, all social evils—war and hunger, prejudice and injustice—would be overcome. The key to universal progress is the government's introduction of a rational system of education. Education will lead to enlightenment; enlightenment will lead to universal happiness.

There was no such agreement about the best form of government. Some *philosophes* like Voltaire were convinced that an enlightened monarchy is the best form of government, for having but one man at the helm will more efficiently bring about justice—an argument Aristotle had used. Other *philosophes*—Thomas Jefferson (1743-1826), for example—thought an enlightened aristocracy would be best. The ruling class Jefferson had in mind was not, of course, titled nobility, but the wise and wealthy plantation owners of Virginia and the less genteel merchants and manufacturers of Massachusetts.

A very few *philosophes* thought the majority of the people should rule. Jean-Jacques Rousseau (1712-1778) was one of them, but his version of democracy bears little resemblance to what we now mean by that form of government. For Rousseau, human beings originally lived in a state of noble savagery. They were free, equal, and happy until some of them began claiming ownership over some part of their natural surroundings. The remedy is that each of these unhappy folk must enter into what Rousseau called a "social contract" with all the others. Individuals must surrender their liberty to the all-powerful sovereignty of the whole. Decisions of the majority should indeed prevail in this political system—or they would if the majority were in fact enlightened. Since that happy condition has not yet been realized, Rousseau relied on what he called the general will: what the majority would choose if it were enlightened. But only those already enlightened could possibly know what those enlightened choices would be. This is clearly a formula for tyranny, and, indeed, modern history has seen a host of dictators—from Robespierre through Napoleon to Hitler and Stalin—who have "known" what is best for the people.

The form of enlightened government that was actually put into practice in the eighteenth century was monarchy—an enlightened monarchy, of course. One of Voltaire's patrons and associates was the brilliant monarch of Prussia, King Frederick II (1740-1786). Frederick applied the laws of reason to statecraft with a remarkable degree of success. He codified Prussian law, abolished torture, and introduced a rational administrative system. He encouraged economic growth by granting subsides to infant industries and built roads and canals to carry to market the goods produced. He also employed the reformed Prussian army to provide protection for both manufacture and market—expanding that market by conquest of neighboring lands.

Frederick fostered public education, thus bringing enlightenment to his subjects. He even proposed, when the Jesuits were suppressed, to enlist them as teachers in his schools. He embraced Prussia's long-standing policy of welcoming exiled French Calvinists, the Huguenots, to his kingdom. In neither case, however, was his decision an expression of sympathy for their religion. His sort of toleration was that of a thoroughly enlightened skeptic who treated all religions equally because they were all equally false.

Frederick's contemporary, the emperor Joseph II, was co-ruler of the Austrian domains with his mother, Maria Theresa, from 1768 to 1780 and sole ruler from 1780 to 1790. In 1784, he wrote to his agent in Rome, Cardinal Herzan: "I have made philosophy the legislator of my empire." On the basis of that enlightened stance he promoted religious toleration for all. For farmers, he introduced greater freedom, a just land-tenure system, and a fairer share of the tax burden. Like Frederick, he reformed the legal and administrative structures and practices of his realm. He went beyond Frederick by introducing a compulsory primary and secondary educational system. He also reformed the curriculum in his universities by stressing "practical" subjects, like law, science, and medicine, at the expense of philosophy and theology.

Although Joseph strove to be a sincere Christian, he declared: "It is necessary that I remove from the domain of religion some matters that never truly belonged to it." "I myself detest superstition," he wrote to Cardinal Herzan, "to it we owe the degradation of the human mind." To reform religion in his domains, he required bishops to take an oath of allegiance to him, realigned diocesan and parish boundaries, and forbad pluralism. He closed existing Church-controlled seminaries and created five state-controlled schools where the education of future priests attained a high academic level. Monasteries dedicated wholly to prayer and meditation Joseph declared wasteful of men and resources. Fortunately for the monks of such monasteries, there were a great many secondary schools without a faculty due to the suppression of the Jesuits. The monks replaced them, but had to leave their monasteries and move to the sites of the schools. All of Joseph's church legislation was intended to reform the Catholic Church, not destroy it, though the popes of the time surely did not see it that way.

F. New Forms of Religion

As Joseph's "enlightened" Catholicism exhibited a new face, so too did the Protestant and Jewish forms of what was called "rational religion." The liberal Protestantism of most "mainstream" or "downtown" churches of today was born in the eighteenth century. From that time, "liberal" theologians have approached the Bible critically, applying to the scriptural books the same sort of historical and literary criticism scholars used in analyzing other texts. Some supporters of "rational religion" went so far as to reject all biblical inconsistencies–the varying stories told in the gospels, for example. They also excised any references to the miraculous, since miracles were impossible and belief in them mere superstition. This left little of traditional Protestantism intact. What the new breed of theologians did accept were those religious teachings which were restatements of rational ethical positions like the Golden Rule's "Do unto others as you would have them do unto you." Traditional practices of religion like prayer seemed to many thinkers to be worse than useless. But, the leaders of liberal Protestantism declared, there are many unenlightened people in the world who need supernatural sanction before they can make proper ethical choices and exhibit enlightened behavior. Those still on their way to education and enlightenment need their faith to guide them.

Liberal or Reform Judaism similarly rejected much that was traditional, most notably the detailed behavioral prescriptions and proscriptions of the Law of Moses. Enlightened Jews gathered in temples on the Sabbath, not in Orthodox synagogues, and the most enlightened of them went to neither. Some Reform Jews saw the Messiah in a novel, enlightened way: as the progress that God had promised and that human beings had attained through reason. Particularly in Germany, where there were larger numbers of Jews than anywhere else in Europe, Jews became assimilated to the middle class life of their gentile neighbors and often took scant notice of their Jewish heritage.

The leader of the Reform Jewish community in eighteenth-century Berlin was a philosopher, Moses Mendelssohn (1729-1786). His gentile friend and philosophic collaborator, Gotthold Ephraim Lessing (1729-1781), was a famous dramatist, art critic, philosopher of history, and ethical teacher. Lessing's 1779 play, *Nathan the Wise*, was set in Jerusalem during the Crusades. The theme of the drama is religious toleration, and the plot features a revealing dialogue between a Muslim ruler and his Jewish advisor. The advisor, Nathan, was modeled on Moses Mendelssohn. Lessing described Nathan–and hence his friend Moses–in this way:

> How free of prejudice his lofty soul
> His heart to every virtue how unlocked
> With every lovely feeling how familiar
> O what a Jew he is! Yet wishes
> Only to pass as a Jew.

Within the parable play, the ruler asks Nathan: "Which is the true religion?" Nathan replies with a story about "a ring of marvelous worth" which was bequeathed by its owner to "the most beloved of his sons." With the ring the son–and his descendants down through the ages–"became the heads and chieftains of their house." At length the ring and its power passed to a man who loved his three sons equally, and so he had two more rings made, both exactly the same as the original. At the father's death the three sons came with their rings to claim the headship of the house, but "the true ring was not distinguishable." "Almost as undistinguishable," Nathan adds, "as to us now is the true religion." A kindly judge declares against the authenticity of all three rings, but urges each brother to strive to exhibit "the virtue of his ring." This can be done through "gentleness and heartiest friendliness, with benevolence and true devotedness to God." This moving plea for religious toleration reflects all the components of the enlightenment approach to religion. All traditional religions are equal in their inadequacy. True values are found not in revelation but as the fruits of reason.

G. The French Revolutions

The Enlightenment that is reflected in the words and deeds of Frederick of Prussia, Joseph of Austria, Moses Mendelssohn, and Gotthold Lessing is a calmer, less radical expression than that of Voltaire, Diderot, and Rousseau. It was the latter group, however, that inspired the explosive movements of revolution which rocked Europe from 1788 to 1815. Remembering that the twin causes of evil, as the Enlightenment saw them, were the Church and the state, politics and religion will be our chief concerns in examining this hectic era–a period crucial to understanding our culture today.

The series of revolutions that shook France at the end of the eighteenth century had its roots in the chronic debt plaguing Louis XVI's government. This monarch, who ruled from 1774 to his execution in 1793, sought to raise taxes to overcome his country's dire financial condition. The nobility of France responded in a very medieval fashion, by demanding that the Estates General–the French equivalent of the English Parliament–be called to consider the question. The Estates General had not been called since 1614–not once during the seventy-two year reign of Louis XIV (1643-1713), who, we remember, ruled by divine right. His grandson and successor Louis XV (1715-1774), ruled by the same right and with the same disregard for France's historic representative assembly. Louis XVI was faced, however, with a demand for taxation only through representation, and so, by agreeing to call the Estates General, he set in motion forces that would eventually overthrow him.

In April 1789, the delegates began to arrive at Versailles, the royal palace outside Paris. These delegates were seated in three groups. The First Estate consisted of the highest ranks of the clergy, the Second Estate comprised the nobility, and the Third Estate represented all others–some ninety-six percent of the population of France. Since each house voted separately, some four percent of the population received two votes, while the rest received but one.

The delegates of the Third Estate arrived carrying lists of grievances, called *cahiers*, for which the king had called. The modest nature of the proposals expressed in these *cahiers* is shown by calls for equality of representation, for freedom from arbitrary imprisonment, for the inviolability of property, and for access to positions of responsibility in both government and the military. Although the religious commitment of the rural majority was clearly expressed in their desire for education in "the principles of religion," that education, the farmers petitioned, should be in public schools. The reform of the Church was clearly their concern: they wanted priests to reside in their parishes, poor relief removed from Church control and made subject to local government, and the sacraments administered without fees being charged.

When each Estate began its deliberations, however, it was not pious farmers who controlled the process. The Third Estate was composed almost exclusively of middle class members: bankers, merchants, literary figures, and, especially, lawyers. These delegates were well aware of the radical reforms demanded by the *philosophes*, and most of them agreed with some or all of the Enlightenment stances. On June 17, 1789, the Third Estate declared itself the National Assembly and charged itself with writing a new constitution for France. One month later, on July 14, a riotous Paris crowd, seeking weapons with which to arm itself, stormed and destroyed a fortress prison called the Bastille. This act frightened the king into submission and provided France with a symbol of a new order celebrated to this day as a national holiday.

The National Assembly, while working on a constitution for France, also assumed the role of legislator. Its "Decree Abolishing the Feudal System" eliminated most of the nobles' privileges. Its "Declaration of the Rights of Man," proclaimed in September of 1789, is a document reflecting middle-class interests: desire for liberty, security, and property, for freedom of speech and of the press, for religious toleration. What religious toleration meant to these men is shown by their confiscation of all church property and by the "Civil Constitution of the Clergy," enacted in July of 1790. The parish clergy were henceforth to be elected by the people–all the people, no matter what their religious preferences or anti-religious convictions. Those who were elected were to swear allegiance to the new order and sever all ties with Rome. To ensure compliance, clergymen were to be paid by the public treasury, a payment administered, of course, by agents of the government. Monastic and other religious orders were abolished, since theirs had been the control of education, now in the hands of an enlightened state. To wean the people away from their traditional religion, a substitute was also offered with the erection of "altars to the fatherland."

On the first of October of 1791, a new constitution and a new government were in place. Things were not really so new, as the Legislative Assembly had been created by the National Assembly and reflected its middle class, enlightened views. Voting for the new Assembly was indirect: male taxpayers of twenty-five years or more voted for electors, who then chose the Assembly delegates, who were required to be property owners. This system ensured that the wealthy and educated members of the middle class would govern, creating a Jeffersonian aristocracy of merit.

During its brief sway, the Legislative Assembly abolished the age-old administrative structure of France that had been based on provinces with traditional names like Champagne and Burgundy. It replaced these relics of the "Dark Ages" with a grid of *départments* of nearly equal size and with names derived from the areas' natural features–mostly rivers, but some mountains as well. History was thus replaced with a natural, therefore rational, and therefore good, political organization. The Assembly also issued a "Decree Against the Non-juring Clergy." This law was directed against those clergymen who, dismayed at the radical ecclesiastical measures of the government, had refused to take an oath of allegiance to that government. Clerics accused of this crime were thereafter to be deported.

The Legislative Assembly did not go farther in its campaign to restructure Church and state, for it was overthrown, in August of 1792, by a Paris mob led by extreme radicals of middle-class origin. New elections, conducted according to universal manhood suffrage, produced the National Convention that then moved to realize the democratic goals of Rousseau. In January 1793, this government executed King Louis XVI by a new, rational means, the guillotine, designed to replace the medieval barbarity of hangman's noose or axeman's blade with a painless–they thought–procedure. The democracy of the Convention quickly turned into a dictatorship by the Committee of Public Safety, twelve men who worked in secret to control the country. This group was soon taken over by Maximilien Robespierre, who presided over the systematic executions of at least twenty-five thousand citizens, many of them merely on suspicion.

On May 7, 1794, the government issued a "Decree Establishing the Worship of the Supreme Being," by which, it was hoped, Christianity would be replaced. The "duties of man," the Decree declared, were "to detest bad faith and tyranny, to punish tyrants and traitors,...and not to be unjust to anyone." Festivals were instituted to replace Christian feast days–festivals of the Supreme Being and of Nature, of the Benefactors of Humanity, to Hatred of Tyrants and Tyranny, to Agriculture, and to Industry. France soon tired of Robespierre's rule and his execution of traitors in the so-called Reign of Terror. In the end, he was himself guillotined.

The reaction which ensued, called Thermidorian after the month (July) of the revolutionary, anti-Christian calendar in which it occurred, was led and controlled by the propertied upper middle class–a return to Jeffersonian aristocracy. Its government, the Directory, was, in turn, overthrown in 1799 by Napoleon Bonaparte, marking the sixth French revolution since 1788. Napoleon employed the most democratic means of all, the plebiscite–a direct vote by each citizen–to support his overthrow of the Directory and, later, his assumption of the office of French Emperor. Robespierrian "democracy" had once again led to dictatorship.

Napoleon was, of course, a brilliant, indefatigable general who conquered all of Europe, save Britain and Russia. But his endless wars required troops. Although Napoleon employed thousands upon thousands of Germans, Austrians, Italians, Spaniards, and Portuguese as cannon fodder, the core of his army was French. Those French soldiers were necessarily recruited from the largest component of the populace: its farmers. Unaffected by the Enlightenment those farmers were almost to a man solidly Catholic. Napoleon, as an enlightened general and ruler, had no use for religion, but he had great need for those who adhered to it. He was convinced that God was "always on the side with the most cannon," but, he counseled his diplomats, "always treat the pope as if he had 200,000 men." Knowing the power of religion over French recruits, Napoleon concluded the Concordat of 1801 with Pope Pius VII (1800-1823).

This treaty acknowledged that "the Catholic, Apostolic, and Roman religion is the religion of the great majority of French citizens." The Church in France was to be completely reorganized. New bishops were to be named by Napoleon and recognized by the pope without any opportunity for dissent. The new bishops were to take an "oath of fidelity" to Napoleon. Church buildings in France were to be "put at the disposal of the bishops," but ownership of churches and church properties remained in the hands of the state–as is the case still today. Caesaropapism, rule of the Church by the state, was now practiced by a man who disdained the supernatural.

An *Imperial Catechism*, issued by Napoleon in 1806, shows the extent and effect of this Caesaropapism. By reciting by rote the answers to questions posed in this catechism, French girls and boys learned how to be good Christians. Asked "what are the duties of Christians...toward Napoleon I, our emperor?", French children would reply in unison: "Christians owe...our emperor, Napoleon I, love, respect, obedience, fidelity, military service, and taxes....We also owe him fervent prayers for his safety." Napoleon, now acknowledged as the "anointed of the Lord," was surely more interested in the military service than in the prayers.

H. The New Force

Napoleon's downfall began in the Russian snowdrifts of the winter of 1812. Of his invading army of some 600,000 men, only one in six returned. His "allies," most of them puppet governments, began to desert him. Even the weak and vacillating king of Prussia, Frederick William III, assembled enough courage, in 1813, to issue an "Appeal to My People," urging resistance to Napoleon and the French.

Frederick William's appeal extended to those beyond his kingdom of Prussia, "to all Germans." There was at the time no political entity called Germany; there never had been one, and there would not be one until 1871. But while there was no Germany, there were Germans, and those Germans had a once glorious past. To that shared history the king appealed in a very unenlightened manner. "Think of the times gone past," exclaimed Frederick William, "remember the blessings for which your forefathers fought...and for which they paid with their blood: freedom of conscience, national honor, independence, commerce, industry, learning."

"National honor" could be achieved, apparently, even if there were no state that represented the whole nation. This national honor was not envisaged as exclusively German: "Look at the great example of our powerful allies, the Russians; look at the Spaniards, the Portuguese....Witness the heroic Swiss and the people of the Netherlands."

Germans could join this heroic band, believed Frederick William: "Faith in God, perseverance, and the powerful aid of our allies will bring us victory....We must fight to a victorious end, unless we are willing to cease to be Prussians or Germans." The only alternatives available, the king declared, are "an honorable peace or a heroic end." "However," he added, "we may confidently await the outcome. God and our own firm purpose will bring victory to our cause and with it an assured and glorious peace and the return of happier times."

This was an appeal to emotion, not to reason. It was an appeal to national pride, not the cosmopolitan uniformity taught by the Enlightenment. It was an appeal to a past scorned by the *philosophes*. It was an appeal to a God whose activity in human affairs the Enlightenment denied. It was the beginning of a new religion, nationalism, that would sometimes be allied with traditional Christianity and sometimes be opposed to it. It would become, in the course of the nineteenth and twentieth centuries, the most powerful alternative to another religion, Marxism–a religion simultaneously in the process of creation.

In October of 1813, at the "Battle of the Peoples," Napoleon was defeated by a coalition that included virtually all the other nations of Europe. In 1815, Napoleon's attempt to regain control of Europe was quashed at Waterloo by Prussia's Marshal Blücher and Great Britain's Duke of Wellington. Nationalism had seemingly defeated the forces of the *philosophes*, but the Enlightenment did not die. It is still very much with us.

XV. RELIGION IN CONSERVATIVE AND ROMANTIC CULTURE

Some Useful Data

1707-1778	Carolus Linnaeus, Swedish botanist
1729-1797	Edmund Burke, Irish politician
1735-1826	John Adams, American president
1743-1826	Thomas Jefferson, American president
1749-1832	Johann Wolfgang von Goethe, German scientist and dramatist
1770-1850	William Wordsworth, English poet
1799-1856	Heinrich Heine, German poet
1786-1859	Wilhelm Grimm, German language scholar
1785-1863	Jakob Grimm, German language scholar
1801-1890	John Henry Newman, English ecclesiastic
1817-1894	Austin Henry Layard, British politician
1811-1899	Robert Lowe, British politician

A. The Conservative Response

On the same day, July 4, 1826, two distinguished American statesmen and former presidents died. They were John Adams and Thomas Jefferson. Though they had been political rivals, their relationship had mellowed after retirement, and correspondence flowed between Adams, living in Quincy, Massachusetts, and Jefferson, at his Monticello home near Charlottesville, Virginia.

On July 15, 1813, Adams had composed a letter to Jefferson in which he shared his musings on the wars and revolutions that had ravaged Europe since 1789. Adams inquired:

> Let me now ask you very seriously, my friend, where are now, in 1813, the perfection and perfectability of human nature? Where is now the progress of the human mind? Where is the amelioration of society? Where the augmentations of human comforts? Where the diminutions of human pains and miseries?

The progress preached by Condorcet, the perfection predicted by all the *philosophes*, including Jefferson, had, to Adams' mind, been dispelled by the horrors of the Reign of Terror and disproven by the famine and slaughter inflicted on the nations of Europe by the revolutionary governments of France. The liberalism of enlightened thinkers had been translated into revolutionary slaughter and these appalling consequences led many to a conservative reaction.

1. The Politics of Edmund Burke

The most influential of those responding was Edmund Burke (1729-1797), who in 1790 published his *Reflections on the Revolution in France*. Burke laid the blame for the damaging effects of that revolution on the abstract theories of the Enlightenment that, in his opinion, had done away with the political wisdom Europeans had gained through ages of experience. He held that *philosophes'* declarations of the rights of humankind were arbitrary and inadequate. Implicit in this conservative critique is a conviction that reason is not capable of knowing everything. Answers to human problems, Burke believed, are best achieved through consulting the wisdom of past generations as well as by considering the impact those answers will have on future generations. Arbitrary and momentary--if apparently rational--declarations of rights put a government in the untenable position of having no sanction for its policies outside the opinions of the governing group. Opponents can always claim that their own policies are more rational and thus superior. This unstable situation leads to the arbitrary cancellation of all human rights. That, thought Burke, is precisely what was happening in revolutionary France.

There are indeed some rights which come to us from nature, thought

Burke. These include the rights to security, justice, and freedom. The way in which these rights are realized, however, should depend on the collective wisdom of many generations. Nations differ because their histories differ, and so the rights of people in various nations take different forms. For example, Burke thought independence should be granted to the American colonies because of their centuries-long experience in self-government. He would have opposed granting immediate and total independence to peoples whom colonial powers had denied administrative and legislative experience.

The form which government should take–whether monarchical or republican, for example–will differ from nation to nation because of their differing historical experiences. Burke was fearful of a democracy without checks on the will of the majority, for observation had convinced him that the majority does not always choose what is in the best interest of all the people. As a conservative he favored a government representative of the interests of each group in the nation, with those interests balanced through compromise.

Much later than the time, 1790, when Burke wrote, conservatives in Great Britain passed, in 1867, an election reform bill which for the first time allowed members of the urban working class to vote. Some members of the Liberal Party vehemently opposed the bill. Robert Lowe (1811-1899) led the fight against extending the franchise based on his Enlightenment principles. "I am a Liberal," he wrote, "and I know that by pure and clear intelligence alone can the cause of true progress be promoted." Lowe warned that giving workers the vote would lead to a graduated income tax and thus to socialism. Sir Austin Henry Layard (1817-1894), Lowe's conservative opponent, claimed socialism would not prevail even if the working class were to vote its own selfish interests. Layard was secure in the knowledge that the balance of powers in the British constitution–between king, the House of Lords, and the House of Commons–would prevent any single group from disregarding the rights and interests of other groups.

Burke had agreed that all a nation's political and economic interests should be represented in the governmental process. He also insisted that governmental power should be as restricted and as decentralized as possible. This was because, as Lord John Acton was to say, "power tends to corrupt and absolute power corrupts absolutely." Implicit in this view is another rejection of radical Enlightenment thought. Human beings are not immune from evil, and the only evil is not ignorance. Humans can know that an action is evil and still choose that evil.

2. *Conservative Culture and Religion*

For conservatives, then, the proper ordering of society is based on more than reason. The heritage of the past provides the restraining concepts necessary for the welfare of both individuals and the community. One effective restraint on aberrant behavior is a legacy handed down from the Middle Ages: the notion of the lady and of the gentleman. As Cardinal John Henry Newman (1801-1890) was to say: "A gentleman is one who would never willingly hurt another person." Another powerful restraint on anti-social behavior, Burke and Newman agreed, is religion. The precepts of religion are a much more effective curb on the human choice of evil than the force exercised by the state–though that is sometimes necessary as well.

Edmund Burke was born in Dublin, but he was not a Roman Catholic. His deep loyalties lay with the Church of Ireland, the Irish branch of the Anglican Communion of which American Episcopalians are now a part. Yet one of Burke's severest criticisms of the French revolutionaries was how they had despoiled and attempted to eradicate the Catholic Church. For Burke, all religions are good, for they restrain immoral behavior. They are also based on faith, a necessary complement to finite human reason. Toleration, according to the *philosophes*, was based on indifference: all religions were obstacles to progress. Toleration for conservatives was based on the truths they believed all religions told and the good they thought all religions fostered. There is a God, conservatives believed, and he acts in time. The history that results is not necessarily progressive, for humans are capable of rejecting the good. Not all conservatives were members of organized churches, but clearly Conservatism would be a powerful force supporting religion in the nineteenth and twentieth centuries. So too would be Romanticism.

B. The Romantic Revolution

1. Goethe and the Daemonic

Johann Wolfgang von Goethe lived from 1749 to 1832. Although he was employed as the chief scientist at the court at Weimar in central Germany and was well known for his significant discoveries in botany, comparative anatomy, and optics, he is best known today for his outstanding contributions to the field of literature. Goethe's autobiography, published over the period 1811 to 1833, is titled *Poetry and Truth*. The work, written in the third person, tells us of a strange force present in the universe:

> He [Goethe] thought he could detect in nature–both animate and inanimate, both with and without soul–something that manifested itself only in contradictions and which, therefore, could not be comprehended under any idea, still less under one word. It was not godlike, for it seemed without reason; not human, for it had no understanding; not devilish, for it was beneficent; not angelic, for it often betrayed malicious delight.

Goethe's struggle with the apparent contradictions in this perceived force led, at least, to a name: "To this principle, which seemed to come in between all other principles and separate them–and yet link them together–I gave the name daemonic."

To give the force a name does not tell us what it is. So Goethe searched history and his own experience for persons who possess the daemonic to an outstanding degree. Among these he singled out Count Egmont, an historical figure little-known in Goethe's or in our own day, but a subject Goethe studied intensely during his extensive historical researches. Egmont was a leader of the Dutch forces in their sixteenth-century struggle for independence from Spain. That struggle, Goethe found, was "in the highest degree dramatic," and Egmont's "greatness as a man and as a hero captivated" him. Goethe saw him as youthful, free "from all fettering restraints," filled with "unlimited love of life, boundless self-confidence, and having a gift of attracting all sorts of people." Although Goethe believed the daemonic is part of all nature–and in our own human nature–it shows itself most obviously in outstanding people, in heroes and heroines: "A tremendous energy seems to emanate from them, and they exercise a wonderful power over all creatures."

In Johann Peter Eckermann's *Conversations of Goethe with Eckermann* (1836), we hear more talk about this daemonic force "which cannot be explained by reason or understanding, which lies not in my nature though I am subject to it." It manifests itself in persons "full of unlimited power of action and unrest" and is "perceptible in events...and throughout nature." Clearly Goethe perceived what the *philosophes* had not: that nature is much more than a rationally constructed machine. The world and the humans who inhabit it are bubbling over with a super-rational force scarce dreamed of by the rationalists of the Enlightenment.

According to Goethe, the existence of that unconscious or super-conscious force is demonstrated by our dreams. That force is released into the conscious world by artists of all sorts, by musicians, painters, and poets. Indeed, there seems to have been a strong current in Romanticism that identified poetry as the true philosophy. "Religious worship" too, Goethe tells us, "cannot dispense with this force, for it is one of the chief means of working upon people miraculously." This daemonic force assumed for some Romantics a quasi-divine status as a sort of pantheistic spirit. As the movement matured, however, most Romantics saw God as transcending nature, not as identical with it. They, unlike the *philosophes*, thought they could communicate with the God of nature. Some Romantics, like Goethe, were not committed to Christianity or any other religion, but they recognized religion as a natural, positive phenomenon. Moreover, most Romantics became active believers as they grew older and, they thought, wiser.

Romanticism was revolutionary. It rebelled against Enlightenment, against what Romantics saw as a world-view that focused on but a narrow part of reality, which stifled creativity with stultifying rules, and which exhibited the crassest sort of materialism. Conservatism, as we have seen, was also a reaction to the Enlightenment. Although Romanticism shared much with Conservatism, the two movements were not the same. Some Romantics were indeed Conservatives, but some were political liberals of a moderate sort. And some followed Goethe in disregarding politics altogether. "The politician will devour the poet," said Goethe–meaning that intense activity in politics would consume the creative energies of the artist.

2. Science and the Origins of Romanticism

The background of Romanticism is strikingly similar to the origins of the Enlightenment. In both cases scientific breakthroughs elicited new modes of thought. For the Enlightenment, we remember, it was the new physics and astronomy of Newton and his generation. Romanticism's creed that reason was not sufficient in understanding reality was based in part on eighteenth-century advances in the life sciences. The first steps taken in botany and zoology had been the collection of biological samples from all over the planet in order that scientists, like Carolus Linnaeus (1707-1778), could classify them systematically. What biologists soon found–although Linnaeus would never admit it–was that neat, orderly arrangements were impossible because the animals and plants were aggravatingly resistant to rational sorting and structuring. This led many scientists, among them Goethe, to wonder if the fault were not with the animals and plants but with human minds. It seemed that those minds could not know everything by the use of reason but insisted on substituting their mental vision of reality for the truly real.

Nature, thought the Romantics, can be known better by experiencing it than by abstractly reasoning about it. A tree can be investigated scientifically, but a complete analysis of its microstructure requires chopping the tree down. In the process, Romantics declared, the most important feature of the tree, its life, is lost. Romantics like Goethe did not reject science as a method of knowing, but they were convinced that all nature was infused with the same daemonic spirit or soul, and thus the daemonic in humans could reach out to commune with nature as well as analyze it.

3. The World of Simple Beauty

Communing with nature, Romantics were sure, could not succeed on a merely abstract level. The nature Romantics experienced was that of unique individuals, and this led to an appreciation of forms of beauty foreign to the aesthetics of the *philosophes*. Enlightenment painting, for example, portrayed serious men and women as young yet mature and as persons reflecting the ideals of classical beauty. They were perfect people set in rationally arranged settings. Romantics were fascinated by the powers of nature, by waterfalls and pounding surf. Their human figures were sometimes old, sometimes young, sometimes ugly. Romantic artists and poets were fascinated by the unique, the singular, the simple. The English author William Wordsworth (1770-1850) offers us an example of a simple poem, written in a simple meter, and using everyday words. The poem, *We Are Seven*, has a rural setting and features an unsophisticated girl:

> I met a little cottage girl.

> She was eight years old, she said;
> Her hair was thick with many a curl
> That clustered round her head.
> She had a rustic, woodland air,
> And she was wildly clad;
> Her eyes were fair, and very fair;
> Her beauty made me glad.

The visitor inquires of the girl the number of her brothers and sisters:

> Then did the little maid reply,
> "Seven boys and girls are we;
> Two of us in the church-yard lie,
> Beneath the church-yard tree."

She rejects the protest of the visitor that there are only five now in her family:

> "Their graves are green; they may be seen,"
> The little maid replied,
> "Twelve steps or more from my mother's door,
> And they are side by side."

The maid sits by the graves knitting her stockings, hemming her kerchief, singing songs to her siblings. And no matter how much the visitor presses his rational objections, the maid maintains the enduring communion among the seven siblings.

4. *The Restless Quest for Happiness*

How does one attain happiness in this romantic world? Goethe offered a comprehensive reply to this crucial question in his powerful drama *Faust* (published in two parts, in 1808 and 1832). Faust, the protagonist of the play, is a middle-aged professor in a sixteenth-century university. He is a man intensely dissatisfied with his life:

> I've studied, alas, philosophy
> And jurisprudence, medicine,
> And worst of all theology,
> From end to end, with labor keen.
> And here I am, for all my lore,
> The wretched fool I was before....
> These ten long years, with many woes,
> I've led my scholars by the nose,
> Have seen that nothing can be known!

Faust has mastered all four disciplines of the medieval university; he has amassed all the knowledge that the rational mind can discover. He rejects it all, both the deceiving faith of his childhood and the meaningless existence of his intellectual maturity. In frustration, he cries out: "No dog would endure such a curst existence! Wherefore from magic I seek assistance."

Faust then sells his soul to Mephistopheles, a demon, in return for the power to obtain whatever he wants. But he is left with the necessity of choosing what he wants. Reason and faith he has rejected as guides; so he embraces, without direction or plan, experiences of all sorts, activities of all kinds. Painfully enough, he knows beforehand that his choices will not bring him happiness. He knows that fame does not last, that gold is more easily lost than gained, that possessions are but deceptions, and that neither action nor sloth bring contentment. He recognizes that overindulging in food and drink and sex brings the boredom of satiation but can also lead to pain. Finding no other options, his ensuing prolonged plunge into a myriad of experiences leaves him weary of life and ready to embrace death.

But when "the gruesome jaws of hell open up" to receive Faust, a band of angels swoops down to seize him and carry him off to eternal bliss. This seems strange indeed, since Faust has not performed one redeeming good deed throughout his wild and reckless career. It is, oddly enough, Mephistopheles who grudgingly discerns the explanation for Faust's salvation: the redeeming power of love. It is love, not the Enlightenment's reason, that will bring happiness to humans.

5. *Romantic Culture and Religion*

Many Romantics embraced a Faustian life of experience and activity free from moral restraint. Like Faust they learned that, lacking a means of structuring that experience, of learning from that activity, their pleasure turned to dust, leaving them frustrated and bored. Goethe's solution was to recapture what was best in the classics of antiquity, particularly its tool in reason, and combine it with the energies released by Romanticism. More often Romantics turned to religion to make sense of life's experiences. Some sought meaning in a Protestantism that Heinrich Heine (1799-1856) identified with freedom of thought, but most of the Romantics who embraced or came back to Christianity chose Catholicism or, in Great Britain, Anglicanism. They were influenced, at least in part, by its aesthetic components: the grandeur of Gothic architecture and the "smells and bells" that enhanced, they thought, the beautiful mysteries of its liturgy.

Romantics reveled in the Gothic, and the early nineteenth century saw a movement in architecture called the Gothic revival. Folk tales from the distant past were collected by the language scholars Jakob Grimm (1785-1863) and his brother Wilhelm (1786-1859). These stories were thought to embody the spirit of the common folk of the Middle Ages and could serve as means of reaching and releasing hidden daemonic forces. Those forces were also to be found in communing with nature–a nature no longer coldly mechanical, but organic, alive, and personified as Mother Nature.

The first half of the nineteenth century was an era much more friendly to religion than the half century preceding it. Conservatism recognized the social utility of religion, and Romanticism saw it as way of exploring the super-rational forces animating the universe. All religions were viewed as positive cultural forces, and thus all religions should thus be tolerated. At the same time, commitment to a particular religion, to an institutional church, became socially acceptable in many circles.

However, Enlightenment ideas would soon return in new forms. Eventually, political Liberalism would prevail over Conservatism, despite the latter's vigorous late nineteenth-century champions. By the end of that century–perhaps before–the enlightened upper and middle classes would be joined in their indifference toward religion by the urban working classes.

XVI. RELIGION AND REACTIONS TO THE INDUSTRIAL REVOLUTION

Some Useful Data

1818-1883	Karl Marx, German philosopher
1815-1898	Otto von Bismarck, German political leader
1878-1903	reign of Leo XIII, pope
1812-1904	Samuel Smiles, English liberal author
1825-1919	Andrew Carnegie, American industrialist
1850-1932	Eduard Bernstein, German socialist
1854-1938	Karl Kautsky, German socialist

The Industrial Revolution began in Great Britain during the late eighteenth century, then spread to the Continent and the United States in the course of the nineteenth century. The institution that made this production revolution possible was the factory. Factories employed newly developed machinery powered by the water flow of rivers and streams and, later, by steam. Factories also employed massive numbers of people who migrated from farm and fields to the new industrial centers–in England chiefly to the Midlands, where cities like Liverpool, Manchester, Sheffield, and Birmingham grew precipitously. There the textile, metals, machinery, and transportation industries spewed forth great numbers of products. Mass production brought down the price of goods, and these goods found ready markets all over the world.

A. The Human Cost

The factory system needed large numbers of workers, most of whom performed simple, routine tasks that required no particular skill. These workers were ruthlessly exploited by the factory owners. The results were so appalling that, in 1832, a committee of the British Parliament was entrusted with the task of ferreting out the ugly details as preparation for remedial legislation. Michael Sadler chaired the committee, and the revealing document this panel produced was called the Sadler Report.

Sadler and his associates found ten-year-old children, boys and girls, worked ninety-six hours a week and more for wages scarcely enough to keep them alive. The effects of this excessive labor–accompanied by frequent and brutal beatings–showed themselves in stunted growth and chronic illness that often left young people unable to work past the age of twenty. The air in the factories was thick with dust, and the machinery had no safeguards against accident. Exhausted children frequently fell groggily into the working machines to be mutilated or killed. Children who spent two hours or more a day trudging wearily to and from work had no time for school, and most remained illiterate. Their Sundays were spent recovering from the physical effects of the week's work, and thus church attendance was impossible.

Money confiscated from the wages of children by their parents went to pay for drink. The working classes of Britain had traditionally drunk beer or ale, but gin soon became their drink of preference, for it was cheaper and offered the quicker effects of a higher alcohol content. Drunken and unemployed adults–and children too debilitated to support them–had but one recourse: to "throw themselves on the parish." Poor-relief laws dating back to the sixteenth century had relied on the individual parishes of the Church of England. The geographical boundaries of those parishes had remained virtually unchanged for centuries, and parishes in newly industrialized areas were too few and far too inadequately funded to care for the crush of sad cases that appeared at their doors.

The workers lived in company-built houses of solid construction but with a monotonous uniformity which went on and on for dreary miles. The real problem with these company towns was that there was never enough housing to go around; so structures built to house one family were rapidly filled with four or five. The problems of fresh water supply and sanitation soon turned these housing tracts into filthy, smelly slums.

Recourse for the workers was nearly impossible. Work stoppages were sometimes organized, but a government heavily influenced by business interests declared that strikes were illegal "restraints of trade." The British Parliament passed Combination Acts that outlawed labor unions. Workers who defied the law by organizing to win better conditions were fired and blacklisted, so that employment elsewhere was impossible. One witness before the Sadler Committee was a physician serving British factory workers. His previous medical practice had been serving slaves employed in the labor intensive Caribbean sugar industry. He declared that the slaves were better housed, better fed, in better health, and better educated than free men working in British industry.

B. The Liberal Response

In 1859 a book titled *Self Help* made its successful appearance. Its author, Samuel Smiles (1812-1904), saw his book reissued over and over again, and it would appear in no fewer than seventeen translations. Its message encapsulated the liberal reaction to the problems attendant on the Industrial Revolution. The message was: do nothing. The state surely should not interfere with the freedom of the market by protecting workers, for "even the best institutions can give a man no active aid." Individuals too should curb their charitable instincts, for "help from without is often enfeebling in its effects." The best thing that institutions and individuals can do for the struggling worker is "to leave him free to develop himself and improve his individual condition."

Smiles contended that self-improvement will lead to success through "the practice of the virtues of industry, frugality, temperance, and honesty." "Industry, wisely and vigorously applied, never fails of success," Smiles wrote. "It carries a man onward and upward, brings out his individual character, and powerfully stimulates the action of others." As for frugality, Smiles continued, there are two classes of people: "those who have saved and those who have spent." He elaborated: "The building of all the houses, the mills, the bridges, and the ships, and the accomplishment of all other great works that have rendered man civilized and happy, has been done by the savers, the thrifty, and those that have wasted their resources have always been their slaves."

The temperance and honesty advocated by Smiles were also virtues emphasized by the Protestant Churches to which many wealthy people belonged. The nineteenth century saw many religious revivals in England and among American Protestants. Methodists and other movements deemed temperance as the key to the reform of society. These groups, like the American Christian Temperance

Union, did not really advocate temperance but rather total abstinence. Even the use of wine in communion services was rejected by the mainstream Protestant Churches in the United States.

Smiles' *laissez-faire* liberalism, his view that prosperity necessitated freedom from economic restraints by government, received theological sanction through the covenant theology that Calvinism–though not Calvin himself–had left as a legacy. The leaders of finance and manufacture who lionized Smiles firmly believed that wealth was a sign of God's favor, an indication of predestination to eternal bliss. "Heaven helps those who help themselves" was a well-worn maxim oft repeated by Samuel Smiles.

Even highly successful industrialists must eventually face impending death. Faced with his end, Andrew Carnegie (1825-1919), the fabulously wealthy founder of U.S. Steel Corporation, arranged to leave some thirty million dollars to his favored benefactions. The recipients were not needy individuals but institutions providing self-help opportunities, like universities and libraries.

It is difficult for many of us today to imagine how the poverty-stricken, overworked wage slaves described in the Sadler Report could have benefited from Smiles' advice. The self-help virtues that he advocated seem impossible for one working ninety-six hours a week. Frugality seems a hollow goal for one barely earning enough to eat. But nineteenth-century liberals could and did point to men like Carnegie who, as a poor immigrant from Scotland, went from working as an assistant to a weaver in a cotton factory to becoming a multi-millionaire captain of industry. Liberals rarely noticed those whom Carnegie left behind.

C. Marxism

Karl Marx (1818-1883) was born into a middle class German family. He was a brilliant student who obtained a doctorate in philosophy and history. His radical views earned him exile from Germany and then France; so Marx spent the last thirty-four years of his life in London, writing voluminously and toiling to build organizations that could realize his comprehensive solution to the suffering of the poor. Marx was an insightful historian: with his work *Das Kapital* (Capital) he advanced significantly the discipline of economic history. He collaborated with his friend Friedrich Engels in the writing of the *Communist Manifesto* of 1848. This clarion call to revolution ended with the much-quoted phrase: "Workers of the world, unite. You have nothing to lose but your chains." That call was grounded in a sophisticated philosophical system: Scientific Historical Materialism.

The last word in this phrase indicates Marx's metaphysics, his view of ultimate reality. As the word indicates, Marx thought that everything is material, made up only of matter. Even ideas, he asserted, are merely the accidental byproducts of the curious physical structure of a material object, the human brain, and the circumstantial challenges with which it is confronted. The only knowledge that can legitimately be stored in that brain is the product of science–and science alone.

To Marx, humans are purely material beings. Human needs are rooted in material goods, and human happiness results from possessing those goods. Because humans are made of matter, their bodies and minds are subject to the laws of matter. They are not and cannot be free. The scientific laws of nature determine their destiny.

Why then did Marx urge the working class to unite in the struggle to overthrow the unjust social order from which they suffered? The Marxist answer is that Marx's cry for action was the product of physical and social forces, not of free will. The workers' response is equally inevitable: they do not initiate the revolution; they are the means by which the revolution carries itself out. This points us toward the lynchpin of Marx's thought, beginning with the arrangement of physical goods that we call economics. For Marx, an economic system inevitably brings forth a social and political system that is dedicated to maintaining that economic arrangement. To put it Marx's way: the state is the instrument by which the owners of the means of production oppress everyone else in order to keep their ownership secure. According to Marx, every social and political order inevitably gives rise to an ideology that justifies the oppression of the majority by the owners of the means of economic production. To put it briefly: economics determines politics, and politics in turn determines ideology.

Marx insisted that economics is always the central determining factor throughout history, but, as the means of production changes, so too do political and social structures–as does the ideology that justifies those changes. Marx asserted that the first organized economic system was agriculture. The owners of the means of production, land, were the political and social rulers in this agrarian system–called by Marx "feudalism." Landowners kept their exploited serfs under control by force and by feeding them a phoney ideology: the Catholic religion. The lords' stooges, the priests, told the serfs that, if they patiently performed their grinding labor, they would be rewarded in Heaven.

The feudal lords were not satisfied. They and their wives wanted luxuries not produced on a farm, however extensive. The production of new forms of wealth, luxury goods, required a new class. In this way, feudal lords inevitably created the artisan, manufacturing, and banking classes that would inevitably evict them from their place of power.

The first–in this case agricultural–structure evoked a "contradiction," in this case the artisan class owning shops that were their means of producing goods. The artisans had an ideology as well. Theirs was Protestantism, which Marx saw as an ideology attacking the restraints the medieval Church put on money making and lending. The result of the economic struggle between landowners and artisans was a "resolution" of contradiction. The new economic system that resulted was capitalism, which by its very success created a new "contradiction." This inevitable and recurring movement in history was described by Marx as dialectical.

In capitalism the means of production is the factory, and so the political and social rulers of the system are the factory owners, the capitalists. They mercilessly exploit the factory workers, the proletariat, and justify their exploitation by their ideology, liberalism. They also train their laborers to work together, and thus unconsciously empower their economic slaves. Beyond that, in the wars that inevitably arise between capitalist countries over colonial markets, the capitalists arm their workers, the proletariat, and train them for battle. Led by their vanguard, the Communists, the proletariat will inevitably rise up, throw off its shackles, and usher in the new age of socialism.

In socialism the factories will be owned by the people who should own them, the proletariat. They will be the new rulers of society. They will exercise their authority through democracy, electing those who know their best interests, the Communists, as their political servants. The primary task of the socialist government will be the suppression of selfishness, that is, capitalism. This will necessitate world-wide domination, since the world cannot be happy until the last capitalist is eliminated, either through education or by force. When that day comes, there will be no further need for government, and the people will be free to enjoy the fruits of their labors.

Prosperity and peace are surely attractive goals. They have been attractive to generation after generation of Marxists who have been willing to lay down their lives for what they regard as the noblest of causes. That cause's inevitable triumph provides both psychological stimulus to, and support for, their efforts as well.

Marxism was clearly a child of the Enlightenment. But Marx made a sophisticated philosophy from what had been little more than the popular point of view of the *philosophes*. Marx transformed the Enlightenment's linear progress toward perfection through rational reflection into a dialectical process of natural forces. The mechanical universe of Enlightenment became a scientific world, and "reason alone" became "science alone" as the means of understanding that world. Marx viewed the rational and freely choosing human being of the Enlightenment as a pawn to economic forces. Marx relegated the enlightened economic theory, *laissez-faire* liberalism, to an intellectual trash bin, but he derived his overriding passion for economics from liberal economists and their intensive concern for profit. Then too, Marx shared with the *philosophes* a disdain for religion and a conviction that education is the most efficacious means of bringing about progress.

Critics of Marxism have pointed out that, if all ideas are the product of economic structures, then Marx's ideas must be the products of his time. What guarantee, they have asked, do we have that the economic structure of nineteenth-century Europe will produce true thoughts while the economic structures of all other times have produced falsehood? Such arguments, even when recognized by Marxists, have been met with indifference. For Marxism has become more than a philosophy; it has become a religion.

Marxism has its saints, the heroes of the revolution. It has its orthodoxy and its heresies–and its Scriptures in the works of Marx. It has as its demons the capitalists; as its priests the party elite; as its feast day May 1; and as its liturgy the never-ending parades that celebrate that workers' feast. It may be that Marxism, in providing a substitute faith and religion, has exercised a more damaging effect on

Christianity than it has through its much vaunted atheism.

D. Social Democracy

During much of the nineteenth century, what we now call Communism was called Socialism. Slowly during that century an alternative reading of Marx emerged that gave birth to the Labour Party in Great Britain and the Social Democratic Party in Germany. We call them, and their like-minded brothers and sisters in other countries, socialists. In a letter addressed to the German Social Democratic Congress of 1898, Eduard Bernstein pointed out that the collapse of capitalism predicted by Marx in 1848 had not occurred, and capitalist economies everywhere showed every sign of burgeoning vitality. Revolution was not the answer to the injustices inflicted on the working class. "Democracy," Bernstein proclaimed, "would function far better." Democracy, Bernstein's colleague Karl Kautsky had earlier written, may be "less dramatic and showy" than revolution, "but it also produces fewer casualties."

The all-consuming struggle of Social Democrats was aimed at universal suffrage. This was accomplished by mid-century–oddly enough, through conservative leadership–in both Britain and Germany. The workers of those countries were then able to outvote other classes. The eventual working-class control of government, Bernstein and Kautsky predicted, would lead to the expropriation of capitalists, the goal of Marx, but an expropriation done peacefully.

This goal would be accomplished by confiscatory inheritance taxes on the estates left by the wealthy to their heirs and by highly progressive income taxes designed so the rich would pay a much greater percentage of their earnings than did the less affluent. The nationalization, through government expropriation, of key industries–manufacturing, banking, transportation, and mining–would soon follow. Working-class people would democratically elect governments that would legislate government ownership. Government bureaus, staffed by technical experts, would run these industries and administer an extensive welfare system. Everyone would be cared for "from womb to tomb," and everyone would be happy.

E. A Catholic Response: Pope Leo XIII

It was not until 1891, more than a century after the horrors inflicted on factory workers had begun, that Catholics heard a pope addressing this problem. To be sure, as we shall see, the popes of the nineteenth century had their hands full with other concerns. But Leo XIII (pope from 1878 to 1903), shared many of those concerns. He also had the energy and the ability to face up to the economic and social challenges of industrialization. His response was an encyclical, a letter to the whole Church, titled *Rerum novarum*, literally "about new things."

Aware of factory workers left alone and defenseless against the inhumanity of employers infected with the unbridled greed of economic competition, Leo rejected the Communist solution to the problem. Doing away with private property, the pope declared, would injure workers. The purpose of all labor, Leo believed, is to procure property, and the law of nature dictates that laborers should be free to retain their property or to dispose of it. This freedom is a large part of what it is to be human. Communists, in depriving people of their natural right to property, act against all "incentives to ingenuity and skill and attack the economic foundation of the family."

The presupposition on which Leo's solution rested was that labor is natural and good–and, indeed, had antedated Adam's Fall, as Adam and Eve had worked as the caretakers of Eden. Leo recalled the competing classes to their duties. Workers should work, not injure the property or persons of employers. Employers should provide their workers an "honorable means of supporting life." This includes keeping the work load reasonable, seeing to it that the work assigned is appropriate to the age and sex of the employee, and allowing workers sufficient days of rest–and thus time to pursue their spiritual welfare. The Church's role in the pursuit of economic harmony is to remind all of what nature and the Scriptures teach: that riches are of no importance to eternal happiness; what counts is rather how one uses wealth.

In meeting the needs of neighbors, each person should actively assist with as much of one's resources as is compatible with the needs of one's own family. If private assistance is inadequate to meet the need, then the Church or some other private agency or association, like a labor union, should step in. The government's role should be restricted to emergency relief and, more importantly, to enacting labor laws to protect the worker.

Leo's encyclical was not well received by liberals or Marxists. Even middle class and well-to-do Catholics were slow in accepting his plan for what he called "distributive justice."

F. A Protestant Response: Otto von Bismarck

Otto von Bismarck was born in 1815 to a family of the small landholding or Junker class. Bismarck is justifiably famous as the architect of the German unification of 1871. It is little known that, as a young man, he joined a small Lutheran group with a Pietist pedigree. The Pietists, we remember, had a strong tradition of social concern and activism, and this provided the basis of Bismarck's enactment of a revolutionary program of social legislation into German law and culture.

In a speech before the German parliament, the Reichstag, Bismarck, as head of the German government, introduced his program of remedial laws to benefit the working class. He declared: "The whole matter centers on the question: is it the duty of the state, or is it not, to provide for its helpless citizens? I maintain that it is the duty not only of the Christian state, but of every state." A state that "desires to demonstrate its practical [application of] Christianity" must pass laws protecting "the poor, the weak, and the old,...for its own sake as well as for the sake of the poor."

Violent opposition to Bismarck's proposals came from both Liberals and Marxists. Bismarck dismissed Marxist opposition as he saw it stemming from their desire to maintain revolutionary fervor by keeping workers dissatisfied and thus disaffected. Liberal arguments Bismarck took more seriously. Liberals denounced him as a Socialist for advocating government "intervention in the marketplace." Bismarck acknowledged "the responsibility of the state for what it does." "But," he continued, "it is my opinion that the state can also be responsible for what it does not do." He accused Liberals, "those who profess horror at the intervention of the state for the protection of the weak," of laying themselves "open to the suspicion that they desire to use their power...to benefit but a part of society and for the oppression of the rest." And yet, said Bismarck, "I am not hostile toward the rightful claims of capital. But I think that the masses too have rights which should be considered." "I wish," he continued, "that we could immediately create a few hundred millionaires"–as long as they behaved responsibly toward their workers–for the whole community, not only the tax collectors, would benefit.

Bismarck's opposition to greedy capitalists and their liberal apologists was joined to criticism of members of his own class, those land owners "who live in town–be it Paris, Rome, or Berlin–and who only require money from their estates and agents." Land owners are delinquent when they lazily reject their obligation to become legislators and thus represent their neighbors. Bismarck believed that the world needs capitalists who are really rich–in concern for others are well as in cash. The world also welcomes "land owners who are really farmers." Members of all classes serve God and neighbor by doing their jobs as best they can.

In addition, all prospering people must "give the working man the right to work as long as he is healthy, assure him of care when he is sick, assure him support in his old age." To this end, and with the support of the Catholic Center Party, this Protestant and conservative Chancellor put through a comprehensive system of social security which the United States was not to achieve for some fifty years. Workers' Compensation laws were passed first for railroad workers (1871) and then extended (in 1884) to anyone suffering from industrial accidents. Health insurance passed in 1883, supported by a fund to which workers contributed one third. A pension plan followed in 1889, to which the state, the employer, and the insured all contributed. Those insured were assessed according to their income level. The plan for the administration of the program clearly shows Bismarck's conservatism. Each state within Germany, not the federal government, would decide whether to administer the fund itself or turn that task over to a local body representing employers, workers, and the state government. With his program Bismarck successfully stemmed the tide of Marxism in his land, but the future would bring victories to the followers of Marx, in Bismarck's land and many others.

XVII. RELIGION IN A SCIENTIFIC AGE

Some Useful Data

1798	Thomas Mathus' *Essay on Population*
1798-1857	Auguste Comte, French philosopher
1804-1872	Ludwig Feuerbach, German philosopher
1805-1872	Giuseppe Mazzini, Italian nationalist
1805-1873	Samuel Wilberforce, Anglican bishop
1808-1874	David Friedrich Strauss, German philosopher
1822-1884	Gregor Mendel, Austrian naturalist
1808-1892	Henry Edward Manning, English Catholic archbishop and cardinal
1809-1892	Charles Darwin, English naturalist
1844-1900	Friedrich Nietzsche, German philosopher
1820-1903	Herbert Spencer, English philosopher
1859-1906	Wilhelm Wrede, German theologian
1863-1914	Johannes Weiss, German theologian
1851-1930	Adolph von Harnack, German theologian
1856-1939	Sigmund Freud, Austrian psychoanalyst
1875-1965	Albert Schweitzer, Protestant theologian
1886-1965	Paul Tillich, Protestant theologian
1886-1968	Karl Barth, Swiss theologian
1913-1969	James A. Pike, Episcopalian bishop and theologian
1884-1976	Rudolf Bultmann, German theologian
1919-1983	John A.T. Robinson, Anglican bishop and theologian
1922-	Shubert Ogden, American theologian
1927-	Thomas Altizer, American theologian
1929-	Harvey Cox, American theologian
1932-	James Robinson, American theologian

A. Evolution

In 1859, Charles Darwin published *The Origin of Species*, which many consider the most important book of the nineteenth century. The background of the man and his book are revealing. Charles Darwin (1809-1892) was the son of a country doctor, whose father, Charles' grandfather, was both poet and naturalist. Young Charles studied medicine at Edinburgh, but his frail constitution prevented him following his father's profession. He also studied theology at Cambridge, but soon found himself more engrossed with biology and geology. One of his teachers at Cambridge urged him to apply for the post of naturalist on a survey ship, the *Beagle*. Darwin spent the next five years of his life, 1831 to 1836, sailing on the *Beagle* and studying and collecting all sorts of flora and fauna. He spent the next twenty years analyzing and classifying his data. By 1858 his manuscript had grown to one thousand pages, which he radically reduced for publication in 1859. In *The Origin of Species*, Darwin did not introduce the theory of evolution; that idea was very much in the air already. What he did do was to propose the theory of natural selection that addressed the question: how does evolution happen?

More than the *Beagle* voyage informed Darwin's formulation. From Sir Charles Lyell's *Principles of Geology* (1830-1833), Darwin gained a sophisticated knowledge of the recently proposed idea of uniformitarianism. According to this notion, the processes we see at work in the world today–like erosion or volcanic eruptions–are the same forces that have always altered the face of the earth. Thus, to account for the Alps, for instance, a process extending over an indefinitely long period is necessary.

From many biologists, his own grandfather among them, Charles had learned about the "artificial selection" practiced by animal breeders who altered the physical attributes of their stock by selective breeding–for color or size or coat length, for example. Darwin was also impressed with accounts of "sports"–we would say mutations–that appeared periodically, such as two-headed calves.

New ideas of history were also in the air. Romanticism saw history as a positive force and as an organic reality, not the lifeless machine proposed by the *philosophes* of the Enlightenment.

Economics also contributed to Darwin's synthesis, specifically the ideas propounded by Thomas Malthus in his 1798 *Essay on Population*. Malthus saw all populations increasing geometrically (2, 4, 8, 16, etc.) at a much more rapid rate than the arithmetically expanding (2, 3, 4, 5, etc.) supply of food. In this analysis Darwin saw the basis for the struggle for survival that he observed everywhere in nature.

Darwin was a meticulous scientist who demanded mountains of evidence to explain how species changed. He had, for example, observed myriad unusual life forms on the visit of the *Beagle* to the Galápagos Islands off Ecuador. He learned that the giant tortoises on those islands could be identified by variations–sometimes slight–that indicated which island they came from. Was it possible that there been an act of special creation for each of these subspecies? That explanation would violate the scientific standard of simplicity enunciated long before by Isaac Newton.

The similarities between species are as astounding, Darwin thought, as the variations within species. Natural selection could account for the "similar framework of bones in the hand of a man, wing of a bat, fin of a porpoise, and leg of the horse." It could explain "the same number of vertebrae forming the neck of the giraffe and the elephant." Embryonic development in all species provided further evidence. Natural selection explains why "the embryo of an air breathing animal or bird [has] gill slits and arteries running in loops, like those of a fish," and why human beings, as embryos, have long tails.

Vestigial organs that have no apparent use, like our appendix, are likewise evidence for our descent from organisms that required them. "The calf," wrote Darwin, "has inherited teeth, which never cut through the gums of the upper jaw, from an early progenitor having well-developed teeth." Evidence from fossils also supports the conclusion that species change. Older fossils, those buried more deeply, are less complex than the related species which succeeded them. As the fossil record reaches upward, the newer versions of animals and plants are discovered to be more diverse and increasingly dissimilar.

All this evidence convinced Darwin that species do change over time. Competition for food ensures those forms that have adapted better to their environment will survive in the struggle for sustenance and thus existence. Darwin did not know how the adaptations occurred. He was ignorant of genetics, since Gregor Mendel's work with sweetpeas in his Austrian monastery was not widely known until about 1900. Darwin did know, however, that successful adaptations were those that enabled animals and plants to win in the struggle for food and thus to pass on their adaptions. Most people agreed.

B. Religious Reactions to Darwinism

There were some who did not agree. Religious fundamentalists, those who held that every word of Scripture is literally true as dictated by God, found Darwin's theories of evolution blasphemous. The extremely long time required for the evolutionary process contradicted, they thought, the age of the world indicated by the Bible. James Ussher, a seventeenth-century Anglican archbishop of Armagh, Ireland, had carefully calculated from the ages of the patriarchs that "the world was created in 4004 B.C." Others added more precise calculations: the date was October 23rd and the hour 9 A.M. Of course the duration of the creation was declared to be six days, a literal reading of the book of Genesis.

The response of another Anglican bishop, Samuel Wilberforce (1805-1873), illustrates a second sort of religious objection to Darwinism. Wilberforce saw in Darwin's work "a tendency to limit God's glory in creation." "The principle of natural selection is absolutely incompatible with the word of God," Wilberforce declared, because it "contradicts the revealed relations of creation to its Creator."

Wilberforce's Catholic contemporary, Henry Edward Manning, archbishop of Westminster from 1865 to 1885 and soon to be named a cardinal, declared Darwin's view of nature to be "a brutal philosophy–to wit, there is no God, and the ape is our Adam."

Darwin made his own point of view clear in his *Origin of Species*: "I see no reason why the views given in this volume should shock the religious feelings of anyone." Such reactions are inevitable, Darwin thought, but can be quickly dispelled. This is shown by the fact that "the greatest discovery ever made by man, the law of the attraction of gravity was also attacked...as subversive of natural and, inferentially, of revealed religion." Darwin's prediction proved true, for gradually virtually all the traditional Christian denominations showed themselves open to evolution and eventually embraced it. Fundamentalist Protestants, especially in the American South, continue to reject evolution and urge that the biblical account of creation replace the teaching of evolution or at least be taught along side it. Most recently creationism, thinly disguised as "intelligent design," has been urged on the schools of several American States.

C. The Neo-Enlightenment

The many scientific and medical discoveries of the nineteenth century, combined with the enormous–if ill-distributed–wealth generated by industrialization, gave rise–in the last half of that century–to a revival of Enlightenment thought. The *laissez-faire* liberalism of Enlightenment economics became immensely popular, as can be seen in the highly successful publications of Samuel Smiles. To this optimistic view was added a darker note inspired by a misunderstanding of Darwin. It was thought that the rich prevail because they are superior in the struggle for wealth. The poor are unfit and so doomed to extinction–economic extinction at the very least. To help the poor through private or public means was, therefore, to fight against the onrushing tide of nature and of history.

Even more concerned with the march of progress was Herbert Spencer (1820-1903), the man who, even before Darwin, popularized the phrase "survival of the fittest." Spencer thought that the laws of evolution applied to the whole cosmos, not only to the realm of biology, but to the physical universe and to human culture and society. Spencer was confident that all things–society and government, industry and commerce, language and literature, science and art–evolve from a homogeneous or uniform condition to a heterogeneous or diverse state. This evolution is a product of a natural force that Spencer formulated in this way: "Every active force produces more than one change–every cause produces more than one effect." The "inevitable corollary" of this law is that "through all times there has been an ever-growing complication of things." This universal "complication" or "differentiation" Spencer called progress–in the same triumphant tone with which Condorcet had announced his Enlightenment theory of progress. Unlike Condorcet, however, Spencer denied that progress could be measured in terms of human happiness. Thus Spencer, who is usually credited with being the outstanding advocate of "Social Darwinism," was rather more concerned with cosmic evolution. Nevertheless, Spencer's system was immensely popular in the decades between 1870 and 1890.

A great many other philosophies owe their origin to Darwin or, at least, to the concept of evolution. Relativism, for example, sees ideas as mere qualities–qualities that enable humans to survive in the struggle for existence or for success. Since there are no absolute truths for a relativist, the definition of "success" is, of course, totally subjective. I am sure that many of us remember a discussion in our college dorm lasting until late at night. In the course of that discussion someone surely prefaced his or her contribution by saying: "Well, that may be true for you, but...." And this relativism leads easily to pragmatism, the conviction that ideas are not right or wrong but merely more or less useful. The definition of "useful" is, of course, the sticking point.

D. Comte and Positivism

Perhaps the most sophisticated application of evolution to the world of philosophy was made by Auguste Comte (1798-1857). The fact that the six volumes of Comte's first major work, the *System of Positive Philosophy*, were published from 1830 to 1842–well before Darwin's 1859 *Origin of Species*–show us how much evolution was in the air at the time.

Comte saw three great stages in the evolution of humankind and of human thought. These stages were the theological, the metaphysical, and the positive or scientific stages. In the theological stage, causation is viewed as spiritual. The supposedly fundamental realities are spirits or gods or God. The events in the theological universe are determined by Will–the capricious decisions of those spirits, gods, or God. The ethics that follow from this view of the universe are straightforward: do the will of the spirits, gods, or God–observe the Ten Commandments, for example. The political structure embraced by people in this stage is military, because those people's first political need is defense from invasion or internal disorder. The theological universe needs a psychological foundation, and the family provides this. The way humans in this stage of evolution learn about truth is through faith.

In the second great evolutionary stage of humankind, the universe is not simply understood as spiritual, but composed of both spirit and matter. In this world events are explained rationally by "abstract essences and occult causes," such as a Prime Mover or Nature. The good now is found in the rational, doing good for one's self and others–for example, following the "Golden Rule." The politics of this stage is "juristic," the rule of "lawyers," by which Comte meant to indicate that the state provides justice. The psychological reference point in this, the metaphysical stage, expands beyond the family to the nation.

In the third, or positive, state of humankind, science provides the only explanation of the sensible world. Since Comte and all thinking scientists know that any reality beyond the phenomena perceived by our senses cannot be known by science, humans must necessarily adopt an attitude of agnostic ignorance. Ethical principles too are unknowable through science, Comte early declared, but through science humans can and do know the laws connecting and governing phenomena. They can thus master the all-important world of appearances and ignore whatever lies behind those appearances. The politics of the positive stage Comte labeled "industrial." By this he meant that captains of industry would be the leaders of a society concerned with the material welfare of humankind.

Comte knew that even a strictly material goal requires a society with a vision and structure through which to realize that vision, and so he, who saw theology as a primitive way of viewing the world, invented a religion for his scientific society. The priests in this religion are sociologists, who apply the methods of science to society. The saints of this society, whose feasts will be celebrated, are the benefactors of humankind, primarily scientists and inventors. The demons are, of course, those who oppose progress. This religion also has its Sacred Scriptures, among them the writings of Newton and Darwin. Though the theories, even the name, of Comte are little recognized today, the principles of his philosophy and a large part of his religion are widely observed, both faithfully and unknowingly.

E. Nationalism

When Giuseppe Mazzini was born, in 1805, Italy was only a geographical designation. There had never been an Italian state. Nevertheless, Mazzini lived long enough, until 1872, to see his beloved Italy freed from foreign control, rid of papal rule in central Italy, and established as a kingdom with an Italian king and parliament. In this victory Mazzini played no small role as leader of a movement called Young Italy and as head of a short-lived Roman republic during the revolution of 1848, but Mazzini's most effective and lasting contributions were his oratory and his skill with a pen.

Mazzini had a vision for all of humanity, not only for Italians. He wrote in his *Duties of Man* (1844 to 1858) that our first duty is "to humanity,...[for] you are men before you are citizens or fathers." Each individual is too weak to serve this cause effectively, and "humanity [is] too vast" to accomplish its ends. God has, however, given us all a means of realizing both the individual's and humanity's goal: "He divided humanity into distinct groups on the face of our globe and thus planted the seeds of nations." Lacking a nation, "you have neither name, token voice, nor rights–no admission into the fellowship of the peoples."

What, then, is a nation? It is not the same as a state, for Italy had existed without a state for millennia. Mazzini knew that a nation "is not a mere territory; a particular territory is only its foundation." A nation is "the idea which rises on that foundation. It is the sentiment of love, the sense of fellowship which binds together all the sons of that territory." The non-rational, emotional nature of nationalism is revealed by Mazzini's characterization of a nation as "brothers entwining right hands round a beloved mother."

Nationalism is one of the most powerful motivating forces of the last two centuries. Like Marxism and Comte's Positivism, it has frequently assumed the character of a religion, often replacing traditional religions like Christianity. All the new mass ideologies–Marxism, Nationalism, and Positivism–demanded unwavering faith and total commitment–just as do religions.

In the nineteenth century, national expansion through aggression was often justified by a racism based, it was thought, on Darwin's survival of the fittest. Victory proved the superiority of a people, race, or nation and justified the subjection of "inferior" peoples. The most notorious twentieth-century example of this biological ideology is the blood mysticism of Nazi Germany that led to the deaths of some six million Jews. Hitler's political party was officially designated the National Socialist German Workers Party. Surely one of the reasons for the rise of Adolf Hitler and his movement was its fusion of widely disparate, indeed contradictory components: social Darwinism, state socialism, and Nationalism.

F. The Protestant Engagement with Modernity

The nineteenth and twentieth centuries were not kind to Christianity. Political attacks on religion came from the rabid anti-clericalism of the Third French Republic (1875-1940), from the repressive atheism of the Soviet Union, and from the religion of racial superiority fostered in Nazi Germany. Another problem was that industrialization forced mass migrations from farm to city and from country to country, dislocating people from traditional social structures and institutions, including churches. Sigmund Freud (1856-1939) and some other advocates of the new science of psychology have seen religion as an illusion created by humans that is inimical to their mental health. Perhaps the force most hostile to religion has been the positivist sociology of Comte. Many sociologists have seen religion in general, and Christianity in particular, as a force opposing progress–a force that needs replacement by a system or a religion stressing secular values.

The reaction of Catholic Christianity to these challenges of modernity has been mixed, and that will be our topic in the next chapter. The reaction of Protestant Christianity has also been mixed. Fundamentalists have rejected much of modern culture and have found meaning and support in a literal reading of their inerrant source of truth, the Bible. Some groups, such as the Salvation Army, have ignored the ideologies that attack Christianity and have worked mightily toward relieving the misery of people suffering from the poverty, alcoholism, homelessness, and starvation that have accompanied modern mass society.

Other Protestants have responded differently to modern culture. "The Protestant is up to date," the Catholic theologian Gustave Weigel wrote in 1960. Protestantism "has an intellectuality. It favors scholarship and has always produced it." Protestant theologians–teaching in universities, seminaries, and divinity schools, and sometimes writing as independent scholars–have engaged modernity with zest and with a challenging profundity sometimes unappreciated by fellow Protestants.

Albert Schweitzer (1875-1965) described a persistent theme in Protestant theology in his book *The Quest for the Historical Jesus* (1906). An early and influential quest of this kind was published in 1835 by David Friedrich Strauss (1808-1874) as the *Life of Jesus*. At the end of his quest Strauss discovered that Jesus was simply a Jewish sage. Jesus as the ideal ethical humanist was presented in *What is Christianity?* by Adolf von Harnack (1851-1930). Harnack sought to cut through the dogmas, the faith formulas, created by churchmen to reach back to the simpler straightforward message of love that Jesus had really taught. Schweitzer's account of the many other such quests for the historical Jesus showed how each biographer "brought the spirit of his own age into his presentation of Jesus."

At the beginning of the twentieth century, Johannes Weiss (1863-1914) and Wilhelm Wrede (1859-1906) explained why this was necessarily so. They demonstrated that the gospels were not historical accounts. They were, rather, highly sophisticated theological works in which the oral tradition bequeathed by Jesus' early disciples had been considerably expanded and altered.

This conclusion formed the basis of Rudolf Bultmann's (1884-1976) *Mythology and the Message of Jesus*. During the 1920s, Bultmann came to the conclusion that the purpose of the gospels was not to present a dispassionate portrait of Jesus, but rather to express what Bultmann called the *kerygma*, the proclamation of early Christian faith in a risen Christ. As a result, Bultmann concluded, "we can now know almost nothing about the life and personality of Jesus." The *kerygma* must be demythologized, he thought, stripped of such unbelievable elements as its three-tiered universe with heaven above and hell below. In our day, Bultmann observed, no one can accept the world view of the gospels. The biblical narratives must undergo demythologization to make Jesus' ethical message relevant to a scientific world view. Following this line of reasoning to its logical end, James Robinson of the Southern California School of Theology has recently pointed out that demythologization threatens to lead to "the conclusion that the Jesus of the *kerygma* could well [himself] only be a myth."

Bultmann's influence has been pervasive. Demythologization advocate and Anglican bishop John A.T. Robinson (1919-1983) urged scholars–in his 1963 book *Honest to God*–to "chip the crust of tradition and myth from Christianity in order to expose the essential message of the gospels." Robinson's intent was seconded by a former Episcopal bishop of California, James A. Pike (1913-1969), who–in his *A Time for Christian Candor* (1963)–encouraged everyone to distinguish "the treasures of God's gifts from the earthen vessels in which they are packaged."

Perhaps the most radical application of the demytholigizing process was made by Shubert Ogden of Southern Methodist University in his *Christ Without Myth* (1961). Ogden suggests that God changes as the cosmos changes. Instead of thinking of God as the immutable Prime Mover of the universe, it makes more sense, Ogden thinks, to describe God as "the ultimate effect." One should think of

God as "the eminently relative One, whose openness to change contingent on the actions of others is literally boundless." The God Ogden describes is a deity few of his fellow Methodists would recognize.

The "Death of God" movement traces its origins, appropriately enough, to an atheist and materialist, Ludwig Feuerbach (1804-1872) and his enormously influential book, *The Essence of Christianity* (1841). According to Feuerbach, religion is merely the human consciousness of the infinite, and "God" is merely a projection of human needs and desires. Feuerbach's goal was "to change the friends of God into friends of man, believers into thinkers, worshipers into workers, candidates for the other world into students of this world."

Another powerful influence on the "God is dead" movement has been the author of that phrase, Friedrich Nietzsche (1844-1900). He saw that the universe in which Darwin's process of natural selection operates is based on random change. This proved to Nietzsche that there is no direction, meaning, or purpose to the universe. The cosmos cannot be known by reason but it can be conquered by those creative individuals with the will to seize and exercise power. All the old value systems of the merely human masses, of those who are "bungled and botched," attempt to restrain the willful creativity of superhuman individuals. This "herd morality" is institutionalized in Christianity and other mass movements, such as socialism. The creative geniuses must be free of these restraints–free to create themselves, free to attain salvation without a savior.

Walking among the dead and dying on a World War I battlefield, Paul Tillich (1886-1965) has told us, "I changed from an idealist to a tragic realist." Tillich, an influential giant in Protestant theology, reached the conclusion that the key to happiness, to salvation, is courage–"The Courage to Be" in the face of life's perplexing uncertainties and meaningless ambiguities. The God of Tillich's universe is the "ground of being" but otherwise unknowable. Potent words–such as "God," "Christ," "Resurrection"–are symbols that should not be taken for the unknowable realities for which they stand.

The God of traditional Christianity is dead, according to Thomas Altizer of Atlanta's Emory University. In his *Mircea Eliade and the Dialectic of the Sacred* (1963), Altizer wrote:

> I want to insist that the original, sovereign, transcendent God truly and actually died in Christ and that his death in Christ has only slowly and progressively become manifest for what it was–the movement of God to man, the movement of Word to flesh.

God becomes, in Altizer's thinking, a forward-moving divine process. This process replacing God is not a static and eternal entity, but rather self-negating and ever changing. Altizer, however, does believe in his own version of Christ: "Wherever there is a moment that is alive, real, and compassionate, that's Christ."

Harvey Cox of Harvard Divinity School welcomed the victory of secularism in his *The Secular City* (1965). Society "no longer looks to religious rules and rituals for its morality or its meanings." Morality and meaning, Cox urges, comes through Christian involvement in social issues. In this way the traditional distinction between the sacred and the secular is overcome and eventually eradicated.

It is doubtful whether many of Cox's fellow Baptists understand his eager acceptance of secularism. It is likewise hard to imagine Ogden's fellow Methodists praying to the God he describes as "the eminently relative One." Many Protestant theologians of the nineteenth and twentieth centuries have come far from the "Faith of our fathers." Among Protestant intellectual giants a lone but powerful voice kept to that faith. Karl Barth (1886-1968) was a sincere Swiss theologian who rejected a simplistic view of predestination and remained true to a sophisticated restatement of Calvinism. In fallen humans, Barth wrote, sin has shattered God's image, and thus they have no knowledge of God's reasons or his will except through revelation. Barth's God is "wholly other," known only through God's self-revelation in Jesus Christ. The Bible, for Barth, contains "divine thoughts about men, not human thoughts about God."

Barth's thought is a sophisticated version of an ancient faith. Among mainstream Protestant thinkers, he is an anomaly. Most liberal Protestant theologians, by way of contrast, have eagerly accepted most of modern culture. Others believe they have murdered by dissection the religion they study. It seems that the secular culture of the modern world has led Christianity along some strange paths, and Christianity has largely ceased to influence the culture in which it dwells.

XVIII. THE CATHOLIC CHURCH FACES THE MODERN WORLD

Some Useful Data

1831-1846	reign of Gregory XVI, pope
1846-1878	reign of Pius IX, pope
1852-1870	reign of Napoleon III, emperor of the French
1878-1903	reign of Leo XIII, pope
1903-1914	reign of Pius X, pope
1857-1940	Alfred Loisy, biblical scholar
1939-1958	reign of Pius XII, pope
1958-1963	reign of John XXIII, pope
1904-1967	John Courtney Murray, American theologian
1963-1978	reign of Paul VI, pope
1904-1984	Karl Rahner, German theologian
1895-1990	Marie-Dominique Chenu, French theologian
1896-1991	Henri de Lubac, French theologian
1904-1995	Yves Congar, French theologian
1978-2005	reign of John Paul II, pope

A. Traditionalists and Progressives

The Catholic Church is not a monolithic structure. It never has been. We have witnessed Bernard of Clairvaux's quarrel with the growth and nascent corruption of the twelfth-century papal court. We have seen the thirteenth-century chasm that divided Thomas Aquinas and Bonaventure concerning the effects of the Fall on human capabilities. We have observed both the institutional schism and the intellectual strife of the fourteenth and fifteenth centuries. Even the Catholic reaction to the Protestant Reformation produced controversy between those promoting a Catholic Reformation and those supporting an anti-Protestant Counter-reformation. We have seen how disparate were the seventeenth- and eighteenth-century Catholic views on spiritual life. It should not surprise us then that modern Catholicism should display two radically different faces to the world.

Commentators on this separation into two camps within Catholicism have often used the labels "liberal" and "conservative." Since the early nineteenth century, "conservative" members of the papal curia have labeled as "liberal" those who strive to be open to modern culture. Such usage hides more than it reveals. In the United States, for example, these two ecclesiastical positions, "conservative" and "liberal," are often identified with conservative and liberal political stances. But American political conservatives declare themselves opposed to "big government," while "conservative" Catholics favor centralization of power in the papacy. American political liberals look to a central body, to the federal government, for social solutions, whereas Catholic "liberals" would emphasize the power and responsibility of all the "people of God" in governing the Church.

Some observers have spoken of those opposing "accommodation" to modernity as "integralists" or "intransigents" or "traditionalists," and to their opponents as "reformers." One difficulty with this is that the reform sought by the latter group, also known as "progressives," is the restoration of traditional–that is, early and medieval–teaching, practice, and structure. "Traditionalists," on the other hand, aim at retaining or restoring a Church organization and theological position developed only in the late nineteenth and early twentieth centuries. Ironically, "liberals" look to ancient and medieval tradition, and find there openness to the world. "Conservatives" have adopted a modern–a very recent–period as the source of their distrustful stance toward the world.

All this fuss about names is at once revealing and confusing. With full understanding, then, that the terms are hardly precise, I shall use the adjectives "progressive," for those Catholics open to the modern world, and "traditionalist," for those concerned that modernity will corrupt Christianity.

B. Ultramontanism and Infallibility

Traditionalists identify the Church with the hierarchy. This hierarchy, the pope through his agents the bishops, rules the Church. Docility is the virtue demanded of the laity. As one joker has put it, the people are to pray, to pay, and to obey–and, of course, to procreate. The Church is a monarchy within which the pope possesses absolute power. This absolute monarch must preserve complete uniformity within the Church, for that is the only possible guarantee of Church unity.

It is ironic that the growth of the papacy into an absolute monarchy should have taken place in a period–the nineteenth century–in which political absolutism was suffering a lingering but fatal illness. The popes of the eighteenth century had been petty Italian potentates, and the bishops of the Church of that time were most often appointed by kings. The French Revolution, the era of Napoleon, and his final defeat finished all that.

After that defeat in 1815, the Congress of Vienna redrew the map of Europe. In Germany, episcopal rule of independent ecclesiastical territories was abolished, and, as a result, Protestants ruled all but two of the enlarged secular states. Rulers who now numbered many Catholics among their subjects found it much easier to deal with a weak papacy than with an aggressive coalition of the bishops within their realms.

The 1815 Peace Treaty restored France to her 1789 boundaries. It also restored a reactionary monarch with the power and determination to name reactionary bishops. Many progressive priests sought a defense against these bishops and appealed to the Roman see situated "over the mountains." From this action came the name for a new ideology, "ultramontanism." The progressive priests who appealed to Rome received a chilly reception, and the ultimate result was a papal condemnation of their leaders.

Yet it was the popes of the nineteenth century who willed the metamorphosis of ultramontanism from a progressive tactic to a traditionalist doctrine. The preeminent pope in this process was Pius IX, whose long reign lasted from 1846 to 1878. Surely the central event in that pontificate was the pope's calling of the First Vatican Council that proclaimed, in 1870, the doctrine of papal infallibility.

In 1854, Pius had prepared the way for that declaration by solemnly proclaiming Mary's freedom from Original Sin, her Immaculate Conception, as Catholic dogma. Pius' declaration was not issued at an ecumenical council. Neither was it created through some other cooperative act with the world's Catholic bishops, some of whom were ordered to assist passively at the proclamation. In effect Pius made what he considered an infallible declaration before the doctrine of infallibility had been approved by any other Church authority.

But approved it would be. Most of the bishops who attended the first Vatican Council supported the notion that the pope could not err when teaching on matters of faith. However, the extreme infallibilists wanted more, declaring that the pope could make pronouncements on behalf of the whole Church on his own authority. Opposing this position were most of the German and Austrian bishops, about one third of the French bishops, and numerous American prelates. These bishops were convinced by history that a papal pronouncement needed the support of the whole Church–expressed through an ecumenical council–to be considered doctrinally binding. A third group considered the timing inappropriate for an infallibility declaration, that should, at the very least, be postponed.

Not surprisingly, Pius favored the extreme infallibilists. During one day's debate, Cardinal Guidi, a moderate infallibilist, proposed to the Council that it was the papal teaching authority, not the person of the pope, that was infallible. He added that papal teaching authority was infallible only when exercised in the traditional way, in collegial conjunction with the world's bishops. That evening, when Guidi reported in to Pius, the pope was furious. He thundered: "I am the Church! I am the Tradition!"

Although a number of bishops packed up and went home when they heard of this papal intransigence, a large majority of the remaining bishops acquiesced. According to the Council's decree, infallibility required the pope to be teaching "from his throne" as "Supreme Pontiff." The topic of his proclamation had to be a matter of "faith or morals to be held by the universal Church." The source of this papal power, the Council declared, was "the divine assistance promised to him in Saint Peter."

Thus the doctrine derived from the document was a matter of teaching authority. It gave the pope no added power over the Church as an institution. On only one occasion has the doctrine of infallibility been invoked, by Pope Pius XII in 1950, when he proclaimed as dogma the Assumption. That doctrine affirmed that Mary, the mother of Jesus, had been taken up body and soul into heaven after her death. The declaration was cheerfully accepted by Catholics–and some Protestants–because they already believed it. No great increase of power accrued to Pius XII through this doctrine. He did not need it; he was already an absolute monarch.

C. The Pope as Absolute Monarch

Vatican I's contribution to the growth of the absolute, monarchical papal power came not through its proclamation of papal infallibility but through a parallel decree. This second statement declared that "by the appointment of our Lord, the Roman Church possesses a superiority of ordinary power over all other churches." "Ordinary power" had previously been the authority exercised by a bishop over his diocese. Nevertheless, the Council insisted that "the power of jurisdiction of the Roman Pontiff, which is truly episcopal, is immediate." The pope's leadership had been long recognized, and his pastoral concern for the whole Church had been universally acknowledged by Catholics. According to this document, however, he also possessed supreme legal power in every bishopric and in all matters concerning the "discipline and government of the Church throughout the world." Bishops were to become little more than agents of the pope.

Pius IX acted to strengthen his control over the bishops. He prohibited their meeting in national councils, lest they discuss independent action. Pius also sent out papal nuncios as resident watchdogs over the bishops of the various countries. Pius encouraged priests and lay people to report directly to Rome any signs of deviation by their bishop.

Pius IX also discouraged dissent by establishing national seminaries in Rome. There the brightest of candidates for the priesthood could live while pursuing their studies in papal universities. They were thus imbued with "the Roman spirit" of Church centralization, a spirit significant for papal control when many of them were made bishops after their return home. The laws of the Church, Pius declared, were eternal, and he enforced those laws from Rome, using bishops as his agents.

Papal control over those episcopal agents became virtually absolute when the pope gained the power to appoint bishops. This did not happen overnight, however, for the weight of nearly two millennia's practice was on the side of election. Since the earliest days of the Church, bishops had been chosen by the clergy and people of their dioceses. Moreover, reformers through the ages had considered episcopal elections the key to the independence and health of the Church.

The beginning of papal appointment goes back to 1801, to the Concordat between Napoleon Bonaparte and the pope. Neither of the parties to the document was aware of the long-term effects of their agreement. It is doubtful whether Napoleon would have cared, since his only purpose in forcing this document from the pope was to assure young Catholic recruits of the legitimacy of their military service. Following the procedure prescribed by the Concordat, Napoleon chose all bishops, and the pope then indicated his approval. Even in the seventeenth- and eighteenth-century days of royal appointment of bishops, the formality of an election had been respected. Now even that weak acknowledgment of tradition was eliminated and for it was substituted the papal voice–a voice quite muted until later in the nineteenth century.

The restoration of the monarchy in France in 1815 brought back the power of the king to appoint bishops without reference to Rome. After the revolution of 1848, Napoleon's nephew, Louis Napoleon, was installed as ruler in France. As the French emperor Napoleon III, he appointed bishops who refused to accept the growing interference of Rome in the French Church. The Third French Republic, the government that succeeded Napoleon III in 1871, continued the policy of appointing bishops, even though the government was bitterly anti-clerical. That anti-clericalism culminated in a law of 1905 that mandated a radical separation of Church and state. This was an opportunity seized on by Pope Pius X (1903-1914), who thereafter filled all episcopal vacancies in France with his own appointees.

In German lands, the process by which the pope gained complete control over the bishops was more complicated. The post-Napoleonic settlement had radically reduced the number of sovereign states in Germany to thirty-nine. In the two countries with Catholic monarchs, Austria and Bavaria, the monarch named the bishops. After the revolution of 1848, however, the Austrian government sought to bolster its support among its Catholic subjects by an 1854 treaty with the Roman Church. In it the Austrian government granted to the pope the power to confirm the state's choice of bishops. More importantly for Rome, the Austrian archbishops were henceforth to be named by the pope.

After 1815, most German Catholics had lived in states with Protestant rulers, and those monarchs did not seek to appoint Catholic bishops. Instead, a far older–indeed medieval–practice was followed: election by the clergymen of the bishop's cathedral–called collectively the cathedral chapter–who represented the other clergy and people of the diocese. In Prussia, the largest of the Protestant states, the king could indicate his preferred choice. In Hanover and most of the smaller German states, the cathedral chapters submitted lists of candidates to the government, from which it could delete those it found unacceptable. All this seems to run counter to the papal efforts to control the Church through its bishops, but these arrangements were a result of treaties between the states and the pope, not the Catholic bishops or people. The Protestant kings of these German states knew of no other way to regularize their relationship with their Catholic subjects than by turning to the pope.

At the beginning of the nineteenth century, Rome viewed the British Isles as mission country. Accordingly, the Catholic churches in England and Scotland were governed by vicars apostolic, who were bishops named and controlled by the pope. When a regular diocesan structure was set up by Roman decree–in England in 1850, in Scotland in 1878–the cathedral chapters were allowed to submit the names of candidates to Rome, but the pope declared himself free to ignore their recommendations.

In Italy, papal control was more obvious. The Law of Guarantees, promulgated by the newly united Italian state in 1871, gave the pope control of episcopal appointments, though the state retained the right of veto.

Throughout the nineteenth century and everywhere in Europe, the popes pursued centralized church power–both directly and openly and by clever maneuvering. The success of their pursuit is indicated by the words of the canon lawyer who wrote in 1911: "The election of bishops by chapters is still, theoretically, the common rule." But, he went on, "in practice...episcopal elections occur now only in a small number of cases."

The Code of Canon Law, promulgated by Rome in 1917, declared directly: "It is the sole right of the [Roman] pontiff to name bishops." In a few dioceses of Germany the traditional practice of episcopal election lived on–but only until 1986. In that year, Pope John Paul II (1978-2005) overrode the rights of the cathedral chapter of Cologne, Germany, to elect its own archbishop. The papal triumph was complete.

D. The Progressive View of the Church and Its Demise

The pontificate of Pope Pius XII (1939-1958) carried the monarchical papacy to new heights. Pius continued to centralize power in the hands of the papal bureaucracy, and he treated the bishops as his vicars, the agents of his will. At the death of Pius in 1958, the cardinals assembled to elect his successor were divided on the question of continuing his extreme form of papalism.

The cardinals chose the seventy-six-year-old Angelo Roncalli, who was considered a conciliatory and moderate man. The cardinals thought his pontificate would be short and anything but noteworthy. They were right about the length of John XXIII's reign as pope: he died after only four years and seven months in the papal office. Nevertheless, during that short time he set in motion what has been described as a "Copernican revolution for the Church" by calling for an ecumenical council, Vatican II.

According to the Council's constitution on the Church, *Lumen gentium* or "The Light of the Peoples," the Church consists of the "People of God" who are all members of a "holy priesthood" by virtue of their baptism. Supporters of this "priesthood of the faithful" did not envisiage the laity as mere helpers to the members of the "ministerial or hierarchical priesthood." Those ministers, the Council asserted, exist only to serve the faithful.

Furthermore, the Council document declared, the bishops are "not to be regarded as vicars of the Roman pontiff, for they exercise the power which they possess in their own right." This doctrine of collegiality also asserted the right of the bishops to participate as a body in the teaching authority and governance of the Church.

These statements were shocking to the bureaucrats of the papal curia, but they had been the universally accepted teachings of the patristic and medieval Church. Those earlier teachings had become known in the twentieth century through a new breed of theologians sensitive to the historical dimensions of Christian thought. The bishops at Vatican II called on scholars like the French Dominicans Yves Congar and Marie-Dominique Chenu and the German Jesuit Karl Rahner, and their work as theological experts strongly influenced the seemingly revolutionary decisions of that body. Traditionalists viewed the theology and the structures of the nineteenth-century Church as having always existed. They were challenged and, for the moment at least, defeated by historically minded progressives–a group which included Pope John XXIII. These scholars knew that the Church had changed and grown as the culture in which it lived had changed and grown. These progressives welcomed encounters with modern culture with the same enthusiasm with which Thomas Aquinas had once embraced all of Aristotle's thought that could be Christianized.

The progressive view of the Church was enshrined in *Lumen gentium*. But, like the fifteenth-century Council of Constance, the Second Vatican Council failed to set up mechanisms to implement its similar reform aspirations, and so in practice little was changed. Real power in the Church remained vested in Rome, in the pope and his papal bureaucracy. Collegiality between bishops and the pope turned out to mean that the pope would call bishops of his own choosing to Roman synods where the agenda was his and the conclusions foregone. Bishops could now meet in national conferences, but the function of these groups was to receive instructions from Rome. The bishops would then submit their implementation plans to the pope, but those plans were often overridden as inadequate.

E. Pope Paul VI on Birth Control

Implied in Vatican II's declaration of the universal priesthood of the baptized was the notion that the laity were not merely objects of clerical rule. Promoting the well-being of all the people of God was the function of their servants, the clergy. And the laity, it was thought, must be consulted on matters of concern to themselves.

How well this was observed was illustrated by Pope Paul VI (1963-1978) in 1968, in his encyclical letter *Humanae vitae (Of Human Life)*. The issue was "artificial" contraception, that is, controlling conception by any means other than sexual abstinence during times of fertility, the so-called rhythm method. Paul was regarded as a moderate progressive at the time of his election in 1963, and that assessment seemed confirmed by his appointment of a commission consisting of scientists and medical doctors, married couples and theologians, to advise him on the question of "birth control." The commission voted overwhelmingly to approve artificial contraception for married couples with children. Paul ignored his commission's finding, however, and his encyclical condemned any form of physical or chemical means of contraception, including, of course, condoms and "the pill."

This traditionalist decision was not well received. The vast majority of the Catholic laity ignored the condemnation, and among lay people the authority of the papacy suffered a devastating blow. Leading theologians condemned the encyclical. Many—perhaps most—priests counseled their flocks in the privacy of the confessional to ignore the document. A large number of bishops, acting individually or in conjunction with national episcopal bodies, rejected the encyclical as bad theology that had been badly arrived at, that is, in an anti-collegial way.

Episcopal resistance did not prevail. Rome has shown its increasing intransigence on this and other matters by appointing only bishops with solid traditionalist credentials. Among the prerequisites for episcopal office is now a firm stance against the artificial contraception widely practiced by the laity of their dioceses.

F. The Church and the Life of the Mind

The positions taken by progressives and traditionalists toward modern thought are derived from their differing anthropologies, their disparate views of human nature. Progressives see humans as basically good, even though they often tend toward selfishness. Consequently, progressives have confidence in human reason and believe that people's choices will generally be good if they are well educated in recognizing that good. Thus, the people deserve to be taught by word and example to become better choosers, better lovers, better Christians.

Traditionalists believe that the Fall has left humans extremely weak and sinful. Human beings, in this view, need rigidly defined and detailed laws and regulations to ensure they will do the right thing. This and strict enforcement of these rules of behavior will "save their souls." This phrase betrays the traditionalists' denigration of the physical and condemnation of the secular world. The world, the flesh, and the devil can be overcome only by strict adherence to the laws the pope lays down for the Church.

The consequences of this traditionalist anthropology came quickly to the surface in the papal pronouncements of the nineteenth century. For example, Pope Gregory XVI (1831-1846) declared his opposition to public health measures and to all such modern inventions as steamboats and railways. He also condemned freedom of conscience, freedom of the press, and separation of Church and state.

Gregory's opposition to modernity was matched and even exceeded by his successor, Pius IX (1846-1878), whose traditionalist exaltation of papal power we have already witnessed. In 1864, Pius extended his traditionalism to the world of thought by issuing his *Syllabus of Errors*. The *Syllabus* condemned any idea that was seen as stemming from modern thought. Pius condemned the notion that "every man is free to embrace and profess that religion which...he thinks is true." He declared false and damnable the proposition that "Protestantism is nothing other than a different form of the...Christian religion." This principle was extended by Pius' condemnation of the idea that people can "attain eternal salvation" in the practice of religions other than Catholicism.

As a consequence of these assertions, it was clear to Pius that it is only proper "that the Catholic religion be treated as the only religion of a state," and any and all other religions be excluded. It follows that Protestants moving into Catholic states should be forbidden the open practice of their faith. In those states, the governments should not have control of public schools, that control being reserved to the Church. This is but one consequence of the condemnation of separation of Church and state.

The tenor of the whole document is contained in Pius' eightieth *Syllabus* condemnation. There he declared damnable the idea that "the Roman pontiff can and ought to reconcile and harmonize himself with progress, with liberalism, and with modern civilization"–surely a splendid summary of the traditionalist position. To ensure that no Catholic teacher or writer should express disagreement with his pronouncements, Pius declared that all the teachings of the Church, not merely those that had been defined infallibly, must be rigidly and absolutely adhered to. It is clear that Pius identified the "teachings of the Church" with his own positions.

We have already met Pope Leo XIII (1878-1903) as the author of a significant response to the problems arising from the industrialization of Europe. Leo also responded to what he perceived as a threat from within the Church, a threat from Catholic scholars whom the pope first labeled as Modernists and then condemned.

This revival of the simmering conflict between traditionalists and progressives was occasioned by late nineteenth-century advances in biblical studies. Biblical scholarship had been pioneered in Germany by Protestant theology professors whose work soon inspired Catholic investigation. Progressive Catholic scholars–mostly German and French–favored freedom of enquiry in all fields because of their confidence in the rational powers and basic good will of human beings. These scholars employed the standard critical tools employed in all scholarly investigation. Their logical analysis of biblical texts was enlivened by a historical sense which recognized that the meaning of words changes over time. The appropriate meaning can best be known, they thought, by identifying the time a document was written and by recognizing the changing cultural context of the text under study by the scholar.

Using this approach, Alfred Loisy (1857-1940), a professor at the newly founded Institut Catholique in Paris, concluded that the Pentateuch, the first five books of the Bible, could not have been written by Moses. He recognized that "the first chapters of Genesis do not contain a [scientifically] exact and reliable [historical] account of the beginnings of humankind." Although these views are commonplace among scholars today, they were bitterly attacked by traditionalists ignorant of historical and critical methods of research. Pope Leo's encyclical on the question declared that there was no possibility of error in the Bible.

Leo's solution to all philosophical and theological questions was to appeal to the thought of Thomas Aquinas. The Aquinas to whom Leo appealed, however, was an Aquinas wrenched out of his historical context and understood as the timeless source of answers to all intellectual questions. Thomas would not have recognized himself in this Neo-Thomism. Nevertheless, in 1880 Leo named Thomas the patron saint of all Catholic universities and insisted that they and all seminaries offer a rigidly ahistorical version of Thomas as their official–and only–philosophic and theological fare.

Leo's successor, Pope Pius X (1903-1914), went still further. In 1906, he affirmed that all Catholics must recognize Moses as the author of the whole Pentateuch–despite the fact that Moses' death was recorded in that biblical source. In 1907, he issued an encyclical that described "Modernism" as the "most pernicious of all the adversaries of the Church" and the source of "poisonous doctrines."

The papal campaign–called the Black Terror–against "Modernism" included the suppression of suspect Catholic newspapers, examination of the mail of seminary professors, and a greatly expanded number of titles being placed on the Index of Forbidden Books. Students–like Angelo Roncalli, the future Pope John XXIII–were liable to suspicion and condemnation for having written essays that spoke of faith in conjunction with scientific research. All priests and those about to be ordained–along with their seminary professors–were required to take an oath against Modernism. As a result Catholic seminaries remained bastions of biblical literalism until the middle of the twentieth seminary. The Neo-Thomist philosophy and theology taught in those seminaries was thought to answer all questions and any attempt at creative thought was discouraged.

In 1909, a papal bureaucrat named Umberto Benigni set up a spy network, called the "Pious Society," with the intent of rooting out all "modernizers" and traces of Modernism from the Church. Vigilance committees and censors were set up in every diocese to detect dangerous speech or writing on such forbidden subjects as democracy or ecumenism. These diocesan committees drew up lists of suspects–including cardinals–that they sent to Rome for papal action. They were urged by Rome to pay special attention to priests who rode bicycles and thus demonstrated their acceptance of modern culture. Victims of this modern inquisition were ousted from their pastoral or teaching positions, and some were driven from the priesthood.

Some forty to fifty years after Pius X dealt the apparent death blow to Modernism, progressive thought reappeared in full flower. The central event in this revival was, of course, the Second Vatican Council (1962-1965). The mood of the time was indicated by the Italian word *aggiornamento*, that had been used by Angelo Roncalli, the future Pope John XXIII, as early as 1957. *Aggiornamento* (renewal, updating, modernizing) set the Council's agenda. The standard for this renewal process was to be sought in the thought of Christian antiquity and the Middle Ages. The word expressing this quest was French, *ressourcement*, meaning "return to the sources."

Ressourcement was a theological activity practiced quietly by a number of scholars in the period before the Council. As we have seen, the leaders in this quest for Church renewal were employed by the bishops at that Council. Before the Council met, however, each of those theologians had been condemned by the Holy Office–the successor to the Inquisition–in Rome. The French Dominicans Yves Congar and Marie-Dominique Chenu were silenced by Pope Pius XII, as were the French Jesuit Henri de Lubac and the German Jesuit Karl Rahner. The scholars whose thought informed the decrees of Vatican II–and who often drafted the documents emanating from that Council–were men who shortly before had been under grave suspicion of heresy. One of these was John Courtney Murray (1904-1967), an American Jesuit who ignored Pius IX's *Syllabus of Errors* by advocating religious freedom. Murray boldly took issue with the head of the Holy Office, Cardinal Alfredo Ottaviani, who had declared that "error has no rights." As a consequence, Murray was notified that henceforth he would have to clear all his writings on the subject of toleration with Rome. Despite this, Murray was invited to assist the American bishops at Vatican II and played an important role in the framing of the Council's *Declaration on Religious Freedom*.

The progressive victories at Vatican II were so unexpected and so impressive that they drew the attention and admiration of Protestant theologians. The leading exponent of traditional Protestantism at the time of Vatican II, the 1960s, was Karl Barth, whom we have met. About that Council, Barth declared in 1963, that, thanks to Pope John XXIII, "we are witnessing a complete reinterpretation of Catholic dogma." He continued: "The thoughts expounded by...modern theologians...are no longer views of a small spearhead minority, but form the very ground swell of Catholic renewal." Little did Barth know that traditionalists would once again prevail.

G. John Paul II

The traditionalist reaction to the progressive thought emanating form Vatican II was led by a Polish prelate, Karol Wojtyla, who was elected pope in 1978 and took the name John Paul II. Assessments of his long pontificate by traditionalists and progressives vary radically, but virtually everyone agrees on his charismatic character and amazing media skills. Less than a week after his election, he invited some 2,000 journalists to a press conference at the Vatican. Frequent audiences for masses of pilgrims to Rome reinforced a rapidly developing popularity which approached the adulation accorded a pop star. This peripatetic pope traveled some 670,000 miles to meet adoring audiences in lands far distant from Rome. John Paul reached out openly, as well, to people of all faiths, of all religions.

Progressive Catholics were less than enthusiastic about the Polish pope. They saw in him a man dead set against any changes in the Church. Though the pope continually professed his support for Vatican II, progressives perceived his beliefs and actions running counter to that Council's spirit and intent. His own intent, they observed, was to strengthen loyalty to papal authority and the centralized hierarchy of the Church. Progressives deeply regretted his uncompromising and autocratic stances on contraception, clerical celibacy, and the ordination of women.

For traditionalists, John Paul II provided much needed discipline and a renewed sense of direction to the Church. John Paul's youthful spirit and active participation in sports such as mountain climbing won over many young Catholics. Traditionalists of all ages were taken with the pope's unabashed assertion of the importance of religion and Christianity. No one could doubt John Paul's forcefulness in asserting what Catholics–and, indeed, all people–should believe and do. His definitions and denunciations of evil seemed all the more convincing in that he had faced–and faced down–evil in the form of the Communist dictatorship in his homeland. John Paul's resolute and largely successful traditionalism received powerful support from his right-hand man at the Vatican, Joseph Alois Ratzinger, his successor as pope.

H. A Church Deeply Divided

The Catholic Church of the early twenty-first century is profoundly troubled. Progressives see the Church as the "people of God"; traditionalists identify the Church with a hierarchy ruled absolutely by the pope. This rule is necessary, claim the traditionalists, because humans are weak and sinful, and thus they need detailed rules to follow and iron discipline when they fail. According to progressives, humans are basically good, but they need the support of a loving community, the Church, to live a life of Christian commitment.

For the traditionalists intellectual inquiry is inadequate in determining the truth and in ascertaining the moral good. The hierarchical Church must supply doctrinal direction and crush dissent in a world in which whatever is new is threatening. Progressives welcome the new in whatever form and are confident that it can be reconciled with Christianity.

What does all this mean for the people in the pew? Most lay Catholics will continue to be divided, though not necessarily hostile, over the means of expressing their religious impulses. Traditionalists will continue to rely on external practices featuring strict observance of detailed rules. They will receive spiritual nourishment from devotions to the Sacred Heart of Jesus and the Immaculate Heart of Mary. Mary will continue to occupy the central place in the hearts of many who will recite the Rosary in her honor by repeating a prayer to her while counting the repetitions on a circlet of beads. Those who are sufficiently affluent will visit the many sites of her supposed apparitions. This devotionalism is not new. It dates back to the Late Middle Ages, although it is now typically expressed in nineteenth-century forms.

What is new in the world of traditional devotionalism is the cult of the pope. Pius IX was the first to foster this devotion to the person of the pope. He did it through friendly strolls through Rome and audiences for distinguished visitors to Rome. The audiences became mass meetings in the twentieth century, ranging from packed halls built for the purpose to outdoor encounters with a pope whisked about in a pope-mobile. In the second half of the twentieth century, popes have traveled away from Rome to receive the acclamation of the people of many lands. The pontificate of John Paul II was often punctuated by television images of the pontiff descending from a plane to kiss the tarmac of airports around the globe. This phenomenon is a marvelous example of how culture–in this case modern material culture–can influence the way Christianity is expressed.

The spirituality of progressives is less spectacular and more interior. It tends to emphasize the interior life through meditation and reading of Scripture. However, it also emphasizes the social character of human beings through charitable works and participation in eucharistic and other liturgical services featuring prayer, singing and, sometimes, dance. The spiritual life of progressives features restraint in external acts and in non-liturgical devotions. Their attitude toward Mary, for example, is reverent but muted, since her Son occupies the central place in their life.

Despite the aggressive actions of radicals ranging from ecclesiastical anarchists to rigorously disciplined traditionalist groups like Opus Dei, I am convinced that schism will not come. Most Catholics will continue their involvement in local church communities. Most will continue to ignore papal pronouncements which impinge on their sexual activity, and some will walk away from the Church–although not necessarily from Christianity.

XIX. RELIGION AND CULTURE IN TODAY'S WORLD

Some Useful Data

1858–1947	Max Planck, German physicist
1879-1955	Albert Einstein, German physicist
1901-1976	Werner Heisenberg, German physicist
1899-1992	Friedrich A. Hayek, Austrian economist
1911-1996	Milovan Djilas, Yugoslav Communist leader

The place of religion in contemporary western culture is complex and confusing–at least to me. The traditional religions that have in the past influenced the culture of the West seem today to be largely ignored in Europe and in the lands inhabited by Europeans in the Americas and Oceania. Even the secular religions bequeathed to us by the nineteenth century, Liberalism and Marxism, have apparently lost their power. The West seems increasingly directionless. It seems to have lost any unifying sense of purpose.

The most powerful cultural unifier for Westerners today is the ubiquitous medium of television, but the fare shown on television is largely bland stuff. Television's entertainment value can be measured by the painful watching of endless hours of homogenous "situation comedies" that neither challenge the mind nor engage the heart. Highly popular "reality shows" highlight and encourage human foibles and follies. Twenty-four hour news channels seem unable to provide enough genuine news to fill out the time available and instead offer the "talking heads" of "experts" who seem to say much the same thing whatever channel one watches. Television touts consumerism as the path to self-fulfillment. The media tell us which cars to buy, what clothes to purchase, and the nature and number of the health products that will restore us. Happiness, it would seem, consists in buying, having, and consuming things.

Young people have replaced the old as the arbiters of western culture. Teenagers have determined the clothing worn, the music heard, and the values promoted. Those values rarely extend beyond the sensual: the gratification of the senses and the indulgence of sexual appetites.

A. The Phenomenon of Fundamentalism

The rejection of traditional values has led many to feel a need for direction, to seek a sense of purpose. That quest has taken the religious form of fundamentalism, especially in America. Many Americans–especially those living in the southern sections of the United States–have embraced a form of Christianity that promises to overcome the lack of meaning and direction in contemporary culture. For fundamentalists of the Protestant persuasion, the Bible, read literally, provides the answers to all human problems and moral dilemmas; it provides an anchor securing the believer in a world of terrifyingly threatening seas.

What the Bible bestows on Protestant fundamentalists, the pope provides to Catholic fundamentalists. Peter's successor is the firm rock to which they can cling in this time of trials. The pope provides to the faithful fundamentalist a trustworthy father figure who will protect his children from a hostile world. Like a father, he educates his children in the unchanging values that, though often requiring heroic and unquestioning response, bring security in the midst of meaninglessness.

Fundamentalism, in whatever form, is a force opposing modern culture. Its tenacity and resiliency may surprise the outsider. It is successful to the extent that it provides its adherents with a psychological stability that makes their lives seem meaningful.

As powerful a force as fundamentalism is in the lives of its adherents, those adherents constitute a very small fragment of the people who see themselves as sharers in western culture. Religion is rejected–more often ignored–by most Europeans. Catholic churches in Italy serve mere handfuls of worshipers–most often elderly women. Likewise, Lutheran services in Sweden are attended by equally few of the aged faithful, though there are a few more men among them than in Italy. Secularism prevails in both Italy and Sweden. Most people of Europe and the other lands where Europeans dwell look to the things of this world for their well-being. By and large they no longer accept even the secular religions of their relatively recent past. The classic liberalism of the Enlightenment and the militant collectivism of both sorts of Marxism–communist and socialist–have lost their appeal. If there is one world view to which most Westerners subscribe, it is an unsophisticated adherence to science. Our quest in this chapter is to seek the shape of our own culture. We shall also ask–if not answer–questions about the possible role of religion, and particularly Christianity, in that culture.

B. The Collapse of Communism

The collapse that we shall explore here is not the fall of the Soviet Union in the early 90s of the twentieth century, though this collapse may well have influenced that fall. We speak here of the moral collapse of a system that–in the middle of the twentieth century–was so strong in both commitment and power that it almost succeeded in world domination. Our study will be of the revealing thought of Milovan Djilas.

Djilas was born in 1911, in Serbia, later a part of Yugoslavia. During World War II, he was a member of the Yugoslav underground, and he both killed and risked death to bring Communism to his people and country. His single-minded dedication to that cause led to membership in the first Communist Politburo to rule his newly liberated land. The leader of the new communist state, Marshal Tito, made Djilas his Vice-President.

In 1954, Djilas used his high post as a base from which to demand the "democratization" of politics in his country. As a result, Tito expelled him from the Communist Party. As an incisive critic of Soviet domination of Eastern Europe, Djilas hailed the Hungarian anti-Soviet Revolution of 1956. This led Tito to clamp him in prison, where Djilas spent "nine cold winters" in the 1950s and 1960s. Before he died in 1996, at the age of 83, he saw the western world acclaim his 1957 work *The New Class*.

In that book Djilas looked back fondly on the idealism that had inspired the young Communists who had fought with him in the underground against Naziism:

> History does not have many movements that, like Communism, began their ascent with such high moral principles and with such devoted, enthusiastic, and clever warriors. They were attached to each other by ideas and suffering. To that attachment was joined the selfless love, comradeship, solidarity, and the warm and open sincerity that can be produced only by battles in which fighters are either fated to win or doomed to die.

These deeply committed young men and women had sought personal happiness and their growth as individuals through "deep devotion to the party, enthusiastic sacrifice for others, protective care for the young, and tender respect for the aged." Djilas declared: "These are the ideals of true Communists!"–and his declaration was delivered with all the determination of an early Christian martyr facing lions in the Colosseum. Communism had supplied Djilas and his comrades with a powerful substitute for the Christianity they had rejected.

However, Djilas discovered that this noble vision and the comraderie that was Communism quickly dissipated when the party took power in Yugoslavia. The "robot-bureaucrats" who came to control the government exhibited "intolerance, servility, opportunism, and self-centeredness." The "former high principles" of party members were "transformed into the intolerant and pharisaical morals of a privileged caste." The heroes of the underground "became self-centered cowards without ideas or friends, willing to renounce everything–honor, name, truth, and morals–to keep their place in the ruling class and the inner circle of the ruling hierarchy."

The fall of capitalism, Djilas found, did not lead to a classless society but to a new ruling class, the bureaucrats. The noble ideal, the glorious vision, the goal for which everything had been sacrificed, proved to be a sham. The world view of Marx–the religion of the triumphant proletariat–had proved itself a hollow idol.

C. The Metamorphosis of Liberalism

In 1944, Friedrich A. Hayek published a book titled *The Road to Serfdom*. According to Hayek, the serfdom into which western culture is sinking is the result of the ever-shrinking freedom caused by ever-growing governmental control. "Instead of freedom and prosperity," Hayek wrote, "bondage and misery stare us in the face."

Friedrich A. Hayek was born in 1899, and as a young man in his 20s he became a leading light in the Viennese school of economics. This group of scholars predicted that tyranny would result from Socialist destruction of "Liberal," free-market economics.

Hayek continued his anti-Socialist crusade as a professor at the University of Chicago and at Freiburg im Breisgau, Germany until his death in 1992. "We have progressively abandoned," declared Hayek, "that freedom in economic affairs without which personal and political freedom has never existed in the past." Hayek put the problem bluntly: "Socialism means slavery, and we have steadily moved in the direction of socialism."

The presuppositions of Hayek's argument are clearly derived from the Enlightenment–especially his profound commitment to the idea of progress. "During the whole of the modern period of European history," he asserted, "the general direction of social development was one of freeing the individual from the ties that bound him to the customary and prescribed ways of pursuing his ordinary activities." This growth in individual freedom led to a "marvelous growth of science," which led in turn to industrial freedom and innovation. "Whenever the barriers to human ingenuity were removed," Hayek wrote, "man became rapidly able to satisfy ever widening ranges of desire." Progress demands freedom and leads to the material prosperity that was Hayek's definition of happiness.

Hayek admitted that total freedom from governmental restraint, "*laissez-faire* liberalism," has led to some "very dark spots in society." Hayek all but ignored the horrors of the eighteenth- and nineteenth-century factory system, but acknowledged the more recent economic dislocations that led to the world-wide Great Depression of the 1930s. These economic obstacles can be overcome if only liberals can desist from their "wooden insistence on certain rough rules of thumb, above all the principles of *laissez faire*." With this Hayek admitted that governmental controls on the economy are, after all, necessary.

Hayek's "fundamental principle," it turns out, was "that in the ordering of our affairs we should make as much use as possible of the spontaneous forces of society and resort as little as possible to coercion." He did not spell out the proper balance between spontaneity and governmental coercion.

It is difficult not to see inconsistency in Hayek's argument. He told us that growth in freedom from governmental restraint has brought us liberty and prosperity. Then he acknowledged that governmental restraint of economic forces and activities is necessary to avoid economic stress. Hayek's optimism, his belief in progress, rivals that of Cordorcet's *Progress of the Human Mind*. "There could be no doubt," he wrote, "that governments possess enormous powers for good or evil, and there is every reason to believe that, with a better understanding of the problems, we should some day be able to use these powers successfully." Knowledge is the virtue that leads to success, to progress in attaining the happiness of prosperity. But Hayek, like the Enlightenment *philosophes* before him, did not account for the evil which has so often prevented prosperity. And, like the Enlightenment, Hayek simply assumed that economic prosperity, the possession of goods, is the only path to happiness. Like the Enlightenment, there is no room in Hayek's liberal view of things for values transcending the material, for religion of any sort.

The sort of liberalism that has carried the day in the West is quite different from Hayek's classical version. This new "liberalism"–as it is called in the United States–is shockingly similar, perhaps identical, to the "socialism" that has prevailed in Europe. In recent history, the "socialist" Prime Minister of Great Britain, Tony Blair, adopted the American President Bill Clinton's "liberal" politics as the standard for the British Labour Party. In both cases, ideology has virtually disappeared, to be replaced by a thorough-going pragmatism.

Both "liberals" in the United States and "socialists" in Europe have long rejected the *laissez-faire* liberalism of the nineteenth century. They consider that whatever progress it brought was in technology, not in human happiness. Modern technology has brought the devastation of war on a scale undreamed of by earlier ages. It has also brought the degradation of the environment and a fundamentally inequitable distribution of wealth.

Neither European socialists nor American liberals have given up the Enlightenment notion of progress, however. The betterment of humankind–conceived almost exclusively in materialistic terms–will be achieved by governmental action and control. That action and control will be planned and executed by ever-increasing numbers of government bureaucrats and technocrats–people who know best how to bring the benefits of progress. Since World War II, European socialism has almost completely abandoned its ideological roots in Marxism. It has placed less emphasis on nationalization of the means of economic production and has reemphasized the growth of the welfare state. Liberalism and socialism have come to the point of being variations on a common theme. For both, ideology is outdated, except for complete trust in the wisdom of the bureaucrats whose knowledge and expertise will bring us ever closer to material happiness. If classical liberalism and traditional socialism have failed, they have been replaced by Comte's vision of a secular, positivistic utopia based on science.

D. Science and Religion

We all believe in science. With good reason. The application of scientific knowledge has brought us a degree of comfort the world has never before known. Science has given us the medical knowledge without which I should have been dead several times over–and I am grateful. Applications of scientific knowledge to transportation have meant that more and more of us travel from place to place, at a greater and greater speed–and for that I am grateful too. The down side of this is that our greater highway speed allows us to kill more and more people as we travel from place to place.

In one sense, the Enlightenment hope has been fulfilled. Material progress is a reality. But whether that material progress has made us happier is at least open to doubt. Science has not reduced the number of murders or the incidence of suicide in our world. Are we any closer to knowing the nature of fundamental reality through science? Can we answer the basic moral or ethical questions through science? Scientists rarely address these questions. Yet a sophisticated attempt to address them has been made by one of the greatest and most renowned of modern scientists: Max Planck.

Most of Max Planck's long life (1858-1947) was spent as professor of theoretical physics at the University of Berlin. He was one of a trio of Berlin physicists who made Isaac Newton's understanding of the universe obsolete. In 1905, Albert Einstein (1879-1955) proposed his Theory of Relativity that denied to time and space and motion the absolute character that the Newtonian world view had assumed and asserted. In 1927, Werner Heisenberg (1901-1976) demonstrated that the more one knows about the location of a subatomic particle, the less one knows about its speed–and vice versa. Heisenberg had discovered that the measurement of physical phenomena alters the objects measured. His Uncertainty Principle implied that there was a definite limit to the knowledge scientists can gain of even the physical world.

Planck's contribution to the revolution in modern physics was made in an address to the Berlin Physics Society on December 14, 1900. The Quantum Theory he there propounded earned him the Nobel Prize in Physics in 1918. Planck addressed the fact that light, when measured in certain ways, does not behave according to the long-standing wave theory. He posited that light was emitted in minute bundles or packets of energy called quanta (singular: quantum). Planck's theory prompted a wholesale overhaul of the fundamentals of physics. Scientists and engineers have transformed his quantum idea into a host of technological marvels–from transistor radios to supercomputers.

In his *Scientific Autobiography* of 1941, Planck addressed the role and meaning of science in modern culture. He began by discussing the nature and needs of humankind. Humans seek knowledge and the power that flows from it, and these science can, to a degree, supply. However, people desire more than this. They want, wrote Heisenberg, a "standard, a measure of their actions, a criterion by which to judge what is valuable and what is worthless." They desire, in short, "an ideology, a philosophy of life, that will assure them of the greatest good on earth: peace of mind." Planck continued: "Religion has failed to satisfy human longing," and so humans "seek a substitute in exact science."

The difficulty with the scientific approach to human happiness, Planck has told us, is that the foundations of "exact science" are not self-evident. We have sought in vain for the objective truths that a "science without presuppositions" would give us. Is there a way out of this dilemma? Planck undertook to answer this question, hoping that the "answer would cast a light on both the meaning and limits of exact science."

Science deals with data, Planck affirmed, through a "logically, mathematically, and philosophically disciplined reasoning," and it is the senses that "furnish science with the raw material for its labors." The difficulty is that sensation and perception differ–sometimes radically–from one person to another, and thus they supply science with subjective–not objective-data.

Most people think of the world that emerges from the application of science to sensation as the "real world." But, warned Planck, this "phenomenological world" always remains a mere approximation of reality. Since humankind is constantly accumulating new sense data, the "phenomenological world is not fixed and constant, but is in a process of constant change." The goal of a scientific world picture that needs no improvement and, therefore, represents ultimate reality, can never be attained. Through science one cannot know the really real, the metaphysical world. Between the phenominological world of science and the metaphysical world, there will always remain "a gaping, unbridgeable chasm." What then?

In Planck's *Religion and Natural Science* (1937), he asked "whether and to what extent a truly religious attitude is compatible with the knowledge gained through natural science?" Planck the physicist answered: "Physical research has established as an incontestable fact that the basic building blocks of the universe," such as electrons, protons, and the like, "are mutually interlinked according to one uniform plan. In other words, every process in nature is subject to a universal and, up to a point, knowable law." The "most adequate formulation" of scientific laws, wrote Planck, "creates the impression in every unbiased mind that nature is ruled by a rational, purposive will." "Thus," he concluded, "our instinctive intellectual striving for a unified world picture demands that we identify with each other the two universal and active, yet mysterious forces: the world order of natural science and the God of religion."

E. A Brief Postscript

Though an impressive affirmation of the compatibility of our scientific culture with religion, Planck's position gives every evidence of remaining the view of a small minority. The possibility of a culture–like that of the High Middle Ages–permeated, directed, and held together by Christianity seems so remote as to be absurd.

I am not disheartened by this. I believe that the creating, sustaining, and sanctifying force in the universe is love–God's love. I believe that God loves each and every individual–whether religious or irreligious, whether Christian or not–with an overwhelming love that will somehow bring about the happiness of each and all–if not in this life, then in another. I believe that God acts in and through all cultures and does not need a throughly Christian culture in which to operate.

The eager affirmation of Christian values, a joyous way of life governed by the basic Christian virtue of love, must today be a matter of personal choice and individual action. We have the knowledge and freedom to affirm these values, to live a life of love. In the end, happiness does not require a Christian cultural environment. Early Christians also lived and flourished in a culture antipathic to their values. Happiness, they believed, ultimately depends on being a good lover, on being open to the gift of love bestowed gratuitously by a loving God. I too believe this.

INDEX OF PERSONS

Abelard, Peter, 11, 102
Acton, Lord John, 195
Adalberon of Laon, 83
Adams, John, 194
Adrian VI, pope, 153
Aelred of Rievaulx, 72, 89-90
Albert the Great, 103
Albrecht von Hohenzollern, 136
Alcuin of York, 40
Alexander III, pope, 100, 108
Alexander V, Pisan pope, 116
Aleyn, Simon, 150
Altizer, Thomas, 221-22
Ambrose of Milan, 25, 56, 99
Anselm of Canterbury, 106
Anselm of Havelberg, 76
Aquinas, Thomas, 11, 79, 88-89, 103-104, 106, 162, 163, 182, 224, 229, 232
Aristotle, 4, 11-13, 22, 99, 101-102, 103-104, 106, 162, 182, 184
Arius, 17, 18
Athanasius, 17, 18
Augustine of Canterbury, 28, 35-36
Augustine of Hippo, 12, 19, 20, 23, 41, 42, 71, 143
Averroës, 103
Barth, Karl, 222, 233-34
Basil of Caesarea, 27
Bede, 35-36
Benedict XI, 112-13
Benedict of Nursia, 27-28, 89
Benigni, Umberto, 233
Bernard of Chartres, 77
Bernard of Clairvaux, 4, 11, 41, 63-64, 69-73, 75, 82, 90-91, 93, 107, 142-43, 163, 175

Bernstein, Eduard, 209
Bérulle, Pierre de, 176-77
Bismarck, Otto von, 210-11
Blair, Tony, 241-42
Boëthius, 11, 99
Boleyn, Anne, 148, 149
Bonaventure, 104, 224
Boniface VIII, pope, 110-12, 113, 118
Boniface, apostle to the Germans, 38-39
Bossuet, Jacques Bénigne, 169-70
Boyle, Robert, 181
Bruno of Cologne, 74
Bultmann, Rudolf, 220
Burke, Edmund, 194-96
Burkhardt, Jacob, 130, 181
Calixtus II, pope, 61
Calvin, John, 143-44, 170, 206
Canisius, Peter, 161
Carafa, Gian Pietro. See Paul IV, pope
Carnegie, Andrew, 206
Cassiodorus, 28
Catherine of Aragon, 147-48, 149
Catherine of Siena, 117
Celestine V, pope, 111
Charles the Bald, 44
Charles the Fat, 45-46
Charles the Great, Charlemagne, 4, 39-42, 44, 45, 56, 59, 147, 154
Charles V, Roman emperor, 148
Charles I, king of England, 176
Charles II, king of Naples, 111
Chaucer, Geoffrey, 83, 89-90
Chenu, Marie-Dominique, 229, 233
Christ. See Jesus
Christian IV, king of Denmark, 167

Cicero, 11, 99
Clare of Assisi, 80
Clement V, pope, 113-14
Clement VII, Avignon pope, 115
Clement VII, pope, 153
Clement XI, pope, 162
Clement XIV, pope, 169
Clement of Alexandria, 9, 11, 19, 132
Clement of Rome, 20
Clinton, Bill, 241
Clovis, 2, 4, 32-34
Comte, Auguste, 1, 217-18, 219, 242
Condorcet, Jean de, 180, 181, 194, 217
Confucius, 161
Congar, Yves, 229, 233
Conrad III, Roman emperor, 70
Conrad of Marburg, 94
Constantine, Roman emperor, 14, 24, 51
Contarini, Gaspar, 154-55
Cox, Harvey, 222
Cunigunda, Roman empress, 57
Cyprian of Carthage, 21
Dante Alighieri, 87, 126
Darwin, Charles, 214-16
Diderot, Denis, 182, 187
Diocletian, Roman emperor, 24
Djilas, Milovan, 239-40
Dominic Guzmán, 78
Eck, Johann, 139, 142
Eckermann, Johann Peter, 197
Edward I, king of England, 112, 119
Edward III, king of England, 119, 121
Edward VI, king of England, 148-49
Egmont, count, 197
Einhard, 39-40, 41-42
Einstein, Albert, 243
Elizabeth, queen of England, 149
Engels, Friedrich, 206
Erasmus, Desiderius, 140-43, 152-53, 155, 156, 175
Eugenius III, pope, 69-70, 75, 76, 107
Eugenius IV, pope, 117, 126
Febronius, 168
Ferdinand II, Roman emperor, 166
Feuerbach, Ludwig, 221
Fisher, John, 148
Francis of Assisi, 72, 77-78, 87
Francis de Sales, 175-76
Franke, Hermann, 172

Frederick II, Roman emperor, 62, 118
Frederick, king of Bohemia, 166
Frederick II, king of Prussia, 184-85
Frederick the Wise, elector of Saxony, 137
Frederick William I, king of Prussia, 171
Frederick William III, king of Prussia, 190-91
Freud, Sigmund, 219
Galen, 98
Galileo Galilei, 4, 104, 162-63
Gauzelin of Paris, 45
Gelasius I, bishop of Rome, 25-26
George III, king of England, 84
Gerbert. *See* Sylvester II, pope
Gibbon, Edward, 181
God, 1, 2, 8-10, 12, 14-17, 19, 20, 22, 23, 26, 28, 33, 36, 37, 41, 42, 53, 57, 59, 69, 71, 72, 73, 77, 83, 85, 87, 88, 90, 92, 94, 103-104, 105, 106, 129, 130, 133, 138, 140-41, 142, 143-44, 147, 159, 163, 169-70, 173, 175-76, 177, 180, 183, 186, 189, 190-91, 196, 197, 215-16, 217, 221-22, 244
Goethe, Johann Wolfgang von, 196-98, 199-200
Gratian, 108
Gregory I, the Great, bishop of Rome, 35-37, 82
Gregory II, bishop of Rome, 38
Gregory VII, pope, 59-61
Gregory IX, pope, 91, 93-94, 108
Gregory XI, pope, 115
Gregory XVI, pope, 231
Gregory of Tours, 32-33
Grimm, Jakob and Wilhelm, 200
Guillaume de Nogaret, 110, 112-13
Gustavus II Adolphus, king of Sweden, 167
Harnack, Adolf von, 220
Harvey, William, 181
Hayek, Friedrich A., 240-41
Heine, Heinrich, 200
Heisenberg, Werner, 243
Henrietta Maria, queen of England, 176

Henry II, Roman emperor, 57-58
Henry III, Roman emperor, 49, 58, 60
Henry IV, Roman emperor, 58-61, 84
Henry V, Roman emperor, 61
Henry VI, Roman emperor, 62
Henry VII (Tudor), king of England, 120
Henry VIII, king of England, 4, 147-48, 149, 156
Henry III, king of France, 166
Henry IV, king of France, 166
Henry of Guise, 166
Heraclitus, 8
Hildebrand. *See* Gregory VII
Hippocrates, 98
Hitler, Adolf, 184, 219
Homer, 9, 11, 12
Hroswitha of Gandersheim, 50
Hus, John, 116
Ignatius of Antioch, 20
Ignatius of Loyola, 159-60
Innocent III, pope, 62-63, 64, 91, 93, 117
Innocent VIII, pope, 136
Irenaeus of Lyon, 21
Jacques de Molay, 113
Jane de Chantel, 176
Jansen, Cornelius, 177
Jefferson, Thomas, 184, 194
Jesus Christ, 1, 8, 9, 12, 14-16, 17, 18, 20, 21, 24, 25, 26, 33-34, 37, 50, 63, 71-72, 73, 77-78, 83, 87, 90, 91, 105, 106, 117, 125, 128-29, 132, 134, 138, 139, 145-46, 155, 156, 158, 159, 161, 169, 173, 177, 180, 220-22, 226, 235
John XII, pope, 49
John XXII, pope, 125
John XXIII, Pisan pope, 116
John XXIII, pope, 229, 232, 233
John of the Cross, 175
John of Salisbury, 84, 89
John Paul II, pope, 228, 234, 235
Joseph II, Roman emperor, 185
Julian "the Apostate," Roman emperor, 24
Julius II, pope, 132-33, 152-53
Justin Martyr, 8-9, 11-12, 19, 132
Justinian, Roman emperor, 34

Kautsky, Karl, 209
Ladislas, king of Naples, 116
Layard, Austin Henry, 195
Leo I, bishop of Rome, 21
Leo III, bishop of Rome, 42
Leo X, pope, 136, 138, 153
Leo XIII, pope, 209-10, 231-32
Lessing, Gotthold Ephraim, 186
Linnaeus, Carolus, 198
Loisy, Alfred, 232
Lothair, Roman emperor, 44
Louis the Pious, Roman emperor, 44
Louis VII, king of France, 70
Louis IX, king of France, 111
Louis XIV, king of France, 168, 169, 187
Louis XV, king of France, 187
Louis XVI, king of France, 187, 189
Lowe, Robert, 195
Lubac, Henri de, 233
Luther, Martin, 4, 136-43, 145-47, 156, 161, 172
Machiavelli, Niccolò, 149
Malthus, Thomas, 214
Manegold of Lautenbach, 84
Manning, Henry Edward, cardinal, 216
Maria Theresa, Roman empress, 170, 185
Marozia, 49
Martianus Capella, 11
Martin V, pope, 126, 152
Marx, Karl, 206-208, 209
Mary, queen of England, 149
Mazzini, Giuseppe, 218-19
Medici, Catherine de', 166
Medici, Lorenzo de', 136
Mendel, Gregor, 215
Mendelssohn, Moses, 186
Murray, John Courtney, 233
Napoleon Bonaparte, 118, 189-90, 191, 225
Napoleon III, French emperor, 227
Nero, Roman emperor, 24
Nevski, Alexander, 120
Newton, Isaac, 181, 243
Nicholas II, pope, 58
Nicholas of Cusa, 126, 128, 142
Nietzsche, Friedrich, 221
Norbert of Xanten, 75-76, 79

Odilo of Cluny, 57
Odo, count of Paris, 45
Ogden, Shubert, 221
Olier, Jean-Jaques, 176-77
Ottaviani, Alfredo, 233
Otto I, Roman emperor, 48-49
Otto II, Roman emperor, 51
Otto of Braunschweig, 62-63
Ovid, 4, 9-12, 131
Papias of Hierapolis, 18
Pashal II, pope, 61
Paul the Apostle, 11, 14, 17, 20
Paul III, pope, 153-54, 155, 156
Paul IV, pope 154-56, 157
Paul VI, pope, 230
Pepin the Short, 39
Pericles, 41
Peter the Apostle, 21, 226
Peter Lombard, 106
Philip IV, the Fair, king of France, 110, 111-13, 118
Philip VI, of Valois, king of France, 119
Philip of Hohenstaufen, 62-63
Pike, James A., 220
Pius VII, pope, 189
Pius IX, pope, 225-27, 231
Pius X, pope, 227, 232-33
Pius XII, pope, 226, 229
Planck, Max, 242-44
Plato, 8-9, 11, 12, 13, 19, 22
Plotinus, 22
Pole, Reginald, 154, 156-57
Porphyry, 11
Proclus, 22
Quintilian, 11, 99
Rahner, Karl, 229, 233
Ramon Lull, 84-85
Ratzinger, Joseph Alois, 234
Ricci, Matteo, 4, 161-62
Richelieu, Armand de, cardinal, 167
Robert Grosseteste, 104, 181
Robespierre, Maximilien, 189
Robinson, James, 220
Robinson, John A. T., 220
Rousseau, Jean-Jaques, 184, 189
Rupert of Deutz, 76
Sarpi, Paolo, 158

Satan, 37, 140, 147
Schweitzer, Albert, 220
Sciarra Colonna, 110, 112
Sigismund, Roman emperor, 116
Simon de Montfort, 93
Smiles, Samuel, 205-206, 216
Socrates, 8, 9, 12, 13
Spencer, Herbert, 216-17
Spener, Philipp Jakob, 172
Stalin, Joseph, 184
Stephen II, bishop of Rome, 39
Strauss, David Friedrich, 220
Sylvester II, pope, 50-51
Tacitus, 30-31
Terence, 50
Teresa of Ávila, 175
Tertullian, 12-13, 26, 99
Tetzel, Johannes, 136-37, 138
Theodoric the Ostrogoth, 34
Theodosius, Roman emperor, 24-25
Tillich, Paul, 221
Tilly, count, 167
Tito, 239
Tyler, Wat, 120
Urban II, pope, 63
Urban VI, pope, 115
Vergil, 11, 12, 131
Voltaire, 182, 183, 184, 187
Wallenstein, Albert von, 167
Walter von der Vogelweide, 86
Weigel, Gustave, 220
Weiss, Johannes, 220
Welf IV, duke, 70
Wesley, Charles, 173
Wesley, John, 173-74
Wilberforce, Samuel, 215-16
William the Pious, duke of Aquitaine, 56-57
Wordsworth, William, 198-99
Wrede, William, 220
Zachary, bishop of Rome, 38
Zeno, Roman Emperor, 25
Zwingli, Huldrych, 145-46

INDEX OF TOPICS

Affectus, 71
Aggiornamento, 233
Albigensian(s), 92-94
Allodial land, 57
American Christian Temperance Union, 205-206
Anglicanism, 149, 200
Anglican(s) 149, 173, 176, 196, 215, 220
Anointing, 62, 107
Anthropology, 23, 36, 140-43, 160, 170, 175, 178, 182, 230-31
Apostolic authority, 19-21
Apostolic life, 75
Apprenticeship, 30, 88
Art, 34, 53, 124, 131, 132-34
Assumption, 226
Astronomy, 98, 101, 198
Atheism, 209, 219
Avignon papacy, 113-14
Baptism, 2, 13, 34, 42, 107, 139
Bible, 10, 12, 16-17, 27, 40, 77, 101, 102, 140-42, 145, 163, 172-74, 183, 215, 219, 222, 232, 238
Bishop(s), 9, 19-22, 25-27, 32, 33, 35, 39, 41, 42, 45, 46, 47, 49, 51, 57-62, 63, 68, 69, 75, 76, 82-83, 99-100, 104, 107, 112, 114, 115, 116, 121, 125, 126, 131, 138, 139, 142, 148, 149, 154, 168, 169-70, 171, 173, 175, 177, 215, 225-28, 229, 230
Black Death, 120-22
Body, 23, 39, 71, 72, 89-90, 92, 132, 146, 160
Bohemia, 50, 126, 166
Book of Common Prayer, 148
Brandenburg, 136, 138, 167, 171

Caesaropapism, 26, 42, 56, 59, 117, 170-71, 190
Calvinist(s), 143, 166, 168, 171, 174
Canon(s) (clergymen), 75-76, 77, 169
Canon law, 99, 101, 107-108, 110, 111, 113, 137, 139, 148, 175, 228
Canossa, 60
Capitalism, 207-208, 240
Cardinal(s), 58, 80, 111, 113, 115, 116, 128, 154-56, 167, 176, 185, 195, 216, 226, 233
Celibacy, 26, 36, 148, 234
Chivalry, 57, 84-85
Cistercian(s), 73-75, 79
Civil Constitution of the Clergy, 188
Clericis laicos, 112, 113
Climate, 3, 52, 110, 122
Cluny, 56-57, 59, 75
Communion (*see also* Eucharist), 2, 20, 128, 139-40, 145-46, 149, 176, 177, 206
Communism, 239, 240
Communist(s), 208, 210, 239, 240
Concordat of 1801, 189-90
Concordat of Worms, 61-62
Confucian(s), 161-62
Congress of Vienna, 225
Conservatism, 194-96, 197, 201, 211, 224
Conversus, conversi, 74-75
Covenant theology, 144, 206
Creed, 1-2, 21, 25
Crosier, 59, 82
Crusade(s), 63-65, 69-70, 91, 93
Cult, 1-2, 235

Daemonic, 196-97, 200
Decretals, 108
Defenestration of Prague, 166
Deist(s), 182
Dialectic, 11, 101, 106, 221
Divine right of kings, 170
Dominican(s), 78-79, 80, 94, 103, 157, 229, 233
Enlightenment, 180-90, 191, 198, 201, 216-17, 239, 241, 242
Eucharist (*see also* Communion), 20, 36, 107, 127, 128, 145, 167
Evangelicanism, 173-74
Excommunication, 60
Faculty (university unit), 100-101, 139
Faith, 8, 9, 13, 14, 15, 22, 25, 26, 38, 56, 90, 92, 93, 103, 104, 127, 141, 149, 162, 183, 200, 208, 217, 219, 220, 222
Feudal(ism), 44, 46-48, 51, 56, 57, 65, 74, 85, 98, 99, 118, 188, 207
Franciscan(s), 77-78, 79, 80, 94, 125, 157
Free will, freedom of choice, 106, 140-43, 207
French Revolution, 187-90, 225
Fundamentalism, 36, 215, 238-39
Gallicanism, 168
Grace, 106, 139, 141-43, 149, 152, 156, 161, 174, 175, 176-77
Gregorian chant, 127
Gregorian reform, 59-61, 74, 83
Gregorian university, 160
Guild(s), 88, 121-22
Heresy, heretic(s), 68, 90, 91-95, 112, 116, 125, 139-40, 142, 143, 149, 153, 156, 158, 162-63, 175, 233
Hierarchy (of being), 22, 23, 71
Hierarchy (of office), 115, 125, 224, 234, 240
History, 3, 11, 16, 17, 20, 32, 33, 40, 68, 73, 75-77, 101, 105, 119, 139, 158, 180-81, 186, 190, 195, 196, 197, 206, 207, 214, 226, 240, 241
Holy Spirit, 17, 19, 22, 129, 146, 147, 163, 168, 172
Horse collar, horse shoe, 3, 52
Humanae vitae, 230

Humanism, humanist(s), 101, 130-34, 141-42, 161, 175, 220
Immaculate Conception, 225
Imperial Catechism, 190
Imperial Theocracy, 57-58
Index of Forbidden Books, 155, 163, 232
Industrial Revolution, 204-205
Infallibility, infallible, 22, 125, 168, 225-26
Inquisition, medieval, 93-95
Inquisition, modern, 233
Inquisition, Roman, 155, 162-163
Inquisition, Spanish, 122
Inspiration, 17, 19, 21, 22
Jansenism, 177-78
Jesuits, 155, 159-61, 168-69, 175, 176, 180, 185
Jew(s), Judaism, 8, 9, 14, 64, 90, 91, 105, 118, 122, 155, 183, 186, 219
Justification, 141, 143-44, 148, 149, 158
Labour Party, 209, 241-42
Law of Moses, 8, 186
Lay investiture, 59-61
Legate(s), 38, 111, 126, 155, 156-57
Liberal arts, 10-12, 25, 40-41, 49-50, 101, 105-106, 160
Liberal(s), 195, 197, 210, 211, 224
Liberalism, 201, 205-206, 208, 216, 231, 238, 240, 241-42
Love, 9, 10, 15, 19, 28, 71-73, 78, 83, 86-87, 90, 91, 121, 133, 138, 175-76, 183, 200, 219, 220, 240, 244
Lutheran(s), 144, 167, 168, 171, 172, 174, 210, 239
Magic, 1-2, 112, 124, 130, 200
Manorialism, 51-53, 146-47
Manuscript(s), 9-10, 177, 214
Marxism, 1, 206-209, 211, 219, 238, 242
Mass, 41, 77, 85, 127, 128, 153, 158, 166, 171, 176
Mathematics, 11, 50, 101, 104
Matrimony, 106, 107
Medicine, 98, 101, 125, 185, 199, 205, 214, 230, 242

Meditation, 27, 69, 74, 75, 79, 82, 161, 172, 185, 235
Messiah, 14, 105, 180, 186
Methodism, Methodist(s), 173-74, 221
Misogyny, 80
Modernism, 231-33
Monk(s), monasticism, 26-28, 35-36, 38, 40, 56-57, 59, 69, 70, 71, 73-75, 76, 77, 82, 90, 91, 131
Music, 11, 101, 127, 128, 238
Muslim(s), 63-65, 183, 186
Myth, 105, 133, 220-21
Nationalism, 1, 190-91, 218-19
Natural selection, 214-15, 221
Nature, 3, 12, 19, 22, 53, 78, 105, 163, 182-83, 188, 189, 194-95, 196-97, 198, 214, 244
Nazi, 219
Neo-platonism, 22, 23
Ninety-five Theses, 136-38
Noblesse oblige, 85
Nun(s), 50, 79-80
Opus Dei, 235
Ordination, 36, 57, 173, 175, 176
Pagan(ism), 8-9, 12, 24, 32, 33, 35-36, 50, 103
Papal curia, 107, 155, 224, 229
Papal States, 39, 111, 152, 155
Peace of God, 57
Peace of Westphalia, 167
Peasants' Revolt 146-47
Penance, 61, 94, 107, 139, 177
People of God, 72, 125, 224, 229, 234
Philosophe(s), 180-84, 188, 191, 197, 198, 208
Philosophy, 8, 9, 11-12, 13, 19, 75-77, 99, 102-104, 127, 133, 185, 199, 206, 208, 217-18, 232, 243
Pietism, Pietist(s), 171-72, 210
Pilgrimage, 28, 50, 70, 72, 73, 128
Pluralism, 136, 154, 173, 185
Poor Clares, 80
Positivism, 217-18
Prayer, 13, 27, 37, 42, 62, 69, 74, 75-76, 77, 79-80, 89, 106, 107, 128, 148, 174, 176, 185, 235

Preaching, 14, 20, 63-64, 69, 77, 78-79, 91, 92, 94, 138, 169, 171, 173, 175
Predestination, 143, 149, 177, 206, 222
Praemonstratenian(s), Prémontré, 75-76
Prevenient grace, 142, 149
Progress, 51, 180-81, 184, 186, 208, 217, 218, 231, 241-42
Proletariat, 122, 208
Protestant(s), 106, 138, 143, 144-46, 148-49, 152, 155, 157, 158, 166-67, 168, 171-72, 185-86, 205-206, 210-11, 219-22, 224, 228, 232, 233, 238
Prussia, Prussian(s), 167, 171, 184, 187, 190-91, 228
Purgatory, 2, 107, 127, 129, 130, 137-38, 140, 148, 158
Puritan(s), 149, 171
Quadrivium, 11, 12, 101
Reason, 1, 2, 8-9, 12, 19, 22, 103, 105, 106, 126, 139, 140, 176, 181-82, 186, 190, 195-96, 200, 208, 221, 231
Reform, 4, 41, 49, 51, 56-63, 65, 73-77, 98-99, 110, 115, 116, 117, 125-26, 128, 137, 139, 152-59, 168, 173, 187
Reform Judaism, 186
Reformed Churches, 143
Relativism, 217
Renaissance, 4, 40, 50, 62, 98, 101, 130, 132, 134, 181
Ressourcement, 233
Retreat houses, 161
Rhetoric, 11, 13, 34, 100-101
Roman law, 94, 99
Sacrament, 93, 106-107, 128, 139, 177
Schism, 63, 65, 69, 90, 115-16, 152, 224, 236
Science, 2, 8, 12, 53, 101-102, 104, 127, 133-34, 161-62, 183, 185, 198, 206, 208, 216, 218, 219, 239, 242-44
Scripture, 5, 11-12, 16-17, 19, 41, 71, 75, 106, 139, 140, 141, 142, 145-46, 148, 162-63, 169

Secularism, 130, 150, 166, 181, 222, 239
Sex, 23, 41, 68, 71, 92, 200, 210
Simony, 59-60, 100, 112, 142, 155
Social Darwinism, 217, 219
Socialism, 195, 208, 209, 219, 221, 241-42
Society of Jesus. *See* Jesuits
Syllabus of Errors, 231, 233
Theology, 4, 62, 70, 76, 79, 101, 102, 103-104, 106-107, 127, 134, 139, 142-43, 144, 172, 174, 178, 185, 199, 220, 229, 230, 232
Toleration, 24, 91, 92, 183, 184, 186, 196, 233
Tradition, 18, 19, 21, 103, 133, 224, 226
Traditionalist(s), 76, 224-25, 230, 231, 234-35
Trent, Council of, 156-59
Trinity, 12, 19, 177, 180
Trivium, 11, 101
Ultramontanism, 225
Vatican Council I, 225-26
Vatican Council II, 229, 230, 233-34
Word (*Logos*), 8-9, 15-16, 19, 105, 177